The Source® for Reading Fluency

Nancy B. Swigert

Skill:	Reading Fluency
Ages:	6 and up
Grades:	1 and up

LinguiSystems

LinguiSystems, Inc.
3100 4th Avenue
East Moline, IL 61244-9700

800-776-4332

FAX: 800-577-4555
E-mail: service@linguisystems.com
Web: linguisystems.com

Printed in the U.S.A.

ISBN 0-7606-0445-2

About the Author

Nancy B. Swigert, M.A., CCC-SLP, is president of Swigert & Associates, Inc., a private practice that has been providing services in the Lexington, Kentucky area for over 20 years. She also serves as president of the Reading Center, a program that provides assessment and intervention for children and adults with reading, spelling, and written language disorders. She has provided training and consultation for numerous private and public school systems concerning these disorders. The Reading Center is an approved provider of supplemental educational services for the No Child Left Behind initiative. Nancy is the author of three other books for LinguiSystems, *The Source for Dysphagia*, *The Source for Dysarthria,* and *The Source for Pediatric Dysphagia*. She is very active in the American Speech-Language-Hearing Association, including serving as its president in 1998 and president of the American Speech-Language-Hearing Foundation in 2004.

Acknowledgments

Thanks to:

- My husband Keith, who understands me so well that he tolerated my working on this book every "free" minute (even on vacation!)
- Melinda Spurlock, who organized and formatted the multitude of materials and compiled many of the practice lists and drills
- Geri Cobb, who ably assisted with formatting and organizing the materials
- Patty Brooks, for sharing her expertise concerning assessment of reading
- The members of the staff at the Reading Center, who reviewed and responded to ideas as they developed: Verity, Sarah, Jennifer, Ashley, and Julie
- Lonnie Wright, MSLS AHIP, and Lori M. Bailey, MSLS, exceptional librarians at Central Baptist Hospital, for helping to find every reference I needed

Dedication

This book is dedicated to all the students who come to the Reading Center and to their parents, who have faith that we can "teach the skills to read . . . one child at a time." A special debt of gratitude is owed to our first student, Taylor, and his mother, Lynn. If not for Taylor's hard work and incredible success and Lynn's confidence that we could teach Taylor how to read, there might not be a Reading Center.

Edited by Mary Conger and Lauri Whiskeyman
Artwork by Dana Regan
Cover design by Mike Paustian
Page layout by Denise L. Kelly

Table of Contents

Introduction

When we launched our Reading Center program several years ago, we found an abundance of materials to help students who were inaccurate readers. We had all become aware of the importance of phonological awareness and its impact on reading. However, we continued to encounter students for whom the use of these excellent materials just wasn't enough. These were the children described by Wolf (1991) as presenting with a naming speed deficit. Despite improvements in their phonological awareness skills and applied decoding skills, they still couldn't read quickly enough and well enough to keep up with their grade-level peers. They were not fluent readers. That was what prompted me to research the theory behind fluency in reading and to compile and develop materials to help these students.

Many of our referrals come when the students are in third or fourth grade. We suppose this is because by third grade, teachers have stopped teaching students how to read and are expecting the students to read in order to learn. The amount of text that students have to read beginning in these grades increases exponentially. In addition, teachers have begun to lecture more in class. These same students who are not fluent readers tend to also be the students who cannot process information quickly enough to take effective notes during class.

What we saw at our center was not unique. Reading rate is a significant problem for children with reading problems. The report of the National Reading Panel (2000) indicated that 44 percent of fourth graders were non-fluent readers. The National Assessment of Educational Progress study (1992) found that 15 percent of all fourth graders (1 out of 7) read "no faster than 74 words per minute . . . a pace at which it would be difficult to keep track of ideas as they are developing within the sentence and across the page" (Pinnell et al. 1995).

Rasinski and Padak (1998) found that students who were referred for special reading help read at a rate that was approximately 60 percent of their instructional level reading rate (passages a level lower than their grade level) and at a rate that was 50 percent on grade level passages.

Lovett's observations (1987) mirror our own: Children with reading rate disorders tend to be referred by middle and later elementary grades when the amount of textual information required for test and project preparation increases and where instruction is more in lecture format. This is when we hear reports of comprehension problems, trouble with note taking and written composition, and a drop in grades.

In addition to the close tie that has been established between reading fluency and comprehension, it has been suggested that dysfluent reading also affects the reader's motivation to read (Meyer and Felton 1999). This is not surprising if you listen to a non-fluent reader read. He certainly must find reading to be extremely frustrating and laborious. This may cause him to avoid reading at all costs.

The Matthew principle (Stanovich 1986) states that better readers read more and thus continue to improve. Reading progress is largely dependent on how much reading is done. Slow, inefficient readers read fewer words per minute. Thus, they would have to read many more hours just to keep up with their peers in amount of text read.

Rasinski (2000) makes the case that speed does matter in reading and that dysfluent reading:

- leads to less overall reading
- is associated with poor comprehension
- leads to reading frustration

Therefore, it is crucial that we identify students who have a reading fluency disorder and address the disorder early and appropriately. In a study analyzing the predictive value of rapid automatized naming in poor readers, Meyer et al. (1998) stated, "The practical consequences of these findings argue for increased emphasis on instructional techniques that stress fluency training in the early grades." We couldn't agree more. We hope that you find the information and materials in this book useful as you strive to help the non-fluent readers you know to become more fluent.

Nancy

Chapter 1

What Is Reading Fluency?

When a student is having trouble with reading, it is initially suspected that the difficulty may be with impaired phonological awareness skills. Much has been written about phonological awareness. There are a multitude of tests that assess phonological awareness and even more products and materials that seek to improve those phonological skills. But what about the student who has adequate phonological awareness skills but is a plodding reader? He can sound out most words encountered, but he reads at a painfully slow rate. He often doesn't recognize familiar "sight" words, though he has encountered them before. He sounds stiff and reads without expression. It is no wonder that by the time the student gets to the end of the passage, he hasn't a clue what the content was. This student may be presenting with a reading fluency disorder not caused by poor decoding skills.

Fluent readers can read text quickly and accurately. In addition, fluent readers read with expression, enhancing the understandability of the passage. There is a noticeable and recognizable difference between a fluent reader and a non-fluent reader. Think of the difference between a fluent speaker and one who speaks haltingly, searching for the correct word, revising sentence structure as the conversation progresses. If you speak a second language, recall how you sounded when you first began to speak that language. Similar descriptions could be given for a non-fluent reader.

Fluent readers

- Quick
- Accurate
- Attend to punctuation
- Use expression
  - Rhythm
  - Intonation
  - Phrasing

Fluent reading might be described as a "lack of trouble with word identification or comprehension" (Leu and Kinzer 1987). A similar definition is found in *A Dictionary of Reading and Related Terms* (Harris and Hodges 1981) as "freedom from word identification problems." Picture the student who reads fluently as being able to read while not being tied to a word-by-word or sound-by-sound process.

Hook and Jones (2002) indicate that fluency involves not only automatic word recognition but also the ability to attend to prosodic features (e.g., rhythm, intonation, and phrasing) at the phrase, sentence, and text level. Wood et al. (2001) state that fluency also involves anticipation of what comes next in the text. This anticipation facilitates reaction time and aids comprehension.

LaBerge and Samuels (1974) were early advocates of the idea that it is not enough to achieve accuracy in reading. They stated that fluent reading is achieved only when all levels from visual to semantic decoding occur automatically. Samuels (1992) explains that reading requires decoding, comprehension, and attention. Fluent reading with good comprehension cannot be achieved if attention is focused on decoding. Once decoding becomes automatic, attention can be focused on comprehension. It is at that point that the reader has become fluent.

Beginning readers are rarely fluent readers. Their attention is focused on individual letters and sounds and on decoding these to figure out what the word is. As readers develop skill, they focus on larger and larger units (e.g., digraphs and word parts). When the student is a fluent reader, the unit of focus is the whole word (Samuels 1992).

The relationship between decoding and comprehension

As the student progresses towards fluency, less and less of his mental energy, or attention, has to be focused on the decoding process. This means that he can begin to focus his attention on comprehending what he is reading.

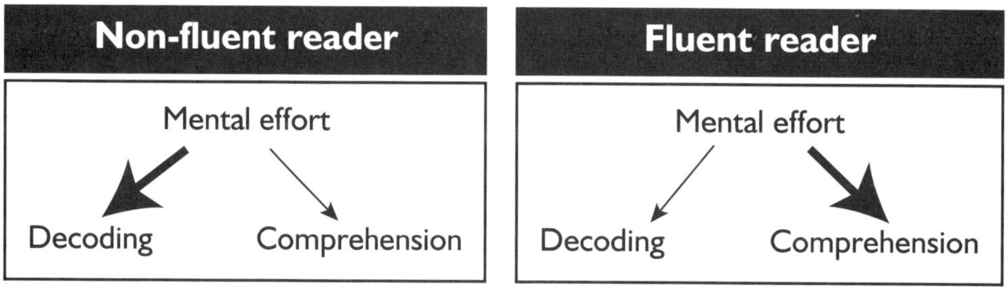

Samuels (1992) states, "The hallmark of fluent reading is the ability to decode and comprehend at the same time." Different studies have exhibited that in general, less fluent readers have poorer comprehension (Carnine et al. 1990, Dowhower 1987, Shinn et al. 1992, Tan and Nicholson 1997).

Perfetti and Lesgold (1977) described the relationship between decoding and comprehension as the bottleneck hypothesis. If decoding is not fast and accurate, there will be a bottleneck for comprehension. This is because decoding operations may share what these authors call the "limited capacity processor" with comprehension. Rather than calling it *mental effort* or *energy*, they refer to it as *memory*. They indicate that the limited capacity processor can only hold so much information in memory.

Automaticity

The term *automaticity* is often used in descriptions of reading fluency. A task is described as automatic when it can be completed without overt attention. Berninger et al. (2001) differentiate between efficiency (speed) and automaticity (direct access). When you finished reading the paragraph above, did you have any recollection of decoding any specific word? Without that overt attention to decoding, you still comprehended what you read. You have reached the level of automaticity in reading, allowing you to focus your attention on comprehending the content. If you are able to do two tasks at once, decoding and comprehending, then one of those tasks has become automatic (Samuels 1992). Samuels points out that automaticity is not achieved simply by reaching an automatic level for decoding. He points out that other "text processing strategies" also have to run automatically. These might include being able to visualize the text, understand a referent, or understand the structure of the text. The relationship between fluency and comprehension is not one way. The more you understand what you are reading, the more fluent you can be when reading the text. Can you be more fluent when reading aloud from an article in your field or when reading from an article on quantum physics?

Shiffrin and Schneider (1977) explained automatic behaviors in terms of features and outcomes of those behaviors. They described automatic behaviors as:

- being difficult to inhibit
- not relying on conscious control and attention
- not utilizing attentional resources when the individual is performing them at the same time as another task.

Nasland and Smolkin (1997) concluded, "Reading . . . (is) a skill that develops to a more automatic level depending on the degree to which the individual can accurately and quickly access phonemic and lexical representations . . . "

Read the following Middle English passage, from Chaucer's *Canterbury Tales*:

> "Somwhat he lipsed for his wantounesse
> To make his Englissh sweete upon his tonge;
> And in his harping, when he hadde songe,
> His yen twinkled in his heed aright
> As doon the sterres in the frosty night."
>
> (lines 266-270)

To read the passage, you probably had to focus some of your attention on decoding many of the unfamiliar words. Even after you decoded some of them, you might have had difficulty understanding what you had read if the words were not familiar to you. For that level of reading material, you have not reached automaticity.

If you were allowed to read that passage over and over again, were taught some of the rules of how sounds are produced in Middle English, and looked up the meanings of the words with which you were unfamiliar between readings, your reading fluency would improve. You'd read faster and with more expression. You wouldn't be satisfied with reading at a level at which you could decode the words if it still took you a long time to do so. You would want to continue to improve until your rate was faster and you could read the passage and impart meaning to the listener. The same is true for students with whom we work. We shouldn't be satisfied when they can read a sentence and correctly decode the words. We should strive to have the student read the material quickly and smoothly.

The double-deficit hypothesis

Why are some children slow readers? What underlying processes are impaired? Perhaps the best-known work is that done by Wolf and Bowers. They first described their theory on the links between naming speed, timing, and orthographic skills in 1993. In their seminal paper on naming speed deficits (Wolf and Bowers 1999), they explained that it had long been believed that a core deficit in phonological processes impedes the acquisition of word recognition skills, which, in turn, impedes the acquisition of fluent reading. They further stated many severely impaired readers have naming-speed deficits (i.e., deficits in the processes underlying the rapid recognition and retrieval of visually presented linguistic stimuli). Their double-deficit hypothesis proposed, however, that the naming-speed deficit was not part of impaired phonological processes, but instead that, "Phonological deficits and the processes underlying naming speed are separable sources of reading dysfunction, and their combined presence leads to profound reading impairment."

Other authors have confirmed the double-deficit theory by isolating reading skills that are more directly related to naming speed than to phonological awareness skills. Cornwall (1992) showed that rapid letter naming added significantly to the prediction of word identification, prose passage speed, and accuracy scores. Manis and Freedman (2001) obtained several findings relevant to the theory. They found that phonological skills and rapid serial naming made differential contributions to particular aspects of word reading skill. They further found that rapid automatized naming (RAN) was most strongly predictive of accuracy and latency measures of orthographic and semantic processing and latency measures of word and non-word reading. Manis et al. (1999) suggest that this differential effect on reading may be because RAN involves arbitrary associations between print and sound (e.g., a letter and its name). They suggest that phoneme awareness is more related to the student learning a systematic spelling-sound correspondence. In addition, they state that RAN has a number of other components that overlap with reading and make it a good predictor of reading skills.

Manis et al. (2000) confirmed naming speed's contribution to measures of orthographic skill compared to phonemic awareness' stronger contribution to non-word decoding. Torgeson et al. (1997) showed unique contributions of both phonemic awareness and naming speed in predicting second and third grade reading when measured in kindergarten and first grade.

Reading skills related to naming speed

- Word identification
- Passage speed
- Word reading speed
- Passage accuracy

What the double-deficit theory means for treatment

Why is it important to consider the theory of separable sources (phonological deficits and processes underlying naming speed deficits) of reading dysfunction? It is important because how a disorder is viewed shapes the way it is treated. Consider an example from medicine. If ulcers are viewed as being caused by stress, then patients are counseled to eliminate or reduce stress in their lives. If ulcers are believed to be caused by a bacterial infection, then medication is prescribed. If the processes underlying naming-speed deficits are really just one of the phonological processes that can be impaired, then the majority of children with reading disorders are well served by improving their phonological awareness skills. However, if Wolf and Bowers' double-deficit theory is accurate, and the processes underlying naming-speed deficits are indeed a separate source of reading dysfunction, then to treat all children with reading disorders in the same way is inappropriate and probably not productive for those children with naming-speed deficits.

This has indeed been demonstrated in several studies (Lovett et al. 1994). Lovett found significant differences in the effectiveness of her program. Specifically, the phonological-deficit-only group showed greater gains on every post-treatment measure than either the naming-speed or double-deficit group. Some of these measures were phonological processing, non-word and word identification skill, and standardized reading measures. The conclusion was that phonological intervention can help some reading disabled children, but some groups of readers have a deficit pattern that require additional or different emphases in intervention.

Children with deficits in the processes underlying naming speed need specific strategies and techniques to try to improve those processes. Children with phonological awareness deficits need techniques to improve their phonological awareness skills. If the child has deficits in both phonological awareness and naming speed, then that child suffers from what Wolf and Bowers describe as *double deficit.* For those children, it is crucial that a combined approach be utilized. Treatment must address their reduced phonological process skills and the processes underlying their naming-speed deficit.

What is naming speed and how is it tested?

Naming speed is tested by having the child name items on a page that contains a series of letters or numbers (colors and objects are used for younger children). A specific letter or number may be repeated many times in the series. These tests are called rapid automatized naming, or RAN. RAN was first designed by Denckla (1972) and further developed by Denckla and Rudel (1974, 1976). In their test, there is an arrangement of 50 stimuli consisting of five symbols repeated ten times. Interestingly, some researchers have shown that having a naming-speed deficit may predict not only reading disabilities, but broader forms of learning disabilities (Berninger et al. 2001, Waber 2001).

Example of a naming-speed task

a t s c k n s k c a s k s c a
t s n c k s n s t c k a s c k
a n t s c k t n a s k c s t a

What skills underlie naming speed?

What skills are required to complete a letter-naming test rapidly? Wolf and Bowers (1999) propose that the cognitive requirements for such a task include:

1. Paying attention to the stimulus
2. Visually processing to detect, discriminate, and identify
3. Integrating the visual features with an orthographic pattern stored in memory
4. Integrating the visual features with a phonological representation stored in memory
5. Retrieving the phonological label
6. Integrating semantic and conceptual information
7. Activating a motor response to articulate the name of the letter

Obviously, a coordination of many processes is required in order to successfully complete the task. A breakdown in any one of the processes can result in slow naming speed.

How does a naming-speed deficit affect reading?

How does an impairment in the processes underlying naming speed result in slow reading? Again, Wolf and Bowers have indicated that there may be three ways this may occur:

1. Impeding connections between phonemes and the orthographic patterns, at word or sub-word levels
2. Limiting the quality of the orthographic codes stored in memory
3. Requiring increasing practice before adequate connections are made

Wolf and Bowers' theoretical description of how processes underlying naming speed result in slow reading implies that intervention needs to:

- Help the student improve the connections between phonemes and their orthographic patterns and between word parts and words and their orthographic patterns. Intervention must not focus just on the phonemic level, but also on helping students improve the speed of recognition of word parts (e.g., onsets and rimes, prefixes and suffixes) and whole words. These connections must occur rapidly and without conscious thought on the part of the student.
- Help the student improve the quality of orthographic codes the student is able to hold in memory. Often the student knows many of the basic codes (e.g., short and long vowels) but does not have other orthographic codes stored (e.g., alternative spellings for the long *e* such as *ea*, or what a blend says: *spr*).
- Provide the student ample practice to help these connections become automatic.

Wolf and Bowers stress helping the student improve speed and accuracy of connections. Apel and Swank (1999) describe these connections as establishing visual orthographic images (VOI). These are mental images of morphemes, syllables, or words that are developed in memory by repeated successful experiences in decoding words. These authors indicate that in normally developing readers, as little as four exposures to a word may be needed to establish a VOI. Once this image of a morpheme, syllable, or word is established, the reader can bypass the slower act of decoding. In children with impaired naming speed, many more exposures to a pattern may be needed.

Word recognition and fluency

Word recognition is crucial in the beginning reader. Early readers learn to recognize the word as a unit. One of the challenges for beginning readers is to understand how these written forms map onto their oral vocabulary. Deficits in word level recognition have been shown to be characteristic of students who are not reading at grade level (Perfetti 1985, Stanovich 1986). Still others state, "The development of rapid word recognition skills . . . (is) the primary factor which distinguishes skilled from less skilled reading performance" (Chabot et al. 1984).

Several theories describe how word recognition develops (Coltheart 1978, Forster 1976, LaBerge and Samuels 1974, McClelland and Rumelhart 1981, Seidenberg and McClelland 1989). At least some of those models recognize that a "framework assumes that reading words involves the computation of three types of codes: orthographic, phonological, and semantic" (Seidenberg and McClelland 1989). When do readers begin to establish VOIs of morphemes and word parts to decode words? Some say that children as young as six or seven may tap their emerging knowledge of morphemes for written language (Treiman and Cassar 1997). By fourth grade, students seem to have a basic knowledge of derived forms (Windsor and Hwang 1997) and by fifth grade, a substantial portion of the child's orthographic representations consist of forms that are derivations of root words (Anglin 1993).

Semantics and fluency

Achieving reading fluency would seem to depend not just on enhancing connections for more efficient orthographic and phonological processing but also on more efficient use of semantics. In their work developing *Retrieval, Automaticity, Vocabulary Elaboration, and Orthography* (*RAVE-O*) (a comprehensive, fluency-based reading intervention program), Wolf et al. (2000) indicate that it is also important to improve the student's semantic knowledge. They state that dysfluent readers cannot afford the time to process different meanings of a word they have read. If students have a rich vocabulary with easy access to multiple meanings of words, they will be able to more quickly retrieve this information during reading. This will help to improve the speed of reading. Obviously, understanding the meaning of words is also crucial to comprehension.

Fluency in connected reading

Attention to all the skills that contribute to fluent reading is important, but we must also help the student apply these skills with the result being increased speed and fluency of connected reading. This involves practice with oral reading, word level drills, and increasing attention to prosodic cues. It is important to remember that when treating component parts, the goal is ultimately to help the student read connected text more fluently.

Naming-speed deficits and ADHD

Denckla and Cutting (1999) summarize the history and significance of RAN as related to students with reading disability. They also report information about similarities in students with attention deficit hyperactivity disorder (ADHD) and RAN deficits.

They caution that much still needs to be learned about rapid automatized naming and challenge that we need to ask, "Who is slow on RAN and why?" They discuss some of the possibilities of where this skill might be neurologically localized. They remind us that it is probably "not possible to assign each deficit of the double-deficit hypothesis neatly to one psychological domain or the other." They state that a variety of linguistic/executive profiles may actually underlie these reading-related deficits.

Van der Sloot et al. (2000) raise the question of whether non-fluent readers who guess at text are really exhibiting a specific reading disorder, or if this might be linked to the same executive deficits which underlie ADHD. Other researchers have completed studies which challenge the tenet that naming-speed deficits are specific to reading disorder and instead implicate these naming-speed deficits for children with ADHD (Tannock et al. 2000). This finding is not surprising, given that others have found that certain difficulties on tasks requiring planning or controlled motor output pertain at least in part to ADHD and cannot fully be accounted for by co-morbid conditions like reading disorders (Nigg et al. 1998).

Are there subtypes of non-fluent readers?

It is likely that we may determine that naming-speed deficit is more complex as we learn more about it. If the model of naming-speed deficit is more complex than that described above, then how intervention is provided would also be more complex. Berninger et al. (2001) elaborate on the concept of naming-speed deficit and indicate they have observed three subtypes of dysfluent readers.

Types of dysfluent readers
Type 1: Processing Rate/Efficiency Impaired • Rarely makes mistakes • Is painfully slow
Type 2: Automaticity Impaired • Is inaccurate and slow • Makes false starts • Hesitates • Fills pauses (e.g., "um") • Repeats • Self-monitors/self-corrects
Type 3: Executive Coordination Impaired • Shows inattention to orthography • Shows inattention to morphology • Shows inattention to serial order of words • Shows inattention to prosody • Shows inattention to self-monitoring of meaning • Rarely self-corrects

Within each of these three subtypes, different processes may be contributing to slow oral reading. In addition, Berninger et al. hypothesize that there is a different brain locus for each of the types. A summary of their description of oral reading in children in each of these subtypes follows.

Processing rate or efficiency of the system

Oral reading is very accurate but painfully slow in children who are processing rate or efficiency impaired. These children rarely make errors and thus are often not identified by schools as having a reading disability. They are the children who may not be able to keep up with assignments in the classroom. The hypothesized brain locus for this type of deficit is the cerebellum, for control of precise timing.

Automaticity of processing

Oral reading is inaccurate and slow with very specific types of errors in children who are automaticity impaired. Errors include false starts, hesitations that are often filled with pauses, and repetitions. These children seem to have adequate phonological awareness skills but have not achieved an automatic level of processing. They do seem able to self-monitor and self-correct. Berninger et al. suggest that this means the children's executive functions are intact. They propose the brain locus for this type of deficit is the striatum and/or insula.

Executive coordination

The third subtype described by Berninger et al. exhibits oral reading that is inaccurate and slow but has an error pattern different from that in the second subtype. These children make errors indicating an "inattention to orthographic and morphological features of words, inattention to serial order of words in sentences, inattention to the prosody or music of the language (Erekson 1999), and inattention to self-monitoring of meaning." They rarely self-correct errors. Berninger et al. hypothesize the brain locus is left frontal for this type of deficit.

Berninger et al. note that some children exhibit errors characteristic of Types 2 and 3, and they indicate this means that both automaticity and executive coordination are affected. It would seem that these children would have even more difficulty becoming fluent readers.

Others describe a different categorization for the types of non-fluent readers. Children described as the guessing subtype of dyslexia are those who read fast and inaccurately, while children with the spelling subtype of dyslexia read slowly and accurately. This latter type of dyslexia, spelling subtype, would mirror Berninger et al.'s Type 1. The guessing subtype of dyslexia probably most closely reflects Berninger's Type 3 description.

Would different subtypes need different treatment?

If we accept Berninger et al.'s more detailed breakdown of types of dysfluent readers, then we must also adjust the intervention provided. They suggest that students in the first type may need work mostly on practicing reading to increase efficiency. However, the second type may need to improve the connections between stimuli and responses and need feedback on their rate and accuracy during reading. Finally, the third type may need instruction in meta-cognitive strategies for self-monitoring and self-correction.

Conclusion

Thus, because the concept of fluency in reading and the relationship to processes underlying naming speed is complex and relatively recent, research continues to yield much new information. The current working definition of fluency provided by Wolf and Katzir-Cohen (2001) summarizes well our current understanding: "In its beginnings, reading fluency is the product of the initial development of accuracy and the subsequent development of automaticity in underlying sublexical processes, lexical processes, and their integration in single-word reading and connected text. These include perceptual, phonological, orthographic, and morphological processes at the letter, letter-pattern, and word levels, as well as semantic and syntactic processes at the word level and connected-text level. After it is fully developed, reading fluency refers to a level of accuracy and rate where decoding is relatively effortless, where oral reading is smooth and accurate with correct prosody, and where attention can be allocated to comprehension."

We know a non-fluent reader when we hear one. The challenge is to figure out how to help that reader become more fluent.

Chapter 2

Testing for Reading Fluency

What does it mean when we say a child reads well? The ability to read involves many different skills. Children who read well are able to:

- read text accurately (i.e., read the words as printed on the page)
- decode new words when they encounter them
- read most words automatically because the words are in the child's sight word vocabulary
- read as quickly as expected of same-age peers
- read fluently with expression
- remember what was read
- understand what was read, including factual recall as well as the ability to infer and draw conclusions

Therefore, an assessment of reading must address all of these areas. When applicable, these skills should be assessed in both silent and oral reading. For example, the ability to decode new words is more easily assessed during oral reading, while comprehension should be assessed in both silent and oral reading.

A child can successfully demonstrate these components of reading if the child has the necessary underlying skills such as the following:

- short-term/working memory
- phonological awareness skills
- rapid naming/retrieval skills
- adequate understanding and use of semantics
- adequate understanding and use of vocabulary
- adequate understanding and use of syntax/sentence structure

Therefore, assessment of reading must address also these underlying skills. A complete reading battery (not including assessment of spelling or written language) may take several hours to administer, with additional time spent scoring and analyzing the results.

See Appendices 2A and 2B.

Because it would not be appropriate to assess a child's reading fluency and ignore the other aspects of reading, this chapter will present information on testing instruments commonly used to assess all components of reading and the underlying skills for reading. Additional information will be provided on the background and rationale for those tests and tools that specifically look at fluency of reading, such as rapid naming and sight word recognition. A list of tests that assess the components of reading can be found in Appendix 2A (page 30). Appendix 2B (pages 31-32) provides a resource guide for all assessments that are cited in this chapter.

Assessing the components of reading

Assessing reading accuracy

Reading accuracy, or how well the child reads the exact words in the text, must be assessed during oral reading. There are standardized tests that assess accuracy. For example, the *Gray Oral Reading Tests* (*GORT-4*) includes subtests on rate, accuracy, and comprehension. The accuracy score is obtained by counting the number of errors in a given passage. Errors include: reading the wrong word, waiting to be told what the word is, taking longer than 10 seconds to sound out the word, self-correcting, adding a word, repeating a word, and skipping a line. Thus, some accuracy errors are errors in decoding; others are repetitions, omissions, insertions, and false starts. Some of these errors may be due to inattention to text, such as misreading a word ending (e.g., *-ed* for *-ing*) or reading a contracted form instead of the two words printed (e.g., *I'll* instead of *I will*). The *GORT-4* allows the examiner to perform a more in-depth miscue analysis, if desired.

The *Phonics Based Reading Test* (*PRT*) is structured in a similar format. The student reads passages aloud, and the number of errors yields an accuracy score. In addition to standard scores and grade and age equivalences, this test is also criterion-referenced and provides an analysis of performance described as frustration, instructional, and mastery. The *Test of Oral Reading and Comprehension Skills* (*TORCS*) also yields an accuracy score from the student's performance on an oral reading task.

Accuracy may also be assessed through an informal analysis, usually called a reading miscue analysis or inventory. Any reading material may be used for such an analysis, though one should note the difficulty level of the text. Children will naturally exhibit more errors with harder text. The examiner makes a copy of the text the student is going to read, so that the errors may be marked on the copy. Thus, the intent of such an analysis is more than counting the number of errors. The analysis provides the basis for teaching strategies.

Weaver (1988) reminds us that not all errors indicate poor reading skills. Some proficient readers change words (e.g., they substitute a pronoun for a noun or change a word that doesn't change the meaning) as they read aloud, and this does not affect their comprehension. Weaver states, "Many proficient readers make relatively few miscues of any sort. However, the most crucial difference between good readers and poor readers is not the quantity of their miscues, but the quality." When using a miscue analysis, the errors are to be described by type. Some types of errors that might be marked in an informal analysis include:

- substitutions of words
- omissions of words
- insertion of a word that is not in the text
- transposition of words in the sentence
- repetition of words or phrases
- multiple attempts to sound out a word
- self-corrections of errors (either immediately or after reading several more words and then returning to the earlier error to make the correction)
- changing the word to a word with a similar meaning

One example of a reading miscue analysis was developed by Goodman and Burke (1972). The Goodman and Burke miscue inventory is fairly complex. For instance, it not only records errors such as substitutions, omissions, insertions, reversals, and repetitions, but it also breaks down the type of repetitions and provides cues for additional markings. These authors suggest that nine areas be addressed for each miscue:

1. dialect
2. intonation
3. graphic similarity
4. sound similarity
5. grammatical function
6. correction
7. grammatical acceptability
8. semantic acceptability
9. meaning change

Johnson et al. (1987) described the role of informal reading inventories. Their description included a system for recording oral reading errors. One example of a system for marking errors is found below. You can devise any system for marking errors as long as it is consistently applied.

Example of miscues marked on a reading passage	
The dog barked ↓	Rising or falling inflection
was (double underlined)	Repetition
saw ~~was~~	Substitution
serly ~~surely~~	Mispronunciation
saw ~~was~~ (sc)	Self-correction
(was) (circled)	Omission
The man/was	Pause (one per second)
big The ^ man	Insertion
H was	Examiner help given
The dog barked ⊙ He saw	Punctuation ignored
perched (wavy underline)	Had to sound it out but got it correct
perc T hed	SLP told student the word
DK	Child states, "I don't know."

Example of miscues marked on a reading passage

Early one morning, mother woke up and got dressed. She woke up her little girl
and her little boy and told them to hurry and get dressed. Mother cooked
breakfast while the children dressed She packed a lunch for them to take
along. Everyone ate quickly because they were so excited. They put on their
coats and hats and grabbed their lunches. Today was the field trip to the farm!

The Reading Recovery program (Clay 1993) uses a tool called *Running Records*. In Reading Recovery, the instructor considers:

- number of errors
- kinds of errors (e.g., substitutions, omissions) and behaviors shown
- cueing systems (e.g., meaning, structure, visual) used and neglected

Allington and Cunningham (1996) provide a nice summary of how *Running Records* are used as a miscue analysis.

Assessing decoding skills

Decoding skills can be assessed in context by analyzing the child's ability to decode a word encountered in text that is not in the child's sight word vocabulary. This is most easily accomplished during oral reading. Decoding can also be assessed at the word level. For example, the *Woodcock Reading Mastery Tests—Revised (WRMT-R)* includes a subtest called *Word Attack*. The student is shown a nonsense word and is asked to read it. Information is then obtained about the child's knowledge of grapheme-phoneme relationships. The *PRT* also uses nonsense words to assess the student's phonics and decoding skills.

For children suspected of having a reading fluency disorder, it is important to note not only how many words or nonsense words the student can decode, but how efficiently she is able to do so. Two students might achieve the same score on the *Word Attack* subtest of the *WRMT-R* but present with very different skills. If one child decodes 18 words correctly and reads each immediately upon seeing the word, that child's skills are very different from a child who can decode 18 words but takes 20-30 seconds trying to figure each one out.

Assessing sight word vocabulary/recognition

Sight word vocabulary is typically assessed by asking the child to read a list of words aloud. It is often called *word identification*. A child's rapid-naming skills tend to predict how well he will do on a test of word identification. The *WRMT-R* includes a subtest entitled *Word Identification* that assesses this skill. The *Diagnostic Achievement Battery—3 (DAB-3)* has a subtest called *Alphabet/Word Knowledge* that also assesses single word recognition. The caveat described about noting how efficiently a student decodes also applies when evaluating his sight word recognition. A student who reads 15 of the 25 words on a list quickly is very different from the student who reads 15 correctly, but who tries to sound out many of the words or takes seconds to think about each word before venturing a guess about what it is. The latter is likely to be the student with a reading fluency disorder.

This is confirmed in a study by Lovett (1987) in which she found that rate disabled subjects had significant impairments in the speed of word recognition. Lovett also indicated that the depressed word recognition time had an adverse effect on a student's ability to read connected text. She found that rate disabled students can identify more words on a task such as reading a list of words than they can in connected text. A student might be able to perform a written language skill competently (though slowly) in isolation, but perform more poorly when completing the same skill in context. Lovett hyphothesizes that this indicates a language overload in context and reduces the student's performance.

The *Test of Word Reading Efficiency (TOWRE)* measures how many words from a graded list the child can accurately read in 45 seconds. The *Spadafore Diagnostic Reading Test* (*SDRT*) includes a subtest on word recognition that consists of approximately 20 words placed at each of 13 grade levels (primer through twelfth grade). This is a criterion-referenced test that yields a grade level score and performance level (i.e., independent, instructional, or frustration).

Assessing reading rate

Reading rate can be assessed for oral and silent reading. The student is asked to read a passage either silently or aloud. The time it takes the student to read the passage is recorded. In oral reading, errors can be recorded as well. One can find references to reading rate typical at different grade levels in reading research. For example, the oral reading rate for first graders should be between 30 to 50 words per minute. Children in second grade should read between 85 and 100 words per minute (plus or minus 15 words). Children in fifth grade should read between 120 and 150 words per minute.

However, these rates do not reflect the number of errors that occurred during that timed reading passage. It is important to consider errors when determining rate. Recording errors allows the examiner to determine not just a words-per-minute (WPM) rate, but a words-correct-per-minute (WCPM) rate. This is a more accurate description of the child's abilities than a simple WPM. For example, a child might read a 100-word passage in 52 seconds for a rate of 115 WPM. However, another child might read the same passage in the same length of time but exhibit 18 errors on those 100 words. These two readers are very different.

Simple WPM rates will not adequately describe their skills. The second child actually read only 82 words correctly in 52 seconds, which yields a rate of 95 WCPM. See Appendix 9M in Chapter 9, (page 249) for more information on how to calculate rate.

Hasbrouck and Tindal (1992) report a large-scale study involving 7000 to 9000 students in second through fifth grade from whom data was collected to establish large-scale oral reading fluency norms. These authors describe oral reading fluency as a combination of accuracy and rate. It is expressed as words correct per minute. That normative data is reprinted in the table on page 21.

Curriculum-based norms in oral reading fluency for grades 2 through 5 (medians)

		Fall		*Winter*		*Spring*		
Grade	Percentile	n*	WCPM**	n	WCPM	n	WCPM	SD*** of raw scores
2	75	4	82	5	106	4	124	**39**
	50	6	53	8	78	6	94	
	25	4	23	5	46	4	65	
3	75	4	107	5	123	4	142	**39**
	50	6	79	8	93	6	114	
	25	4	65	5	70	4	87	
4	75	4	125	5	133	4	143	**37**
	50	6	99	8	112	6	118	
	25	4	72	5	89	4	92	
5	75	4	126	5	143	4	151	**35**
	50	6	105	8	118	6	128	
	25	4	77	5	93	4	100	

n* = number of median scores from percentile tables of districts (maximum possible = 8)
WCPM** = words correct per minute
SD*** = the average standard deviation of scores from fall, winter, and spring for each grade level

From "Curriculum Based Norms in Oral Reading" by Jan E. Hasbrouck & Gerald Tindal, *Teaching Exceptional Children*, Spring 1992, pp. 41-44.

Of course, a WCPM can only be obtained on oral reading. On silent reading, a simple WPM can be calculated. However, little normative information is available on silent reading rate. Citations indicate that students typically improve their silent reading rate by 10 to 20 words per minute a year. By high school, students should have a silent reading rate of 200 WPM (plus or minus 20 words).

The *GORT-4* has a subtest on rate; thus, a separate standard score, grade equivalent, age equivalent, and percentile can be obtained. However, it will not provide a words-per-minute or words-correct-per-minute score. The *PRT* allows you to derive a words-correct-per-minute score and gives criterion-referenced information about those rates for each age level, indicating whether the rate indicates frustration, instruction, or mastery level.

Assessing fluency

Unfortunately, there is no standardized test that will determine if a reader can read connected text fluently or non-fluently. Several tests (*GORT-4* and *PRT*) combine the child's reading rate and reading accuracy score into what is called a *fluency score*. Although rate and accuracy are important components of fluency, fluency is really more than just reading accurately and quickly. In their 1995 report, the National Center for Education Statistics summarized the results of their Integrated Reading Performance Record of fourth grade students and stated, "Fluency appears to be more than simply the sum of its parts."

Fluency must be assessed by having the child read aloud and describing what the child sounds like. There is no normative data available, and it is important to remember that beginning readers do not sound fluent. However, by the end of second grade, a proficient reader should sound fluent when reading an "easy" book (one in which the student knows 90 to 95 percent of the words without having to sound them out). This would hold true for subsequent grade levels when reading an easy passage. Fluency is important at any grade level and should not be ignored until later grades.

A checklist might be used to capture the kinds of errors the child is making. Such a checklist might include some of the types of errors described in the paragraph on assessing accuracy (page 19), for the less accurate a child is, the less fluent he is (although, see later discussion concerning students who are accurate but slow). These errors might include:

- substitutions of words
- omissions of words
- insertion of a word that is not in the text
- transposition of words in the sentence
- repetition of words
- repetition of phrases
- self-corrections of errors immediately after reading the word incorrectly
- self-corrections after reading a few more words of the text
- changing the word to a word with a similar meaning

The checklist should also include other factors that appear to contribute to the perception of reading non-fluently, including:

- not showing evidence of gaining meaning from text
- lacking intonation
- failure to use appropriate phrasing

The National Assessment of Educational Progress (NAEP) developed an *Integrated Reading Performance Record Oral Reading Fluency Scale* that attempted to describe levels of fluency. This is a four-point scale that ranges from Level 1, where the reader "reads primarily word-by-word. Occasional two-word or three-word phrases may occur, but these are infrequent and/or they do not preserve the meaningful syntax" to Level 4, where the reader "reads primarily in larger, meaningful phrase groups. Preservation of the author's syntax is consistent. Some or most of the story is read with expressive interpretation."

As can be seen, this scale focuses on several elements:

- attention to accurate phrasing

- intonation and stress to emphasize phrasing
- adherence to author's sentence structure
- expressiveness

This scale does not include errors of accuracy, arguing that even the most fluent of readers make errors as they read, and this does not detract from their comprehending the passage.

Two other informal measures for checking if the student is reading fluently or automatically are to:

- ask him to retell what he remembers about a passage. If he remembers the key elements, he is probably automatic.
- compare his listening comprehension with oral reading comprehension of a similar passage. If they are about the same, he may have achieved automaticity.

See Appendix 2C (page 33) for a *Scoring Guide for Fluency and Expression* (Hoyt 2000). Use this during assessment to record your impression of the student's fluency. The checklist includes factors that contribute to the perception of fluency.

See Appendices 2C and 2D.

In Chapter 1, information was provided about Berninger et al.'s theory of different types of dysfluent readers (page 14). Completing a checklist based on those types of dysfluent readers will provide more detailed information about the child's reading fluency and could also shape the type of intervention provided. See Appendix 2D (page 34) for such a checklist.

Assessing comprehension

Many standardized tools exist to assess reading comprehension. The examiner should select instruments that assess the ability to remember the information (probably most frequently by assessing factual recall), as well as the ability to infer and draw conclusions. The latter is, of course, largely tied to the student's underlying language skills. A discussion of receptive language tools is beyond the scope of this chapter, but it is often necessary to assess a child's language skills to determine why he is having trouble understanding the text read.

The examiner should also choose instruments that assess comprehension of what is read silently, as well as passages read orally. Sometimes a discrepancy will be noted. For instance, if a student is really struggling to read aloud, comprehension may suffer. When that same student reads silently, he may skip hard words rather than stopping to try and decode them. The student may have enough understanding of the topic to be able to answer the questions without having completely read the passage.

The *GORT-4, PRT*, a subtest on the *DAB-3*, *Test of Early Reading Ability* (*TERA-3*), and *TORCS* all assess comprehension of text read aloud. On most of these tests, the questions require factual recall, as well as making inferences and drawing conclusions.

Other tests measure comprehension of material read silently. The *Gray Silent Reading Test* (*GSRT*) and a subtest on the *DAB-3* tap the student's comprehension for factual recall, inferences, and drawing conclusions. The *WRMT-R* yields both a word comprehension and passage comprehension score.

The word comprehension score is derived from three subtests: *Synonyms, Antonyms*, and *Analogies*. These subtests can be analyzed by subject area (e.g., vocabulary related to science or social studies). The *Passage Comprehension* subtest uses a cloze technique. The student must read a sentence or short paragraph and tell a word that makes sense in the blank. This may occur at any point in the passage.

The *Test of Reading Comprehension (TORC-3)* requires the student to read a variety of tasks silently and answer questions or follow directions to determine comprehension. The *TORC-3* assesses both general vocabulary and vocabulary specific to the areas of mathematics, social studies, and science. It also has subtests for *Syntactic Similarities*, *Sentence Sequencing*, and *Paragraph Reading*.

For young children, *TERA-3* has a subtest entitled *Meaning*. This subtest measures comprehension of words, sentences, and paragraphs, as well as relational vocabulary, sentence construction, and paraphrasing.

Assessing the underlying skills for reading

Assessing short-term memory

In order for a student to learn sight words and to hold a word in memory while working to decode it, the student must have adequate short-term and working memory. Short-term memory refers to temporary storage of the information that is being processed. Because it is a temporary storage system, the short-term memory has a limited capacity, and the information cannot be held in that memory for very long. This is called *rapid decay*. Work by several researchers has shown that stimuli are held in short-term memory for no longer than approximately 30 seconds each (Collins and Loftus 1975, Anderson 1980, Lindsay and Norman 1977).

Breznitz (1997) describes the roles which have been attributed to verbal short-term memory in reading. Short-term memory does the following:

- provides a buffer storage system during the process. The buffer storage is used for decoding of unfamiliar words as the student applies graphemes to phoneme rules and sound blending.
- integrates lexical information with the word identification process (e.g., when an unfamiliar word is incompletely decoded or there are multiple pronunciations to choose from)
- integrates information within the sentence and between sentences. This may be attributable to working memory, which is different than short-term memory. Working memory is responsible for active, temporary processing functions (Breznitz 1997).

Other research (Cornwall 1992) has shown that a child's score on a memory task can predict the child's word recognition scores. Therefore, there are many reasons to test short-term memory.

Short-term memory is often assessed via digit repetition, although repetition of other sequences is used as well. The *Comprehensive Test of Phonological Processing* (*CTOPP)* has a measure of short-term memory which is called *phonological memory*. Phonological memory is described as a *phonological loop*. A phonological loop records the most recent two seconds of auditory information and provides the articulatory control process to refresh information already in the loop so it can be stored for longer than two seconds. The authors of the *CTOPP* state that deficits in phonological memory do not necessarily lead to poor reading of familiar material. They may more likely impair decoding of new words, particularly words that are long enough to require decoding bit by bit (e.g., multi-syllabic words). Deficits may also impair listening or reading comprehension for more complex material. The *CTOPP* composite phonological memory is assessed via two subtests: *Repetition of Digits* and *Repetition of Non-words* (i.e., nonsense words of increasing length).

It is interesting to note that memory variables appeared to be more closely related to phonemic awareness than to naming speed (Torgeson et al. 1997, DeJong and Van der Leij 1999). Bowers (2001) points out that, "Variance on tests of either short-term memory or more complex working memory does not seem to overlap with the unique variance contributed to reading by naming speed."

Assessing phonological awareness

Phonological awareness (also sometimes called *phonemic awareness*) is described as the awareness of words, syllables, and phonemes. It is the ability to focus on and manipulate the parts of a word, including phonemes and syllables. These skills may include:

- isolation/identification of phoneme at the beginning or end of the word
- phoneme categorization
- phoneme blending
- phoneme segmentation
- rhyming discrimination
- rhyming production
- sentence segmentation
- blending onset + rime
- phoneme deletion

Tests of phonological awareness add significantly to the prediction of word attack, spelling, and reading comprehension scores (Cornwall 1992, Bowers et al. 1988, Bowers and Swanson 1991). Manis et al. (1999) demonstrated that phonemic awareness was more related to the learning of systematic spelling-sound correspondences.

Many testing instruments are available to assess phonological awareness skills in children of different ages. The *CTOPP* has a phonological awareness composite derived from two or three subtests, depending on the age of the student. For five- and six-year-old children, the three subtests are *Elision*, *Sound Blending*, and *Sound Matching*. For children seven and older, the subtests utilized are *Sound Blending* and *Elision*. There are supplemental subtests on other phonological awareness skills such as *Reversal*, *Blending Non-words*, *Segmenting Words*, and *Segmenting Non-words*.

The Phonological Awareness Test includes subtests on *Rhyming*, *Segmentation*, *Isolation*, *Deletion*, *Substitution*, and *Blending*. A screening version of this test, *The Phonological Awareness Profile,* assesses *Rhyming*, *Segmentation*, *Isolation*, *Deletion*, *Substitution*, and *Blending*. The *Test of Phonological Awareness (TOPA)* can be used with students in kindergarten through second grade to measure a child's awareness of individual sounds in words. The *Lindamood Auditory Conceptualization Test (LAC)* is criterion-referenced and measures the ability to discriminate one phoneme from another and to segment a spoken word into phonemic parts.

A recent study (Catts and Hogan 2002) concludes that assessing phonological awareness is much more important in early grades and not as important in later grades. They state that in kindergarten, testing phonological awareness gives some unique and clinically relevant information about the child's subsequent word recognition skills. In that regard, those tests are useful to provide information for early identification and intervention planning. Even in the primary grades, phonological awareness and word recognition are related. The authors state, "By at least second grade, phonological awareness becomes highly correlated with knowledge and use of sound-symbol correspondence and is difficult to measure independent of phonetic decoding. Regardless, its measurement offers little unique information, and thus should not serve as a primary measure for reading problems." They think that more information is gained from a measure of phonetic decoding, as it gives information "about both decoding and phonological awareness abilities." They do acknowledge, however, that, "Follow-up assessments of phonological awareness (most often with informal probes as opposed to a formal test) in some cases highlight areas of particular weakness in our intervention."

In contrast to Catts and Hogan's view, additional testing of phonological awareness can help in making a determination about the type of intervention to be provided to the student. In addition, additional testing helps with the delineation of which type of reading disorder the student presents (e.g., single deficit versus double deficit). Of course, including a measure of decoding is also important.

Assessing rapid automatized naming

Rapid automatized naming (RAN) or retrieval is assessed by having the student name items that are well-known to the child as quickly as possible. Well-known items are used because the task is not to see if the child knows the name of the item, but to see how quickly the child can retrieve that name. Recent research suggests that RAN may tap into both the language domain (visual and verbal) as well as the executive domain (processing speed) in making its contribution to reading (Denckla and Cutting 1999).

Denckla and Rudel (1974, 1976) demonstrated that children with reading disorders perform differently than children without reading disorders on the speed with which they name numbers, letters, color patches, and line drawings of objects. They were the first to refer to this task as *Rapid Automatized Naming* (RAN). The task was actually first described in 1966 in a paper by Geschwind and Fusillo from their work with an adult who they described as having "pure alexia without agraphia."

The task used by Denckla and Rudel included five target items arranged in five rows of ten items. Spring and Capps (1974) performed similar research and presented some evidence that these differences might be associated with the dysfunctional rehearsal and memory processes of these children. Cornwall (1992) found that in children with severe reading disabilities, rapid letter naming helped to predict word identification and prose passage speed and accuracy scores.

Wolf and her colleagues (Wolf 1984, Wolf et al. 1986) built on this work and showed that naming speed tests for colors and objects predicted reading levels through kindergarten, but after that only numbers and letters continue to predict reading from kindergarten through second grade. Other researchers have shown that naming speed is correlated with several other reading measures, including speed of identifying print words (Biemiller 1977-78, Lovett 1987). Meyer et al. (1998) found that naming speed deficits persisted at least through eighth grade. They suggest that children who have difficulty acquiring basic reading skills in early elementary school and who are deficient in rapid serial naming "can be expected to lag well behind their peers for years to come." Interestingly, adults who had reading disorders as children continue to be slower namers as adults (Felton et al. 1990).

Manis et al. (1999) summarized many of the findings about RAN and indicate that it has been found to be closely associated with:

- word reading accuracy (but not non-word reading)
- word reading latency
- reading rate
- reading comprehension
- orthographic skill

The *CTOPP* has a *Rapid Naming* composite comprised of two subtests. For children ages 5 and 6, the two tasks used are color naming and object naming. For students ages 7 through 24, letters and numbers are used. The student is instructed to name these items pictured on the page as quickly as possible.

Some authors describe assessment of fluency-based measures that are different from the standard rapid automatized naming tasks. For example, Kame'enui et al. (2001) described fluency-based measures they used that included measures developed by Kaminski and Good in 1996 which were called *Dynamic Indicators of Basic Early Literacy Skills* (DIBELS). These included *Letter Naming Fluency*, *Onset Recognition Fluency*, *Phonemic Segmentation Fluency*, and *Nonsense Word Fluency*.

Since the double-deficits hypothesis is a relatively new concept in reading, much research continues to take place concerning the hypothesis and the relationship of rapid automatized naming to the disorder. For example, Waber (2001) found in one study, "Although the RAN reliably predicts reading rate independent of accuracy, and it appears to measure processing speed, rate itself does not appear to be the determining component." This author, among others, points out that slow naming speed is characteristic of children with learning impairments in general and is not specific to dyslexia. She hypothesizes that naming speed will likely be found to reflect different underlying processes in different children. For more information concerning current research in this area, read *Dyslexia, Fluency, and the Brain* (2001) by Maryanne Wolf.

Assessing semantics

There are many tools available for children of different ages to assess their comprehension of word meaning (semantics). These include *The WORD Test-R (Elementary), The WORD Test—Adolescent, Language Processing Test—Revised (LPT-R), TOSS-P (Test of Semantic Skills—Primary), TOSS-I (Test of Semantic Skills—Intermediate), Test of Language Competence (TLC),* and subtests of the *Clinical Evaluation of Language Fundamentals (CELF-3).*

Assessing vocabulary

This is another area well known and understood by speech-language pathologists (SLPs). Both receptive and expressive vocabulary can be tested. However, in reading, it seems most pertinent to know what the child's receptive skills are. The *Peabody Picture Vocabulary Test—Third Edition* (*PPVT-III*) is a receptive test of vocabulary as is the *Receptive One-Word Picture Vocabulary Test (ROWPVT)*. The *Expressive One-Word Picture Vocabulary Test (EOWPVT)* provides a look at the child's expressive skills. The *Comprehensive Receptive and Expressive Vocabulary Test (CREVT-2)* assesses both receptive and expressive skills.

Assessing understanding and use of syntax/sentence structure

Good readers tend to be more sensitive to constraints of the text, such as sentence structure. Therefore, a good understanding of sentence structure may aid the student in gaining fluency and speed. When text is easier or more predictable, the student's eyes can pause more briefly on each word (Adams and Henry 1997). Good readers, however, do not skip text because of familiarity with syntax. The *CELF-3* has a receptive subtest called *Sentence Assembly* that requires the student to unscramble words and phrases to make two different sentences. This yields some information about the student's grasp of syntax.

Assessing other language areas

The SLP may choose to assess other areas of language comprehension and expression that may have an impact on a particular student's ability to read fluently.

Summary

Determining if a student has trouble with reading fluency is not achieved by looking at a single test score. Instead, multiple pieces of information are gathered and analyzed to reach this conclusion. Listening to the student read and comparing how that student sounds to same-age peers without reading difficulties may provide the easiest way to determine that the child does not read fluently. The standardized measures must then be administered and analyzed to try to determine causes for the non-fluency and to establish a treatment plan.

List of Appendices for Chapter 2

Assessing the Components of Reading

Area being assessed	Tests to consider
Reading accuracy	*Gray Oral Reading Tests (GORT-4)* *Phonics Based Reading Test (PRT)* *Test of Oral Reading and Comprehension Skills (TORCS)*
Decoding skills	*Woodcock Reading Mastery Tests—Revised (WRMT-R)* *Phonics Based Reading Test (PRT)*
Sight word recognition	*Diagnostic Achievement Battery-3 (DAB-3)* *Spadafore Diagnostic Reading Test (SDRT)* *Test of Word Reading Efficiency (TOWRE)* *Woodcock Reading Mastery Tests—Revised (WRMT-R)*
Reading rate	*Gray Oral Reading Tests (GORT-4)* *Phonics Based Reading Test (PRT)*
Fluency	*Gray Oral Reading Tests (GORT-4)* *Phonics Based Reading Test (PRT)*
Comprehension of text read aloud	*Diagnostic Achievement Battery-3 (DAB-3)* *Gray Oral Reading Tests (GORT-4)* *Phonics Based Reading Test (PRT)* *Test of Oral Reading and Comprehension Skills (TORCS)* *Test of Early Reading Ability (TERA-3)* *Woodcock Reading Mastery Tests—Revised (WRMT-R)*
Comprehension of vocabulary and text read silently	*Diagnostic Achievement Battery-3 (DAB-3)* *Gray Silent Reading Tests (GSRT)* *Test of Early Reading Ability (TERA-3)* *Test of Reading Comprehension (TORC-3)* *Woodcock Reading Mastery Tests—Revised (WRMT-R)*
Short-term memory	*Comprehensive Test of Phonological Processing (CTOPP)*
Phonological awareness	*Comprehensive Test of Phonological Processing (CTOPP)* *Lindamood Auditory Conceptualization Test (LAC)* *Test of Phonological Awareness (TOPA)* *The Phonological Awareness Profile* *The Phonological Awareness Test*
Rapid automatized naming	*Comprehensive Test of Phonological Processing (CTOPP)*
Semantics	*Clinical Evaluation of Language Fundamentals (CELF-3)* *The WORD Test-R (Elementary)* *The WORD Test—Adolescent* *Language Processing Test—Revised (LPT-R)* *Test of Language Competence (TLC)* *Test of Semantic Skills—Primary (TOSS-P)*
Vocabulary	*Comprehensive Receptive and Expressive Vocabulary Test (CREVT-2)* *Expressive One-Word Picture Vocabulary Test (EOWPVT-R)* *Peabody Picture Vocabulary Test—Third Edition (PPVT-III)* *Receptive One-Word Picture Vocabulary Test (ROWPVT-R)*
Understanding and use of syntax/sentence structure	*Clinical Evaluation of Language Fundamentals (CELF-3)*

Resource Guide of Assessment Instruments Cited

***Clinical Evaluation of Language Fundamentals* (CELF-3)**
Ages: 6 through 21
The Psychological Corporation
19500 Bulverde Road
San Antonio TX 78259
1-800-872-1726

***Comprehensive Receptive and Expressive Vocabulary Test* (CREVT-2)**
Ages: 4 through 89
Pro Ed
8700 Shoal Creek Blvd.
Austin TX 78757-6897
1-800-897-3202

***Comprehensive Test of Phonological Processing* (CTOPP)**
Ages: 5 through 24
Pro-Ed
8700 Shoal Creek Blvd.
Austin TX 78757-6897
1-800-897-3202

***Diagnostic Achievement Battery—3* (DAB-3)**
Ages: 6 through 14
Pro-Ed
8700 Shoal Creek Blvd.
Austin TX 78757-6897
1-800-897-3202

***Expressive One-Word Picture Vocabulary Test* (EOWPVT)**
Ages: 2 through 18
Academic Therapy Publications
20 Commercial Blvd.
Novato CA 94949
1-800-422-7249

***Gray Oral Reading Tests* (GORT-4)**
Ages: 6 through 18
Pro-Ed
8700 Shoal Creek Blvd.
Austin TX 78757-6897
1-800-897-3202

***Gray Silent Reading Tests* (GSRT)**
Ages: 7 through 25
Pro-Ed
8700 Shoal Creek Blvd.
Austin TX 78757-6897
1-800-897-3202

***Language Processing Test—Revised* (LPT-R)**
Ages: 5-0 through 11-11
LinguiSystems
3100 4th Avenue
East Moline IL 61244-9700
1-800-PRO-IDEA

***Lindamood Auditory Conceptualization Test* (LAC)**
Ages: early preschool through adult
Pro-Ed
8700 Shoal Creek Blvd.
Austin TX 78757-6897
1-800-897-3202

***Peabody Picture Vocabulary Test—Third Edition* (PPVT-III)**
Ages: 2 1/2 through 90+
AGS
4201 Woodland Road
Circle Pines MN 55014
1-800-328-2560

***Phonics Based Reading Test* (PRT)**
Grades: 1 through 6
Academic Therapy Publications
20 Commercial Blvd.
Novato CA 94949
1-800-422-7249

***Receptive One-Word Picture Vocabulary Test* (ROWPVT)**
Ages: 2 through 18
Academic Therapy Publications
20 Commercial Blvd.
Novato CA 94949
1-800-422-7249

Resource Guide of Assessment Instruments Cited, *continued*

***Spadafore Diagnostic Reading Test* (SDRT)**
Ages: 6 through adult
Academic Therapy Publications
20 Commercial Blvd.
Novati CA 94949
1-800-422-7249

***Test of Early Reading Ability* (TERA-3)**
Ages: 3-6 through 8-6
Pro-Ed
8700 Shoal Creek Blvd.
Austin TX 78757-6897
1-800-897-3202

***Test of Language Competence* (TLC)**
Ages: 5 through 18
The Psychological Corporation
19500 Bulverde Road
San Antonio TX 78259
1-800-872-1726

***Test of Oral Reading and Comprehension Skills* (TORCS)**
Ages: 5-4 though 14-11
Academic Therapy Publications
20 Commercial Blvd.
Novati CA 94949
1-800-422-7249

***Test of Reading Comprehension* (TORC-3)**
Ages: 7 through 17
Pro Ed
8700 Shoal Creek Blvd.
Austin TX 78757-6897
1-800-897-3202

***Test of Semantic Skills—Primary* (TOSS-P)**
Ages: 4-0 through 8-11
LinguiSystems
3100 4th Avenue
East Moline IL 61244-9700
1-800-PRO-IDEA

***Test of Semantic Skills—Intermediate* (TOSS-I)**
Ages: 9-0 through 13-11
LinguiSystems
3100 4th Avenue
East Moline IL 61244-9700
1-800-PRO-IDEA

***Test of Word Reading Efficiency* (TOWRE)**
Ages: 6 through 24
Pro-Ed
8700 Shoal Creek Blvd.
Austin TX 78757-6897
1-800-897-3202

***Test of Phonological Awareness* (TOPA)**
Grades: K through 2
Pro-Ed
8700 Shoal Creek Blvd.
Austin TX 78757-6897
1-800-897-3202

The Phonological Awareness Profile
Ages: 5 through 14
LinguiSystems
3100 4th Avenue
East Moline IL 61244-9700
1-800-PRO-IDEA

The Phonological Awareness Test
Ages: 5 through 14
LinguiSystems
3100 4th Avenue
East Moline IL 61244-9700
1-800-PRO-IDEA

The WORD Test-R (Elementary)
Ages: 6-0 through 11-11
LinguiSystems
3100 4th Avenue
East Moline IL 61244-9700
1-800-PRO-IDEA

The WORD Test—Adolescent
Ages: 12-0 through 17-11
LinguiSystems
3100 4th Avenue
East Moline IL 61244-9700
1-800-PRO-IDEA

***Woodcock Reading Mastery Tests—Revised* (WRMT-R)**
Ages: 5 through 75+
AGS
4201 Woodland Road
Circle Pines MN 55014
1-800-328-2560

Scoring Guide for Fluency and Expression

_____ **5**

The reader reads with expression.

The rate matches the style of the text.

The reader adjusts tone and emphasis to reflect meaning.

The reading reflects an understanding of audience.

Pauses are used for emphasis.

Self-corrections and fix-up strategies are employed so smoothly the listener does not notice them.

_____ **3**

There is some expressiveness in the reading.

There is an attempt to match the rate to the text.

The reader may over-exaggerate tone in an attempt to be dramatic.

The reader is concentrating so much on the print that there is only some connection to the audience.

There are pauses for word recognition rather than to emphasize meaning.

Disruptions may occur as the reader attempts to implement reading strategies.

_____ **1**

The reader reads word-by-word in a monotone.

There is no evidence of changes in tone, speed, or inflection to match meaning.

The pace is slow and not reflective of the text.

There are frequent pauses for sound outs, repeats of words, and time to look at pictures to construct meaning.

Note: If a child exhibits characteristics at one level and some characteristics at a different level, you might assign him a score between those two numbers.

Appendix 2D

Types of Dysfluent Readers Checklist

Name ______________________________ Date ______________

Check each characteristic observed during oral reading. Information in parentheses after each type indicates the approach to intervention.

Type 1: Processing Rate/Efficiency Impaired (Practice reading.)

_____ Rarely makes mistakes

_____ Is painfully slow

Type 2: Automaticity Impaired (Improve connections between stimuli and responses; give feedback on rate and accuracy during reading.)

_____ Is inaccurate and slow

_____ Makes false starts

_____ Hesitates

_____ Fills pauses (e.g., "um")

_____ Repeats

_____ Self-monitors/self-corrects

Type 3: Executive Coordination Impaired (Instruct in meta-cognitive strategies for self-monitoring and self-correction.)

_____ Shows inattention to orthography

_____ Shows inattention to morphology

_____ Shows inattention to serial order of words

_____ Shows inattention to prosody

_____ Shows inattention to self-monitoring of meaning

_____ Rarely self-corrects

Adapted from Berninger et al. 2001

Chapter 3

Treating Reading Fluency

After identifying a student as having a reading fluency disorder, you must establish an appropriate plan for intervention. In the framework of the double-deficit hypothesis, you will encounter students who have a deficit in naming speed only (i.e., fluency only) and children who also have phonological awareness/processing deficits (Wolf and Bowers' classic double deficit). The third type of student in the framework, the one with adequate naming speed but poor phonological awareness, is not addressed in this book. Therefore, your treatment plan for the child with deficits in both phonological processing and naming speed (double deficit) would require much more emphasis on activities to improve phonological awareness and processing than your treatment plan for a child with naming speed deficits only.

The activities described in this book for improving fluency have been selected based on a model called the connectionist theory (Adams 1990, Seidenberg 1990). This theory, or model, indicates that the reading process involves parallel activation of three subsystems:

- phonological
- orthographic
- semantic

This theory indicates that weaknesses beyond the phonological level (i.e., orthographic and semantic) are also responsible for part of the student's difficulties with fluency. Therefore, we will address activities designed to improve the student's skill in each of these three areas.

As the model would indicate, for either type of child (fluency only or double deficit), phonological awareness skills cannot be ignored. In the development of their comprehensive, fluency-based reading intervention program, RAVE-O, Wolf et al. (2000) state, "The double-deficit hypothesis' two-fold emphasis on phonological skills and on fluency and automaticity builds on past treatment models of phonological awareness and decoding skills, but it adds to them a new stress on rate of processing in each component skill and reading outcome." Thus, for all children with reading deficits, it is important to address their phonological awareness (and/or their decoding skills) to the degree indicated. Some children with significant phonological awareness (or decoding deficits) will need much work on building the basics of phonological awareness skills. If those children also have naming-speed deficits and are therefore likely perceived as non-fluent readers, those children will need additional work on activities designed specifically to increase fluency.

Students with naming-speed deficit only (fluency only) are perceived as non-fluent, in part because they have not achieved a level of automaticity with their phonological awareness/decoding skills. Therefore, one cannot treat fluency in a vacuum, ignoring the importance of helping the fluency-only student achieve automaticity with phonological processing. That is why many of the activities described in this chapter and in the subsequent chapters will include those that should help the student achieve an automatic level with these processing skills.

An example of this type of student is one who can complete phonological awareness activities such as blending and deletion, but who does so with great effort and/or in a much longer time than same-age peers. This type of child will often achieve an adequate score on tests of phonological awareness and/or word attack because these tests do not account for the length of time it takes the student to complete the task. This might be exhibited by long latencies before attempting the task or by a struggle with multiple attempts and self-corrections. They demonstrate the skill, but obviously not at an automatic level.

For the fluency-only child with adequate phonological awareness skills but impaired naming speed/fluency, intervention needs to address phonological awareness skills only to increase the speed with which the child can complete such activities (i.e., helping the child achieve automaticity). The majority of time in intervention must be spent on the activities specifically designed to increase fluency (e.g., repeat reading, page speed drills).

Type of deficit	Intervention		
	Develop basic phonological awareness skills	Address phonological awareness skills to achieve automaticity	Use activities to improve fluency of reading
Adequate phonological awareness skills and poor rapid naming/fluency (fluency only)		X	X
Poor phonological awareness and poor rapid naming/fluency (double deficit)	X	X	X

The development of basic phonological awareness skills will not be addressed in depth in this book, as there are many commercially-available materials to address the development of these skills in students of all ages. Instead, this chapter will discuss ways to use such materials to help a student achieve automaticity. The materials cited are but a few examples of the materials available. These examples are provided in order to help you develop expertise at using phonological awareness materials for the student with adequate phonological awareness skills who needs to achieve automaticity.

In addition, this chapter will discuss the importance of increasing the student's ability to recognize written letter patterns and syllable patterns. Although these two skills might be included under the heading of phonological awareness skills, they are highlighted because they are essential skills if a student is to achieve automaticity. Additional materials are provided in subsequent chapters.

This chapter will also address other activities designed to improve fluency. When applicable, the evidence basis for these activities will be cited. These are activities for which there are few, if any, commercially-available products. Activities such as repeat reading, improved stress and intonation drills, improved word identification tactics, page speed drills, and other activities to increase attention to text are discussed here. Many of these activities have been designed to address the different types of errors made by the non-fluent reader.

Building phonological awareness skills

To organize a discussion of adapting materials to build automaticity, we will use the list of phonological awareness skills in Chapter 2 (page 25):

- identification of phoneme at the beginning and end of word
- categorization of phonemes
- blending phonemes in a word
- segmenting words
- rhyming discrimination
- rhyming production
- segmenting sentences
- blending onset + rime
- phoneme deletion

Because some of the skills listed above are basic and are developed by very young students, we will not address them here. Instead, we will address those phonological awareness skills that seem most important for achieving levels of automaticity. They are as follows:

- blending phonemes in a word
- segmenting words
- blending onset + rime
- phoneme deletion

When using materials that are designed to build phonological awareness with a student who has adequate phonological awareness skills but has not achieved automaticity, the materials are used as designed with two exceptions:

- The student must complete the activities multiple times until he is able to do so quickly and automatically.
- After some level of quickness is achieved, the student should be asked to complete the activities under time constraints to force automaticity. This is especially important with students for whom the "wheels seem to turn slowly." This type of student seems to process all material slowly and deliberately and needs to be forced to speed up processing.

A list of computer games and other materials to help build automaticity of phonological awareness skills can be found in Appendices 3A (pages 46-47) and 3B (page 48).

See Appendices 3A and 3B.

It is important to remember that phonological awareness skills are not taught for the sake of achieving better phonological awareness skills. Rather, as the National Reading Panel Report (2000) points out, "Acquiring phonemic awareness is a means rather than an end. Phonemic awareness is not acquired for its own sake, but rather for its value in helping children understand and use the alphabetic system to read and write. That is why including letters in the process of teaching children to manipulate phonemes is important."

Blending phonemes in words

There are many materials that help students practice blending sounds into words. You must determine the level at which your student needs to work to achieve automaticity. The types of syllable structures yield a natural continuum against which to compare your student's skills:

- VC up
- CV pie
- CVC cat
- VCC ask
- CCV stay
- CCVC stop
- CVCC cats
- CCVCC stops

Your student should be able to blend any of those types of syllables when the word is read to her phoneme by phoneme (e.g., */k/ /a/ /t/ /s/*). Her brain should be able to hear the individual sounds in the syllable and blend them into a cohesive unit.

Some materials add a visual component to the blending activity. For instance, they have the student manipulate colored blocks to represent each of the sounds in the syllable. Use of colored blocks is an abstract activity that some children find quite challenging. A more concrete adaptation is to have the student blend the phonemes when they are represented by graphemes. Still other approaches use motor movements to represent each of the sounds the student has heard. For instance, the teacher might clap for each phoneme he says to help the children hear the different parts of the syllable.

Thus far, we have described blending activities as consisting of the instructor saying the sounds and words, the student listening, and the student responding verbally. Blending, or any of the other phonological awareness skills mentioned on pages 39-40, can become an auditory-visual activity if manipulatives are utilized. Although it is a somewhat artificial categorization, in this book we will describe phonological awareness skills that utilize letter patterns presented visually in the section *Increasing speed and accuracy of decoding/word attack skills* on page 41. This delineation does not imply that utilizing letter patterns changes the activity from a phonological awareness activity to a decoding activity. It is really impossible to separate these two skills once the child is reading. In the pre-reader, when phonological awareness skills are presented totally through the auditory mode, it is easier to see the differentiation. However, even for young children, it is noted that teaching phonological awareness with letters helps students acquire phonological awareness more effectively than when the skills are taught without letters (National Reading Panel 2000).

Blending activities do not have to be done only with real words. Nonsense syllables can be used as well. In fact, for the older student who is already familiar with the spelling of words, using nonsense syllables may free the student to concentrate on the sounds being heard.

Blending activities can be done with multisyllabic words. However, this is a bit redundant. By the time students' brains can hear up to five phonemes (CCVCC) and blend them into a cohesive syllable or word, working on the skill at higher levels does not appear to yield much extra gain.

Segmenting syllables or words

Most materials that address sound blending also address segmentation. That is because segmenting is the opposite skill to blending. Segmentation is the ability to take apart a syllable or word and pronounce it phoneme by phoneme. For older children who are already spellers, it is sometimes more difficult for them to segment a word than it is to spell it. For example, when asked to segment the word *pie*, the student is likely to say *p - i - e*. She may need instruction in understanding the difference between the sounds in a word and the letters in the spelling of the word. This is another instance in which beginning with nonsense syllables may be helpful before asking the students to segment real words.

Segmentation seems to be a particularly important skill for spelling. In order to be able to spell a word the student has heard pronounced, it is necessary to be able to break that word into its component sounds. In addition, segmenting is crucial to decoding unknown words when encountered in text.

Materials that use manipulatives, such as blocks or letter tiles, seem particularly well-suited to working on segmentation skills. This manipulation forces the student to select a block or letter tile to represent each sound that is heard. This visual representation of segmentation is helpful to many students. Clapping or tapping by the student for each sound heard as she divides the word into its component phonemes can also be helpful.

Blending onset + rime

Being able to blend individual phonemes into a syllable/word and being able to break that syllable/word into its individual phonemes (segmentation) are very important skills. However, students don't begin to achieve automaticity in reading until they move to the level of recognizing larger parts of words instead of individual phonemes. At the most basic level, and occurring in very young students, is the ability to blend an initial sound with a common word ending. This is referred to as *onset + rime*. The rime is the common word ending. For example, the rime can be the ending for the words: *fit*, *hit*, *pit*, *mit*, *lit*, *sit*, *bit*. The ability to blend onset + rime is what makes young children able to rhyme. Preschool children who delight in making up nonsense rhyming words are demonstrating the ability to blend an onset + rime.

Of course, using an onset with two phonemes (as in a blend *st* or in a digraph *sh*) is a little more difficult than using an onset with a single consonant. When completing onset + rime activities, it is acceptable for the student to produce a nonsense word. However, it is important to point out to the student that although she has produced a word that rhymes, it is not a real word.

Examples of onset + rime

Onset	Rime	Words
b f p sp	in	bin fin pin spin
d l s tr sh	ip	dip lip sip trip ship
c m dr st	op	cop mop drop stop

In the vocabulary of the reading specialist, *onset + rime* is often called a *word family.* Numerous materials exist that help the student practice blending the initial sound with the word ending. These materials are often available at school supply stores and are certainly available in reading catalogs (Appendix 3C, page 49).

See Appendix 3C.

Phoneme deletion

On a phoneme deletion task, the student is asked to listen to a word, then to delete one of the phonemes and tell what word is left. For example, the student is instructed to say the word *stop.* Then the student is asked to "say the word *stop,* but don't say the /*s*/." The student is expected to be able to determine that what remains after deleting the phoneme /*s*/ is the word *top*. This is a very basic phoneme deletion example. The chart below provides other examples of how a phoneme deletion task can become more complex.

Say:	**Say it again, but don't say:**	**What the word becomes**
blend	/l/	bend
cast	/s/	cat
break	/r/	bake
sweater	/s/	wetter
box	/k/	boss
place	/l/	pace

Organizing your approach to working on phonemic awareness skills

Should you work on one phonemic awareness skill at a time until it is mastered at the level of automaticity? Or is it advisable to work on the development of all of the skills at the same time? You'll probably need to make this determination based on your student's ability. If you're working with a student who has a double deficit, and she is mastering these phonological awareness skills at the basic level, there is some evidence to indicate that you will achieve a larger effect when focusing on one or two skills rather than a multi-skill approach (National Reading Panel 2000). However, when you're working with a fluency-only student who already demonstrates competence in phonological awareness skills, it would seem appropriate to use a multi-skill approach.

How do you create time pressure to "force" automaticity?

Use either a stopwatch or a timer that counts down and then alarms as a helpful tool with any timed activity. Two approaches to timing an activity follow:

- **Counting up**: Select a given number of stimuli (e.g., a column of 10 or a list of 20) and time how long it takes the student to complete these. Then have the student complete an equal number of stimuli (e.g., another column of 10 or another list of 20) and, once again, time how long it takes the student to complete the set. The goal, of course, is for the student to shorten the time on subsequent trials.

Following the premise upon which repeat reading is based (see Chapter 9), it may be beneficial to have the student repeat the same set of stimuli several times in a row. For example, have the student complete a set of 10 syllables on a segmentation task. Time how long it takes her to complete this task. Then, have the student complete the same set of 10 words again on the segmentation task. Time her again. This should help build her confidence and is particularly helpful with the student who needs to be forced into automaticity.

- **Counting down**: When counting down, you should use the timer that has an audible alarm at the end of the allotted time. A preset time is determined and set on the alarm. For instance, you'll ask the student to work for one minute. The student then begins the activity and continues working until the alarm sounds. The goal is to see how far along the student has gotten before the allotted time is up. You might read a list of nonsense syllables to the student one sound at a time and ask her to blend the sounds and tell you what the syllable is. When the alarm goes off, mark on the list how many words the student was able to complete in the minute. Then try the task again, with either the same set of stimuli based on the premise described above, or with a different set of stimuli. See if the student can get further in the minute.

Increasing speed and accuracy of decoding/word attack skills

Decoding, or word attack, skills are closely related to phonological awareness skills. Decoding is the ability to look at a syllable or word and sound it out. Tests of phonological awareness add significantly to the prediction of word attack, spelling, and reading comprehension scores (Cornwall 1992, Bowers et al., 1988, Bowers and Swanson 1991). Manis et al. (1999) demonstrated that phonemic awareness was more related to the learning of systematic spelling-sound correspondences, which is a necessary part of word attack/decoding. In fact, Catts and Hogan (2002) indicate that by at least second grade, phonological awareness becomes highly correlated with knowledge and use of sound-symbol correspondence and is difficult to measure independent of phonetic decoding.

Word attack/decoding activities will use the printed letter or letters (graphemes), whereas phonological awareness skills do not always use the grapheme. Some of the activities listed in the section previously concerning phonological awareness will also be mentioned in Chapters 4, 5, and 6. The National Reading Panel Report (2000) stresses the importance of using print when working on these skills. The more easily a child is able to recognize larger parts of the word, the more quickly she will be able to decode what she is reading. Moving the child beyond reading at the letter-by-letter level is essential if the child is to achieve automaticity.

Chapters 4, 5, and 6 will describe activities to:

- increase the speed of reading written letter patterns
- increase the speed of reading simple and complex syllables
- increase the speed of recognition of syllables in multisyllabic words

These chapters will discuss the rationale for these activities as well as provide materials that can be used. The chapters will also highlight other commercially-available materials, including software, that addresses these skills.

Increasing speed of sight word identification

Another important avenue to achieving automaticity is to build the child's sight word vocabulary. Fluent readers decode very few words. Instead, they continually commit more and more words to their sight word vocabulary. One of the most noticeable features about non-fluent readers is that they may recognize and read a word in one line and fail to recognize the same word when it occurs later in the passage. Obviously, they have not committed that word to their sight word vocabulary. Still other non-fluent readers seem to recognize the words, but it takes that extra second or two to do so when they are reading connected text.

Therefore, the more words a student can quickly and easily recognize (i.e., those that are included in her sight word vocabulary), the more fluently the student will read. There are several published lists that are often used to build sight vocabulary. The most common are the Fry 1000 Most Common Words list and the Dolch list. Activities in Chapter 7 will help build a student's sight word vocabulary.

Increasing speed of word retrieval

Many authors believe that skillful reading of words requires not only good understanding of orthography and phonology but also of meaning and context. Having a good grasp on meaning is easier for the student who has adequate word retrieval skills and a good understanding of multiple meanings of words. Some researchers have wondered whether a naming-speed deficit is actually a reflection of broader word-finding problems, one that might be exhibited on a test of confrontation naming. Research has yielded mixed results in an attempt to answer this question. Several researchers argue for the importance of working on word retrieval, as improving these skills may generalize to other processing speed tasks.

There are a multitude of materials and strategies for helping a student improve her word retrieval skills. This is typically a language-based activity. However, it does have some impact on fluency of reading related to the student's facility with multiple meanings, in particular. When a student encounters a word with multiple meanings, she must decide which meaning is applicable in this particular situation. The more efficiently the student can accomplish that, the more efficiently and fluently she can continue reading the text. Activities in Chapter 8 will focus mostly on words with multiple meanings.

Increasing speed and fluency of connected reading

This is where, as the common phrase puts it, "the rubber hits the road." The goal of all the activities described thus far and those which will be described in Chapter 9 is to make the student more fluent when reading. Many studies cited in the literature describe how important it is to work with students using connected text, in addition to the activities described thus far. Chapter 9 will describe activities that will help different types of non-fluent readers. For example, some students will need to improve their ability to attend to orthography and morphology as well as the serial order of words. Other students will need to improve their ability to self-monitor and self-correct. Still others may need to pay closer attention to prosody or to monitoring the meaning of what is being read.

Coordinating activities to work on improved fluency

How do you know what to work on when? This is very individualized, but there are some general guidelines depending on the type of disorder presented by the child.

For the child with a double deficit, begin with heavy emphasis on phonological awareness skills, making sure to pair the printed letter with the auditory task as often as possible. For students in first and second grade, the phonological awareness activities will be of utmost importance if this has been identified as a deficit area. For children in third grade and up, this work will probably take the form of decoding activities (which will also build phonological awareness skills). At the same time, you can start word identification activities and perhaps some connected reading. Some younger students may be so non-fluent that they cannot start work on connected reading until later in treatment. You may have to begin with echo reading (Appendix 9B, page 238).

The next skill to address would be the quick recognition of letter patterns. You do not have to wait until this is established to begin work on syllable patterns. As the child begins to show some mastery of letter pattern and syllable pattern recognition, you can introduce word retrieval activities. Work on multi-syllabic words will need to wait until the child has mastery over many syllable patterns. Continue to work on letter patterns and syllable patterns as needed. Work on phonological awareness skills (or decoding), sight word recognition, word retrieval, and connected reading continues throughout treatment. The flow sheet below illustrates how these treatment activities might be integrated.

Double-deficit student

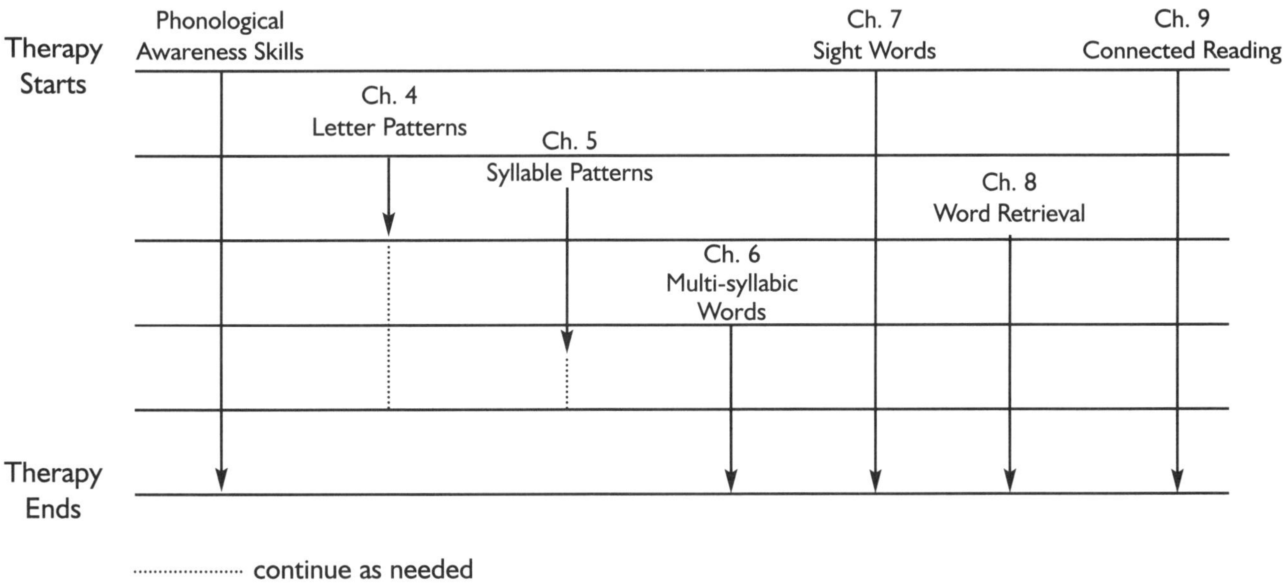

The pattern of intervention might be somewhat different for a child with a fluency-only disorder. One major difference is that much less time will be spent on phonological awareness skills, as fluency-only children already have adequate phonological awareness skills. You will address the phonological awareness skills only to achieve greater speed and automaticity. Work on letter pattern recognition can begin at the start of therapy, as can work on sight word recognition, word retrieval, and connected reading. Work on syllable pattern recognition should begin after letter pattern recognition has become more automatic, and multi-syllabic work will begin after some level of automaticity has been achieved with syllable patterns. The flow sheet on the next page shows how these activities might be integrated for a fluency-only student.

Fluency-only student

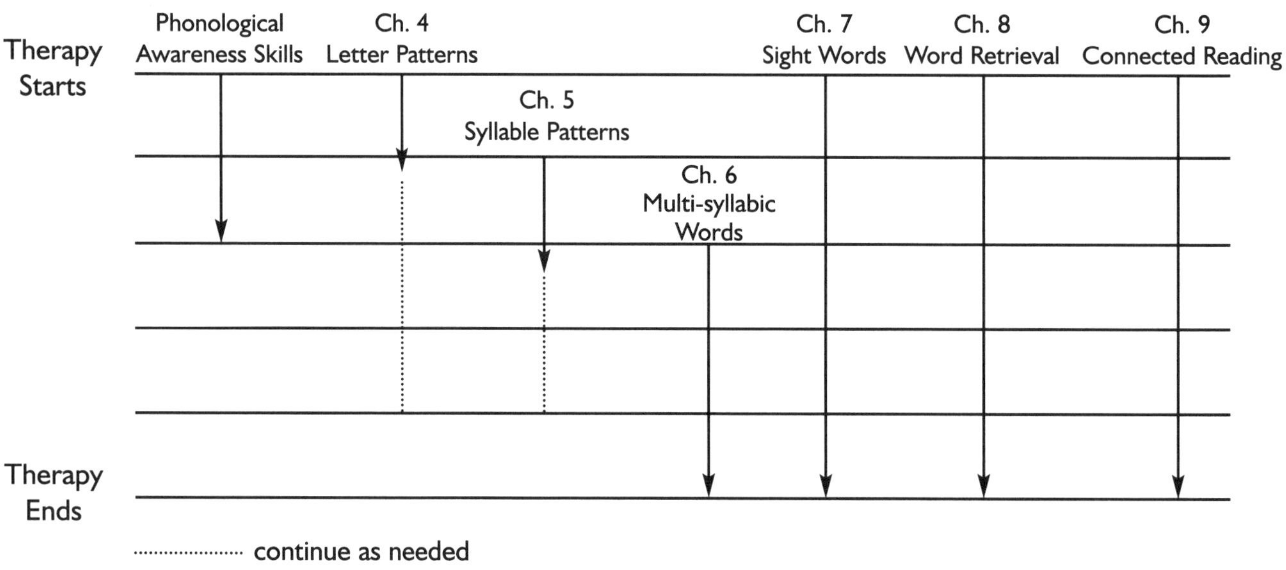

Keeping the student motivated

When using the activities in any of the subsequent chapters, you might use the reinforcement sheet *I'm Working Hard to Be a Better Reader* (Appendix 3D, page 50). You can use this sheet to collect data on any individual skills (e.g., page speed drills, words in sight word vocabulary, how many word families can be quickly recognized). You can also write in the dates of therapy and reward the student for an overall good therapy session by filling in the path to the bookmobile.

See Appendix 3D.

List of Appendices for Chapter 3

Computer Games

Games	Phoneme blending	Phoneme segmentation	Onset+ rime	Sound deletion	Timed
Earobics Step 1					
Katy Caterpillar	X				X
Rap a Taps		X			X
Rhyming Frog			X		X
Earobics Step 2					
Duck Luck	X	X	X	X	X
Paint by Penguin		X			X
Pesky Parrots	X			X	X
Earobics Adolescent/Adult					
Connectivity	X				X
Get Rhythm		X			X
Rhyme Time			X		X
Lexia PB—Level 1					
Bridge		X			X
Consonant Castle	X	X	X		
Lexia PB—Level 2					
Change		X			
Lexia PB—Level 3					
Pirate Ship	X				
Super Change		X			
Word Stairs	X				
Lexia SOS—Level 1					
Consonant Blast	X	X			
Short Vowel Trap	X	X			X
Lexia SOS—Level 2					
Find and Combine	X	X			
Letter Switch	X	X			
Lexia SOS—Level 3					
At the Mall		X			
Sea Hunt	X	X			X

Chart continued on next page.

Computer Games, *continued*

Games	Phoneme blending	Phoneme segmentation	Onset+ rime	Sound deletion	Timed
Reading Blaster—Ages 4-6					
Clam Shell	X				
Sand Dollar				X	
Hidden Pics				X	
Reading Blaster—Ages 6-7					
Toy Train	X				
Reading Blaster—Ages 7-8					
Volcano Drop			X	X	
Reader Rabbit—Learn to Read with Phonics					
Dandy's Tree House	X	X			
Decorator Crabs	X	X			
Falling Peacenuts	X				
Grandpa's Moat	X	X			
Kelp Forest			X		
Reader's Basement			X		
Roaring Heights		X			

For information on where to obtain these materials, see the Resources list on pages 260-262.

Other Materials

Materials	Phoneme blending	Phoneme segmentation	Onset+ rime	Sound deletion	Timed
Blend It, End It			X		
Lindamood Phoneme Sequencing Program (LiPS)	X	X			
Phonemic Awareness Activities for Early Reading Success	X	X	X		
Phonemic Awareness Word Recognition	X	X	X		
Seeing Stars	X	X	X	X	
Silly Sounds Playground	X	X	X	X	
Sounds Abound	X	X		X	
The Phonological Awareness Kit (Primary)	X	X		X	
Word Families			X		

For information on where to obtain these materials, see the Resources list on pages 260-262.

Reading Catalogs

AGS
4201 Woodland Road
Circle Pines MN 55014-1796
1-800-328-2569
www.agsnet.com

Carson-Dellosa
PO Box 35665
Greensboro NC 27425-5665
1-800-321-0943
www.carsondellosa.com

Didax
395 Main Street
Rowley MA 01969-1207
1-800-458-0024
www.didaxinc.com

Gander Educational Publishing
412 Higuera Street
Suite 200
San Luis Obispo CA 93401
1-800-554-1819
www.ganderpublishing.com

Jamestown Education
4255 West Touhy Avenue
Lincolnwood IL 60646-1975
1-800-323-4900
1-847-679-2497
www.glencoe.com/gln/jamestown

LinguiSystems, Inc.
3100 4th Avenue
East Moline IL 61244-9700
1-800-776-4332
www.linguisystems.com

Pro-Ed
8700 Shoal Creek Blvd
Austin TX 78757-6897
1-800-897-3202
www.proedinc.com

Remedia Publications
15887 North 76th Street, No. 120
Scottsdale AZ 85260
1-800-826-4740
www.rempub.com

Riverside Publishing
425 Spring Lake Drive
Itasca IL 60143-2079
1-800-323-9540
www.riversidepublishing.com

Steck-Vaughn Publishing Co.
PO Box 690789
Orlando FL 32819-0789
1-800-531-5015
www.steckvaughn.com

I'm Working Hard to Be a Better Reader

Name ______________________________

Help the students get to the bookmobile.

Chapter 4

Increasing Speed of Reading Written Letter Patterns

Normal readers begin to recognize letter patterns rather than letters as individual units. This ability helps them to increase their speed of reading. The ability to detect letter clusters in words is related to better reading (Berninger 1987, Berninger et al. 1991).

How well students recognize these letter patterns is associated with how frequently they have seen the patterns occur in their own reading (Bowers et al. 1994). With brief practice, normal beginning readers can recognize a specific letter pattern faster than they can sound out a new pattern. This is sometimes called *learning to read by orthographic analogy*. Learning to read by orthographic analogy means that normally-developing readers read a word like *peak* and can then read a word like *beak* without direct instruction because they make the analogy between the rime patterns.

Unfortunately, brief practice does not yield the same results in reading disabled children (Reitsma 1983). Poor readers have been shown to consistently demonstrate slow speed of access to lexical items (Meyer et al. 1998). Children with severe dyslexia cannot transfer their knowledge of these patterns easily to new words (Lovett et al. 1990), meaning they will need much more work with letter pattern exposure. Berninger and her colleagues have done several studies indicating that it is important to work on recognition of letter clusters (Berninger 1987, Berninger et al. 1991).

What are some things that might interfere with a child developing adequate letter cluster codes?

- The child cannot discriminate the sound unit.
- The way the child processes the letter cluster interferes with forming a clear orthographic image.
- The child is slow to recognize individual letters.
- The child uses poor strategies, such as guessing the word based on the first letter.
- The child has lack of exposure to print (Bowers and Wolf 1993).

Berninger et al. (1991) found that a child's ability to rapidly name digits on the RAN was significantly correlated with both reading skill and letter cluster recognition.

Samuels (1985) explained how children move from looking at individual letters/sounds to recognizing a larger letter pattern as a unit. He explained perceptual learning as occurring in three stages:

1. **Feature Discovery** The child discovers which aspects of the stimulus make it distinctive.
2. **Unitization** The distinctive features have been identified and are now joined together with practice and are seen as a unit.
3. **Automatic** The stimulus identification occurs quickly, automatically, and accurately.

The student's accuracy nears 100 percent as soon as he enters the second stage: unitization. However, learning should not be considered completed at this stage. The student must continue to move toward and into the automatic stage.

The techniques described here are just a few of the ways you might address increasing the student's speed of recognition. These activities actually have two goals: increasing the speed with which the child can visually recognize a part of the word and increasing the speed with which the child can then decode or recognize what that letter pattern says.

Increasing speed of recognition of consonant combinations

You may need to help the student build automaticity in recognition of two-letter consonant patterns (digraphs) and other consonant patterns. The chart below lists consonant combination patterns that commonly occur. Appendices 4A and 4B (pages 59-61) contain rhymes and silly stories with letter patterns for students to practice.

Digraphs and consonant combinations	
Initial position	ch- sh- th- (voiced and voiceless) wh-
Initial position consonant + vowel	qu-
Final position	-ck -tch -dge -ng

See Appendices 4A and 4B.*

Students should also be taught to quickly recognize consonant blends. These typically occur in the beginning of words, but there are also common word-ending blends. The chart below lists consonant blends that commonly occur. Appendices 4C and 4D (pages 62-69) contain rhymes and silly stories with blends and consonant combinations for students to practice.

Consonant blends and consonant combinations	
Initial position (though they may also cross syllable boundaries)	bl- cl- fl- gl- pl- sl- cr- dr- br- gr- pr- tr- sk- sl- sp- sc- st- sn- sm- sw- tw- scr- spr- str- spl-
Digraph in blend, beginning	shr- thr-
Digraph in blend, ending	-nch -rch
Two letter combinations (silent letter)	kn- gn- wr- -mn (end)
Final position (though these may also cross syllable boundaries)	-ft -nt -lf -lt -ld -lk -lp -lm -mp -nd -st -sk -xt

See Appendices 4C and 4D.*

*You can also look through the lists in Appendices 4L (pages 81-93) and 4M (pages 94-99) and choose words with target digraphs, consonant blends, or consonant combinations.

Increasing speed of recognition of vowel patterns

If students don't have a good grasp of what each single letter vowel sound is, then they need more basic work developing phonological awareness skills and those sound-symbol relationships. There are many materials designed to address basic vowel recognition. The student with a fluency problem may need work on basic vowels so those materials can be used. In particular, you may need to review the concept of short versus long vowels, since many reading/spelling rules depend on knowledge of this concept. For example, knowing the difference in the words *luck/Luke*, *bit/bite*, or *dim/dime* depends on the child knowing what short and long vowels are.

In this section, we focus on increasing the student's speed and accuracy of recognizing two-letter vowels. Some of these two-letter combinations make only one sound (they represent only one phoneme), while others represent two different sounds or phonemes. These are summarized in the chart below and in the charts on the next page. Appendices 4E, 4F, and 4G (pages 70-73) contain two-letter vowel combinations in silly stories, nonsense syllables, and real words for students to practice.

See Appendix 4E.

Two-letter vowel combinations that have two or more spellings but make only one sound	
the long e sound	ee* (as in *feet*) ea* (as in *beat*)
the *oy* sound	oy (as in *boy*) oi (as in *oil*)
the long *a* sound	a/silent e* (as in *made*) ai* (as in *paid*) ay (as in *day*)
the *aw* sound	au (as in *cause*) aw (as in *claw*)
the long *o* sound	oa* (as in *boat*) o/silent e* (as in *rode*)

*Some of these are included in Appendices 4L (pages 81-93) and 4M (pages 94-99). Look through the lists and choose those with the target vowel sound.

See Appendix 4E.

Two spellings	Two sounds			
ew sometimes spelled eu*	/u/	neuron	new	grew
	/ju/	few	feud	
ue*	/u/	blue	glue	Sue
	/ju/	cue		

* You may need to highlight that the *ew* and the *ue* are two spellings, and each can say two different sounds: /u/ or /ju/. In addition, *ew* can appear as *eu* for the /ju/ sound. Students will expect the *ue* to always say /ju/, as in *you*.

See Appendices 4E, 4F, and 4G.

Two-letter vowel combinations that represent two different phonemes (sounds)	
ea	the long e sound (as in *seat*) the long *a* sound (as in *great*)
ow, ou**	the *ow* sound (as in *house*, *down*) the long *o* sound (as in *show*, *four*)
ie**	the long e sound (as in *chief*) the long *i* sound (as in *pie*)
ei	the long e sound (as in *seize*) the long *a* sound (as in *vein*)
oo**	the *oo* sound (as in *boot*) the *oo* sound (as in *foot*)

** Only the vowels *ou/ow*, *i*, and *oo* have practice lists in the appendices, because there are so few words with alternate pronunciations for the other vowels.

r- and *l*- controlled vowels

There are three ways to spell the *er* sound: *er*, *ir*, and *ur*. Students need ample practice recognizing these alternate spellings. Two other vowel sounds have vowel + *r* with predictable pronunciations. These are *ar* and *or*. There are less common spellings that change the way the letter combinations sound (e.g., *ear* can be *er* as in *earth* or *air* as in *wear*; *er* can be *air* as in *berry*; and *ar* can be *air* as in *marry*).

Words that end in -*l* may change how the short vowel is pronounced. This is particularly true for words ending in -*all* (the vowel sounds more like short *o* than short *a*) and -*ull* (the word may sound like a short *u* in *dull* or more like the vowel sound in *pull* and *full*). Speed drills to practice *r*- and *l*- controlled vowels are found in Appendix 4H, pages 74-75. (See pages 56-57 for information on page speed drills.)

See Appendix 4H.

Other letter patterns for alternate spellings

There are other letter patterns that are important for the child to recognize as well. These are often alternative spellings that confuse the child when they are encountered in text. Some examples of alternate spellings are as follows: *f* spelled like *ph* (*phone*) or *gh* (*laugh*), *ie* spelled like *igh* (*high*), *ks* spelled with an *x* (*fox*), *sh* spelled with *ch* (*chiffon*), or *k* spelled with *ch* (*chrome*). Also, some spellings change the way the word sounds. For example, words ending in *-nk* sound like *-ngk* (*thank*). You should select the ones to address based on the age of the child (e.g., a first grader may not need to recognize *-ight*, but a third grader certainly does). Silly stories with other letter patterns can be found in Appendix 4I, page 76.

See Appendix 4I.

A special note about *b*/*d* reversals

Although the letters *b* and *d* are not truly a pattern but individual letters, some children have a great deal of difficulty and continue to make errors recognizing these. Therefore, some specific strategies for increasing accuracy and speed are indicated. One strategy to use when children encounter this reversal is to remind them that when they see a letter *b*, a straight line is the first thing their eyes see. They should squeeze their lips tight into a straight line, and their mouth naturally produces the *b* sound. This tip is used in the LiPS Program (Lindamood 1998).

Another strategy is to remind the student that the letter *b* looks like a baseball bat with a ball lying next to it. You have to pick up the bat first, before you can hit the ball. The student can then be told that the letter *d* looks like a doorknob sticking out of a door. If he reaches with his hand toward the letter *d*, he would grab a doorknob. This may help the student differentiate between the two letters.

For more practice with *b*/*d* reversals, use the rhyme and silly story in Appendix 4J (page 77) and the page speed drills in Appendix 4K (pages 78-80).

See Appendices 4J and 4K.

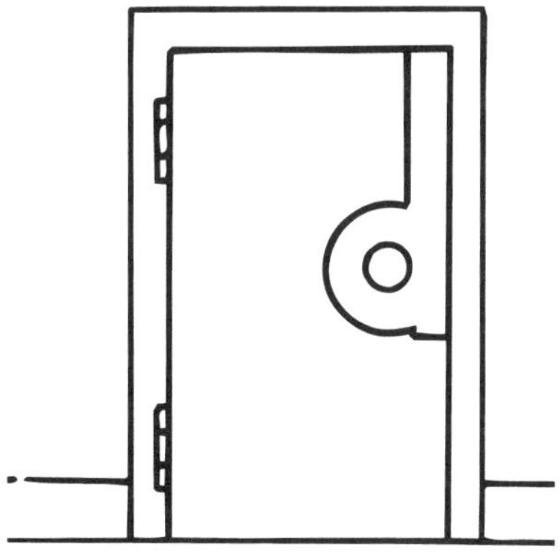

Onset + rime letter patterns

In Chapter 3, we described activities (including the use of word families) which help the child learn to blend onset + rime. This auditory activity is easy to transition from a phonological awareness activity to a decoding activity when written letter patterns are presented. The word families materials mentioned in Chapter 3, page 40, provide a wealth of information for working on visual recognition of onset + rime.

These rimes are logical letter patterns to address with the child. Building quick recognition of many common rime endings will immediately expand the number of words the child can automatically recognize. This work can overlap with work on syllable patterns in Chapter 5, as most rimes represent the V + C syllable pattern.

Teaching children to recognize these onset + rime letter patterns can have a direct impact on their reading skills. Training at this level transfers to untrained words. Children learn to read words when these sublexical connections are taught. Interestingly, using onset + rime is not necessarily more effective than teaching alphabetic principle in improving reading. However, use of onset + rime (i.e., pairing the spoken and written syllables) was found by Berninger et al. to be more effective in helping students spell real words and transfer the spelling of words (Berninger et al. 1998, Berninger et al. 2000).

If the activity involves writing (e.g., having the student write down as many onset + rimes as he can think of), you may want to point out those which are not spelled correctly. For example, if you are using the rime *ine* and the student writes the word *sine* (meaning the word *sign*), you should accept that. The student has "heard" that the word *sign* contains the target ending sound. Simply tell the child that it does indeed sound like *sine*, but it is spelled differently. Depending on the age of the child, you might discuss this alternate spelling at the same time.

Onset + rime is presumed to be a relatively easy thing for the student to learn. Goswami (1993) confirmed this in a study that showed beginning readers only transferred pronunciations that corresponded to rimes in words (e.g., *bug-rug*). The study also found that as reading progressed, students were able to transfer the pronunciation for the vowel grapheme (e.g., *beak-heap*; *beak-bean*). The word lists and card games in Appendices 4L (pages 81-93), 4M (pages 94-99), and 4N (page 100) can be used to develop practice materials.

See Appendices 4L, 4M, and 4N.

Focusing

Hansen and Eaton (1978) summarized research into different methods of treatment for reading disorders. They described a method called *focusing*, in which the child is simply asked to focus on his common errors. For example, focusing was used to help a child with *b*/*d* confusion. They suggest that strategies such as focusing would probably be of most benefit to children who have a good grasp of basic decoding skills but who evidence consistent errors on certain symbols or words. This seems very similar to the advice offered by Berninger et al. (2001) in their description of different types of dysfluent readers. They suggest that for the Type 3 non-fluent reader, instruction in meta-cognitive strategies to improve self-monitoring and self-correction would be helpful. This is because those students are inattentive to orthography.

Hansen and Eaton provided an example of a 14-year-old who was only 69 percent correct in recognizing the letters *b* and *d*. The intervention simply involved the teacher writing a keyword for each of those letters on the page and asking the student to pay careful attention. Within two days, the student scored 100 percent on recognition of these two letters and continued to score 100 percent after intervention.

Page speed drills

Page speed drills present a page of stimuli to the student that will allow practice recognizing and decoding any number of patterns. Page speed drills can be devised for individual letter recognition, letter pattern recognition, syllable recognition, or whole word recognition. Ask the student to use a finger to follow the line of text or use an index card to cover all but the line he is reading. Time how quickly the student can read the stimuli. Accuracy is stressed. The student might read the same page speed drill several times to see if he can improve his speed and accuracy. The goal each time is to decrease the time it takes to read the list and decrease the number of errors.

As described by Fischer (1995, 1999), the student should read the sequences as fast as possible and see how far he can go in one minute. Fischer suggests that for beginning students (6- and 7-year-olds), the goal is to read 30 words correct per minute, but by the middle of third grade, the student should be able to read 60 words correct per minute.

The possibilities are endless for the targets on page speed drills. They should be designed specifically for the student to provide practice on patterns that are difficult for him. Although page speed drills are first used in this chapter, you will find page speed drills in other chapters as well. The page speed drills in Appendix 4O (page 101), 4H (pages 74-75), and 4K (pages 78-80) provide several examples of drills for students who need to practice letter patterns and *b*/*d* confusion.

See Appendices 4O, 4H, and 4K.

How to use the appendices in this chapter

The appendices in this chapter include materials you can use to help students increase speed and accuracy of recognition of the letter patterns discussed in this chapter. Any of these can be used to help a student improve phonological awareness and decoding. To improve fluency and to achieve a level of automaticity, remember the following:

- Have the child read the stimuli multiple times.
- If the student reads something incorrectly, correct the error.
- Have the student pre-read the stimuli (e.g., poem or story) to make sure he can read all the words (or nonsense stimuli) before beginning the activity.
- Introduce an element of time. Use a stopwatch or timer and see if the student improves the time it takes to complete the activity on successive trials.
- Copy the stimuli onto index cards to make flash cards so the timing of presentation of the stimuli can be controlled. This works best with stimuli that are word length (e.g., onset + rime) or two words (e.g., two contrasting pronunciations of a word or nonsense syllable) rather than with sentence or story level stimuli.
- Use commercially-available computer games and materials for practice (Appendix 4P, pages 102-103 and 4Q, page 104).
- PowerPoint software can be used for any length stimuli to control the speed of presentation (Appendix 4R, page 105).

See Appendices 4P and 4Q.

See Appendix 4R.

Note: Not all of the appendices will be appropriate for all ages of children because of the level of vocabulary included.

List of Appendices for Chapter 4

Rhymes with Letter Patterns for Consonant Combinations/Digraphs

These rhymes contain words that may not be familiar to readers who are younger or who may be more impaired. Read a line and have the student repeat it. Or copy the page and have the student use a highlighter to mark the letter pattern you are practicing (e.g., *ch*). If the student can't read the words, read to the student while he follows along and raises his hand each time he hears and sees the target sound.

ch-/sh-

Chip, choose, chew,
Ship, shoes, shoe.
I can find the words with *ch* and *sh*, can you?
Chip, ship,
Choose, shoes,
Chew, shoe.
I can find the words with *ch* and *sh*, can you?
Ship, chip,
Shoes, choose,
Shoe, chew.
I can find the words with *ch* and *sh*, can you?

th- (voiceless)

Think, thank, thin,
Tink, tank, tin.
I can find the words with quiet *th*, can you?
Think, tink,
Thank, tank,
Thin, tin.
I can find the words with quiet *th*, can you?
Tink, think,
Tank, thank,
Tin, thin.
I can find the words with quiet *th*, can you?

th-

Those, then, there,
Hose, hen, hair.
Words with noisy *th*, I know where.
Those, hose,
Then, hen,
There, hair.
Words with noisy *th*, I know where.
Hose, those,
Hen, then,
Hair, there.
Words with noisy *th*, I know where.

wh-

Which one went there?
Why do we care?
When did he go there?
Why do we care?
What did he do there?
Why do we care?
Where is he when he's there?
Why do we care?
When is he coming back?
Why do we care?

qu-

Quick, quit, quite,
Kick, kit, kite.
Some words have *qu*, am I right?
Quick, kick.
Quit, kit.
Quite, kite.
Some words have *qu*, am I right?
Kick, quick,
Kit, quit,
Kite, quite.
Some words have *qu*, am I right?

-ck/-ke

Back, tack, rack,
Bake, take, rake.
Ck or *k* at the end, which does it take?
Back, bake,
Tack, take,
Rack, rake.
Ck or *k* at the end, which does it take?
Bake, back,
Take, tack,
Rake, rack.
Ck or *k* at the end, which does it take?

Rhymes with Letter Patterns for Consonant Combinations/Digraphs, *continued*

-ch/-tch

Peach, beach, leach,
Patch, batch, latch.
Ch or *tch*, which does it match?
Peach, patch,
Beach, batch,
Leach, latch.
Ch or *tch*, which does it match?
Patch, peach,
Batch, beach,
Latch, leach.
Ch or *tch*, which does it match?

-dge/-ge

Fuge, buge, truge,
Fudge, budge, trudge.
Ge or *dge*, you be the judge.
Fuge, fudge,
Buge, budge,
Truge, trudge.
Ge or *dge*, you be the judge.
Fudge, fuge,
Budge, buge,
Trudge, truge.
Ge or *dge*, you be the judge.

-ng

Bang, song, thing,
Bring, sang, sing.
Ng has a nice ring.
Bang, bring,
Song, sang,
Thing, sing.
Ng has a nice ring.
Bring, bang,
Sang, song,
Sing, thing.
Ng has a nice ring.

Silly Stories with Letter Patterns for Consonant Combinations

Silly stories can be used in the same way as rhymes. Adapt as appropriate for the age of the student. Have the student highlight the target letter pattern in the passage. Then have the student read the passage aloud, paying close attention to the target letter pattern. If the student routinely misreads the pattern (e.g., usually says *s* for *sh*), have the student read the passage again and pronounce all the target sounds as the commonly-made error sound (e.g., read all the *sh* sounds as if each was really an *s*). This further draws the student's attention to the pattern he is working on.

ch-

My dog Chip loves to chew. He will chew on cheese, especially cheddar cheese. He will chew on chips and on things he finds at the beach. He will chew anything in his reach. But Chip gets in trouble if he chews on chairs.

sh-

What shape is the ship? The ship is shaped like a shoe. I wish the ship were shaped like a fish. It looks like it has a sharp point on the end. If the ship hits a sharp rock, it could sink. That would be a shame. It would take a lot of cash to fix the ship after a crash.

th-

I think that my thumb is swollen. I either hit my thumb with that thick board, or I stuck my thumb with the thistle. I can't hold my pencil to do the math, because my thumb is so sore.

wh-

Where, *what*, *when*, and *why* are question words. When we are in the car, we ask lots of questions. We ask where we are going. We ask what time will we get there. We ask when we are going to stop for something to eat. We ask why it takes so long. When we ask who are we going to see, the *wh* doesn't make the *w* sound, it makes the *h* sound.

qu-

Please quit quacking like a duck. If you don't quit, I will quickly run and tell the queen. It is quite annoying to hear you quack. Please be quiet! That quacking is as loud as an earthquake. Quiet, please!

-ck

Jack went out the back door to take a walk. He wants to walk to his friend's house to see his new truck. They will talk for hours. They might even draw a picture of the truck with chalk on the sidewalk. They'll have to draw where there is no crack in the walk.

-tch

When I tried to reach the latch, I felt a scratch on my leg. I tore my jeans and now they need a patch on the knee. My mom will stitch them up with a nice patch. Then I can play catch and dig a ditch and dress up like a witch.

-dge

Madge loves to eat fudge. She likes chocolate fudge and peanut butter fudge. If she passes a store selling fudge, she won't budge until we go in and buy some. Once we even had to trudge across a bridge to find the fudge store. We always keep some in our fridge. The only person she will share her fudge with is the judge who lives next door.

-ng

The king loves to sing. The king will sing about anything. He once sang a song about another king who wanted to bring his queen to see a shiny ring. The king who likes to sing made up a silly song, and all the words were wrong. The only thing the king likes better than singing a song is playing a game of ping pong.

Rhymes for Blends and Consonant Combinations

These rhymes contain words that may not be familiar to readers who are younger or who may be more impaired. Read a line and have the student repeat it. Or copy the page and have the student use a highlighter to mark the letter pattern you are practicing (e.g., *spr*). If the student can't read the words, read to the student while he follows along and raises his hand each time he hears and sees the target sound.

bl-/cl-/fl-

Bleat, cleat, fleet,
Blue, clue, flew.
I see words with *l* blends, do you?
Bleat, blue,
Cleat, clue,
Fleet, flew.
I see words with *l* blends, do you?
Blue, bleat,
Clue, cleat,
Flew, fleet.
I see words with *l* blends, do you?

gl-/pl-/sl-

Glip, plip, slip,
Glide, plied, slide.
Find the words with *l* blends, don't let them hide.
Glip, glide,
Plip, plied,
Slip, slide.
Find the words with *l* blends, don't let them hide.
Glide, glip,
Plied, plip,
Slide, slip.
Find the words with *l* blends, don't let them hide.

fr-/cr-/dr-

Fried, cried, dried,
Fry, cry, dry.
I can find words with *r* blends when I try.
Fried, fry,
Cried, cry,
Dried, dry.
I can find words with *r* blends when I try.
Fry, fried,
Cry, cried,
Dry, dried.
I can find words with *r* blends when I try.

br-/gr-/pr-/tr-

Trim, grim, prim,
Bray, gray, tray.
Lots of words have *r* blends, wouldn't you say?
Trim, bray,
Grim, gray,
Prim, tray.
Lots of words have *r* blends, wouldn't you say?
Bray, trim,
Gray, grim,
Tray, prim.
Lots of words have *r* blends, wouldn't you say?

sk-/sl-/sp-

Sky, sly, spy,
Skit, slit, spit.
I see words with *s* blends, I can do it!
Sky, skit,
Sly, slit,
Spy, spit.
I see words with *s* blends, I can do it!
Skit, sky,
Slit, sly,
Spit, spy.
I see words with *s* blends, I can do it!

sc-/st-/sn-

Scoop, stoop, snoop,
Scare, stare, snare.
More words with *s* blends, do you know where?
Scoop, scare,
Stoop, stare,
Snoop, snare.
More words with *s* blends, do you know where?
Scare, scoop,
Stare, stoop,
Snare, snoop.
More words with *s* blends, do you know where?

Rhymes for Blends and Consonant Combinations, *continued*

sm-/sw-

Smile, swile, smell,
Sweet, smeet, swell.
Some are real words, can you tell?
Smile, sweet,
Swile, smeet,
Smell, swell.
Some are real words, can you tell?
Sweet, smile,
Smeet, swile,
Swell, smell.
Some are real words, can you tell?

tw-

Tweak, beak, bill, fin,
Twist, fist, twill, twin.
Which words have a *tw* in them?
Tweak, twist,
Beak, fist,
Bill, twill,
Fin, twin.
Which words have a *tw* in them?
Twist, tweak,
Fist, beak,
Twill, bill,
Twin, fin.
Which words have a *tw* in them?

scr-

Scram, scrub, screech,
Scratch, scrape, scream.
Lots of words with *scr*, or is it a dream?
Scram, scratch,
Scrub, scrape,
Screech, scream.
Lots of words with *scr*, or is it a dream?
Scratch, scram,
Scrape, scrub,
Scream, screech.
Lots of words with *scr*, or is it a dream?

spr-

Sprinkle, spruce, spray,
Sprinkled, spruced, sprayed.
Regular or past tense, *spr* is here to stay.
Sprinkle, sprinkled,
Spruce, spruced,
Spray, sprayed.
Regular or past tense, *spr* is here to stay.
Sprinkled, sprinkle,
Spruced, spruce,
Sprayed, spray.
Regular or past tense, *spr* is here to stay.

str-

Strap, strong, strip,
Straw, strange, string.
Finding *str* is an easy thing.
Strap, straw,
Strong, strange,
Strip, string.
Finding *str* is an easy thing.
Straw, strap,
Strange, strong,
String, strip.
Finding *str* is an easy thing.

spl-

Splice, splash, splutter.
I'm all a-flutter.
Splice, splash, splutter.
Don't put the *spl* words in the butter.
Splice, spash, splutter.
I'm all a-flutter.
Splice, splash, splutter.
Let's eat some peanut butter.

shr-/thr-

Shrimp, shrug, three,
Shred, threw, thread.
I found these words in my head.
Shrimp, shred,
Three, thread.
These words are going around in my head.
Shrug, threw,
Thread, shred.
I can't even forget them when I go to bed.

Rhymes for Blends and Consonant Combinations, *continued*

-nch/-rch

Don't lurch on the porch.
Don't punch your lunch.
You'll be in trouble, that's my hunch!
Don't perch on the torch.
Don't scorch your lunch.
You'll be in trouble, that's my hunch!
Don't search for the birch.
Don't crunch the bunch.
You'll be in trouble, that's my hunch!

kn-/gn-

I know a gnat
Who knows how to gnaw.
He liked to munch on the dog's paw.
I knew a gnat
Who knew how to gnaw.
That nasty gnat I knew
Sure could gnaw,
But he got squished by the dog's paw.

wr-

I'd like to write about a boy
Who was never wrong.
He said that he had hurt his wrist,
But he was ever so strong.
If he hurt his wrist in a wrestling match,
The match must have been very long!

-mn

A hymn is a solemn song.
To scream a hymn would be wrong.
Stand by the column and sing the hymn.
When you sing a hymn, don't stand in a gym.
A hymn is a solemn song.
Sing it seriously and you can't go wrong.

-ft/-nt

When I smell paint, I feel faint.
Then I sprint to find a mint.
If I can't,
I look for an ant.
If I can't find an ant,
The only thing left
Is to hop in a raft
And go buy a craft.
A craft in a box I can lift
And turn it into a gift.

-lf/-lt/-ld

Half, halt, hold, calf, colt, cold.
Blends can come at the end, that's what I am told.
Half, calf, halt, colt, hold, cold.
Blends can come at the end, that's what I am told.
Calf, half, colt, halt, cold, hold,
Blends can come at the end, that's what I am told.

-lk/-lp/-lm

Stay calm, take a walk.
Have a gulp, then we'll talk.
Stay calm, let out a whelp.
Pick up the film, I'll get help.
Stay calm, don't spill the milk.
Don't balk, we'll find the silk.

-mp

We went to camp
One morning when it was damp.
We had to jump
Over the dump.
I got a cramp
When licking a stamp.
That made me a grump,
So I sat down like a lump.
Then I walked with a limp
To go buy some shrimp.

-nd

We heard a band
While we sat on the sand.
The band sounded so grand
That I just had to stand.
I hope you don't mind
When I tell you about my find.
While I stood on the sand,
Listening to the grand band,
I found a round mound on the ground.
I could stand on the mound
To see the grand band.

-st/-sk/-xt

Let's have a blast!
You can go last.
Who is next?
I'll look in the text.
Make a fist first.
Then quench your thirst.
You can have a drink from the flask.
Put on your mask.
It's an easy task.

Silly Stories for Blends and Consonant Combinations

Silly stories can be used in the same way as rhymes. Adapt as appropriate for the age of the student. Have the student highlight each target letter pattern in the passage. Then have the student read the passage aloud, paying close attention to the target letter pattern. If the student routinely misreads the pattern (e.g., usually says *br* for *dr*), have the student read the passage again and pronounce all the target sounds as the commonly- made error sound (e.g., read all the *dr* sounds as if each was really a *br*). This further draws the student's attention to the pattern he is working on.

bl-

Don't blame me for your blue lips. You ate too many blueberries, and that's what made your lips turn blue. When I blink my eyes, your lips look almost black from the blueberries. You picked so many blueberries that you have a blister on your finger. Get a blank piece of paper, and we'll make up a story about eating blueberries.

cl-

Do you know how to clean a clock? Our clock won't chime, it just goes "clack." I climbed up to the shelf to try and fix the clock, but it still clacks. I am not clever enough to fix the clacking clock. If you can clean the clock and stop the clack, I will clap and clap.

fl-

Mr. Flynn flies the flag every day. He flies the flag at his house, and he flies the flag at school. He even flew a flag on his boat in the summer. He would flip if he forgot to fly the flag one day. He can hang the flag in a flash because he has a lot of practice hanging the flag.

gl-

Bob is glad that he is going to learn how to hang glide. He thinks gliding will be fun. He can't learn today because it is a gloomy day. He has to learn to glide on a sunny day. If he breaks his glider, I guess he can glue it back together.

pl-

Please don't plant that plum tree near the door. I love plump purple plums, but I don't want the plums falling on the porch. Let's plant the plum tree by the window so we can watch the plums grow. When the plums are ripe, we can pick them and put them in a plastic basket and then place the basket on the table. Then we can eat plump plums every day.

sl-

Slow down before you slam into the tree! You are riding your bike so fast you might slide on the wet spot. Then you will slam into the tree and slice open your leg. The street is slippery. You will slip and fall. Slipping and sliding is no fun at all. Please slow down.

br-

Did Bruce bring the pizza to the party? Who brought the bright blue cups? My brother brought peanut brittle. Peanut brittle sticks in my braces, so I brought bread and jelly. I was going to bring my new game, but I broke it right after breakfast.

cr-

Did you cry when you crashed into the wall on your skates? Did you crack your helmet in the crash? Did you crumple your skates in the crash? Did the big crow fly down and make you crash?

Silly Stories for Blends and Consonant Combinations, *continued*

dr-

Don't drop the water on the dry floor. When my nice dry floor gets wet, it drives me crazy. Pour the water down the drain. Don't let it drip on the floor. Don't let it drip on your dress. Don't let a drop drip from the cup.

fr-

Do you think it is freezing in this room? It's so cold that if we try to fry the egg, the egg will freeze. If the egg freezes, I will frown. It's so cold, the picture frame might crack. If the frame cracks, I will frown.

gr-

Grab the green ball and we'll go outside and play with the dog. We can throw the green ball across the green grass. The dog can grab the green ball and bring it back. If we don't throw the ball to him, he might growl. If you throw it over the fence, I'll groan.

pr-

Do you know what the prize is for winning the game? One time the prize was a big pretzel. One time the prize was a present all wrapped up. One time the prize was a prune. No one wanted that prize! We all pretended we didn't know how to play the game because no one wanted that prize.

tr-

Joe tried hard to catch the train. He ran as fast as he could, but he tripped on the steps and fell. The train went past him on the track and did not stop. Joe is in big trouble because he missed the train. He won't be home in time to train his dog. He wanted to train his dog to do a new trick.

sc-

When Jake played soccer, he scored a goal. The other teams were scared to play Jake and his team because he scored so much. Then one day, he fell and cut his arm and had to leave the game. At first he had a big scab on his arm. Now the scab is gone, but he has a big scar.

sk-

One night a skinny girl was looking up at the sky. She could name lots of the stars in the sky. She hardly skipped any, but she did have to ask for a little help. It took a lot of skill to name all the stars in the sky. After she named the stars, she put on a mask and skipped home. On her way she saw a skunk, so then she ran as fast as she could.

sl-

Becky slammed the door and ran outside. She was going to climb on the slide, but she slipped on some green slime in the grass. She slid into the slide and bumped her head. She was so mad, she slapped the slide.

sm-

Patch was one smart dog. He could smell a storm coming and bark a warning. He could smash an egg with his paw. He was small and looked like he was smiling. He had a nice, smooth coat.

sn-

My friend Rick is from far away. He thinks snails make a good snack. He likes to sneak up on me, and he snoops in my locker. Sometimes he will snatch my lunch from my locker. I have to chase him to get it back. When he snaps his fingers, his dog Snoops comes running.

Silly Stories for Blends and Consonant Combinations, *continued*

sp-

Sometimes my little brother likes to play spy. He turns out the lights because he thinks spies should be spooky. Sometimes he plays spaceman and spins around until he is dizzy. Sometimes he pretends to be a clown and hangs a spoon on his nose or paints his face with sparkles.

st-

Three boys stood on the line to start the race. They ran fast up a steep hill, down the steps, and around the stop sign. One boy had to stay behind to stand at the finish line. The boy who stepped over the finish line first was the star.

sw-

Here are some things you can do on a summer day. You can swim in the swimming pool or just swish your feet in the water. You can swat the flies who try to bite you. You can eat sweet things like watermelon. You sweat when you get hot. When you sweat, you have to run from a swarm of bees.

tw-

Tom and Tim are twins. They have twin beds, twin bikes, and twin book bags. They have twin hats, twin coats, and even twin watches. The twins love to play *Twister*. It is their favorite game. They get all twisted up when they play *Twister*. You can't tell one twin from the other.

scr-

The screen door at our house is a mess. The cat scratches the screen door when he wants to go out. The dog scrapes the screen door when he wants to come in. My little sister even scribbled on the screen door with her crayons. Now guess who has to scrub the screen door? Me!

spr-

There's a spry old man who lives on our street. He lives in the house with the spruce tree. Every day he sprinkles the spruce tree with water so it will grow. Every spring he spreads tree food around the spruce tree so it will grow. I hope the spry old man's spruce tree grows very tall.

str-

Last month a stray dog came to our house. He was dragging a piece of string. The stray dog was black with a streak of white on his back. He needed a home, so now the stray dog is ours. We named him Stripe because of the streak on his back. Now Stripe isn't a stray anymore.

spl-

What a splendid splash the rock made when I threw it in the pond. The water splashed on me. The water splashed on the grass. The water splashed on the tree. The water splashed on my bike. It was a splendid splash.

shr-

A shrew looks a little like a mouse. A shrew looks a little like a mole. A shrew has a shrill cry that sounds like a shriek. A shrew has sharp claws that can shred a piece of paper. A shrew likes to dig. A shrew likes to hide. I wonder if a shrew would eat a shrimp.

thr-

I have three best friends. My three friends live close by. We like to throw rocks in the pond. One time we threw three rocks at the same time and made a big splash. We like to run through the woods and hide. We like to throw our hats in the tree. Then we climb up and get them.

-nch

Last summer our family went to a ranch. We learned a bunch of stuff on the ranch. We learned how to use a wrench and how to dig a trench. The best part about the ranch was that we ate a bunch of food for lunch.

-rch

One Sunday in March, when we drove to church, we saw a bird on a perch in a birch tree. The bird would lurch at a bug and then fly back to the perch in the birch. We also saw an arch on our drive in March.

kn-

I know a story about a knight in shining armor. He knew how to ride a horse. He knew how to fight. He even knew how to knead bread. He had a lot of knowledge. He became a knight when he kneeled down in front of the queen. She said, "I know a good knight when I see one."

wr-

What's wrong with writing a list? When I write a list, it hurts my wrist on my right hand. Maybe I am holding the pencil wrong. I wrote a list of birds that started with wren. I wrote a list of sports that started with wrestle. I wrote a list of things that a car can do that started with wreck. After all those lists, my right wrist really hurt from all that writing.

gn-

Gnaw is a word that is kind of like chew. Gnaw is a word that is kind of like bite. Gnaw is a word that is kind of like tear. You can gnaw on an apple. You can gnaw on a bone. But don't gnaw on a gnat. Yuck!

-mn

On Monday we had a big assembly in the gym at school. It was a solemn event. A teacher gave a speech in the gym. We sang a song that sounded like a hymn. Then we marched outside and stood by the column in the front of the school.

-ft

One day after class we talked about the best gift we ever got. Tammy said her best gift was a soft sweater that her craft teacher gave her. Ted liked the raft he got as a gift. I was the only one left. I couldn't decide what I would call the best gift, so I was swift and ran ahead.

-lk

A walk and a balk are baseball words. Ted knows what they mean. Ted will talk about baseball all the time. He will draw baseball pictures with chalk. He will stalk you down and make you play baseball. When I see Ted, I walk the other way so I don't have to talk about baseball.

-lt

Alex had a stomachache. She loosened her belt but still felt bad. She was supposed to ride her new colt and teach it not to bolt across the field. Her dad bought her a malt, but she let it melt. She felt too sick to drink it. Her dad gave her a flower, but she let it wilt. Poor Alex. She never felt so bad.

-ld

I bet if you are bald, your head will get cold. I bet if your room has lots of mold, you will catch a cold. I bet if you forget to fold your clothes, your mom will say, "I thought I told you to fold those clothes." I bet if you are bold, you will run across the field. I bet on your birthday, you will be 9 years old.

Silly Stories for Blends and Consonant Combinations, *continued*

-mp

When Sam went to camp, he fell down the ramp and got a bump on his head. Then he walked with a limp. He didn't see the hump on the ramp. Because of his limp, he couldn't help dig up the old tree stump. He had to sit by the lamp at the top of the ramp and watch us work on the stump.

-nd

The wizard held a magic wand in his hand and waved it over the land. Everyone in the land soon found a bag of gold on their front steps. They didn't mind this find. Some used the money to start a band. The band marched across the land. If you asked, the band would lend you a horn. You could play in the band if you could bend your fingers on the keys.

-st

You must try this game. It is the most fun of all the games. You have to move fast across the last level to find the lost key. There is so much mist it is hard to see. You might get lost too. You have to be the first one through the mist to find the key and hold it tight in your fist. If you do, you get the most points.

-sk

Your task is to find the elephant's tusk. There is a lot of risk in this task. You should probably wear a mask while you look for the tusk. The tusk might be in the forest. The tusk might be by the lake. When you find the tusk, whisk it right back to the elephant.

-xt

I have a textbook for math and a textbook for social studies. I have a textbook for science and a textbook for English. Next week I will get a new textbook for art and a textbook for history.

-nt

I want to tell you a story about when we went to the beach. We had to rent a house near the beach so we could walk to the ocean. I sent all my friends a postcard. I sent Clint two postcards and a box with a mint and some gum in it. When we went to the beach, we got a dent in our car.

-lp

My uncle is a lot of help. When he comes to visit, he will help with anything. He knows a lot of things too. He showed me where my scalp is and taught me how to gulp air and burp. He has climbed a tall mountain called an alp. He said it was so cold up there he had to yelp.

-lf

Ralph is my friend who knows how to play golf. He taught himself how to golf. I wish I could teach myself. Ralph has a shelf in his room full of cool stuff. There is a toy elf, a calf, and a wolf on that shelf. There is even a shell he found in the gulf when he went to the beach.

-lm

Juan has been on a sailboat. He says you have to stay calm. The front of the boat is the helm. You have to be very calm and stand still in the helm. The helm could be made of elm. If you go on a sailboat, take a camera and some film to take a picture.

Silly Stories for Two-letter Vowels

Silly stories can be used in the same way as rhymes. Adapt as appropriate for the age of the student. Have the student highlight the target letter pattern in the passage. Then have the student read the passage aloud, paying close attention to the target letter pattern. If the student routinely misreads the pattern (e.g., usually says *oi* for *ou*), have the student read the passage again and pronounce all the target sounds as the commonly-made error sound (e.g., read all the *ou* words as if the *ou* were really an *oi*). This further draws the student's attention to the pattern he is working on.

the long e sound spelled as ee or *ea*

Mr. Treen, the coach, drove his jeep to the pool. He put the keys under the seat. He had promised to meet the team at the deep end of the swimming pool. He said he would leap into the pool if the team had a winning season. Their record was 10-4, so the team was in for a treat, seeing Coach Treen leap into the deep water!

the *oi* sound spelled as *oi* or *oy*

The boy's mother promised she would buy him a new toy if he would just try the soybeans which had been boiled in oil. She said the toy could be his choice. But just to annoy his mother, the boy would not take a bite of the soybeans. He didn't like them boiled in oil or boiled in water. So the boy didn't get a toy!

the long *a* sound spelled as *ai*, *ay*, or *a*/silent e

It was a gray day on October 9th, the date when the family decided to take a hike on the trail from the mailbox to the lake. Jay and Jake decided they didn't want to go. "They say it may rain," said Jake. "We don't want to be on the trail when it rains," said Jay. Their dad said Jay and Jake could stay at home and paint the mailbox or rake the yard or bake a cake. It didn't rain that day, so Jay and Jake were sorry that they had not gone on the hike up the trail.

the *au* sound spelled as *au* or *aw*

The weather was awful when Shawn and Haun decided to haul the wood from the barn to the house. Shawn picked up a log and turned around. He accidentally hit Haun in the jaw with the log. Haun fell down and crawled around crying, "You broke my jaw." After that, Haun could only drink from a straw because his jaw was wired shut.

the long o sound spelled as *oa* or o/silent e

Todd the toad had a load of bones to take to the dog in the castle. The toad could take a boat across the moat to the castle. He could pull the load of bones in the wagon up the road all alone. He could ask the frog to loan him the car and load the bones into the trunk and drive the car on the road all alone. What should the toad do?

***ea* pronounced as long e (as in *seat*) or long *a* (as in *great*)**

One day a Great Dane took a seat at the table. He was ready to eat a big piece of meat. For a Great Dane, a piece of meat is a real treat.

Silly Stories for Two-letter Vowels, *continued*

***ow* pronounced as *ow* (as in *down*) or long *o* (as in *show*)**

Did you know it was going to snow? Let me show you how to drive the plow so we can clear the snow from our school downtown. We could blow the snow away or make snowballs and throw them slowly, but the teacher frowns on playground clowns.

***ie* pronounced as long e (as in *chief*) or long *i* (as in *pie*)**

There was a pie-eating contest at the fair. The chief of police won the contest. I couldn't believe it because I thought it was a tie between the chief and my teacher. I was sure the chief ate one pie and she ate one pie. But he said he ate two pies. Who should we believe? Did someone tell a lie?

***ei* pronounced as long e (as in *seize*) or long *a* (as in *vein*)**

Did you receive either a letter or a box in the mail? Did the box have a book about the human body? Did it have a picture of a vein in the arm? If you didn't receive it, who did? Did someone seize the box you were supposed to receive?

***oo* pronounced as *oo* (as in *boot*) or *oo* (as in *foot*)**

One time I read a cookbook that taught how to cook lots of different good foods. You needed a spoon to stir the food and a broom to clean up your mess after you cooked.

***eu* and *ew* pronounced as *oo* or *u* /*ju*/**

A few boys in our class got into a feud when a new student said she knew how to spell *neuron*. They said nobody knew how to spell *neuron*. The little argument grew into a big feud. And do you know what? The new girl knew how to spell *neuron*!

***ue* pronounced as *oo* (as in *blue*) or *u* /*ju*/ (as in *cue*)**

One day Sue wore her new blue dress to school when we had art class. Right on cue, she spilled glue on her new blue dress. She didn't have a clue what to do. After art class, Sue had to go to the library because her books were due.

Say It Both Ways—Nonsense Syllables for Alternate Pronunciations of Vowel Sounds

These lists contain nonsense syllables with vowel patterns that have alternate pronunciations. Write the headers (i.e., the two possible pronunciations of the vowel sound) on index cards. Have the student pronounce/read the syllables with each possible pronunciation.

ou **and** ***ow*** **can say** ***ow*** **as in** ***cow*** ***ou*** **and** ***ow*** **can say** ***long o*** **as in** ***show***	***ie*** **can say** ***long i*** **as in** ***pie*** ***ie*** **can say** ***long e*** **as in** ***chief***	**oo can say oo as in** ***boot*** **oo can say oo as in** ***foot***
bouch	biep	booch
bouf	biesp	bood
boush	blie	boop
clow	clie	boops
drow	diech	boosk
fout	dief	cooch
foux	diest	coom
frow	fiem	dooch
goub	fiep	doofs
goup	fiesh	doot
houch	gie	floop
housp	giesh	foop
hout	gliek	goot
joum	grie	hoom
joup	hien	hoon
jour	jie	joom
jow	jiek	looch
louch	jiesh	lood
loug	liemp	loosh
scow	liest	loosp
splow	rie	ploop
spow	smie	poon
sprow	snie	smoon
stoup	stie	smoots
strow	stieb	snook

Real Word or Not

These lists contain words with two-letter vowel combinations that can be pronounced in two ways. One way makes a real word. Write the headers (i.e. the two possible pronunciations of the vowel sound) on index cards. Have the student read each word both ways and decide which pronunciation is the real word.

ow **pronounced** ***ow*** **as in** ***now*** ***ow*** **pronounced** ***oe*** **as in** ***grow***	***oo*** **pronounced** ***oo*** **as in** ***boot*** ***oo*** **pronounced** ***oo*** **as in** ***foot***	***ie*** **pronounced** ***ie*** **as in** ***pie*** ***ie*** **pronounced** ***ee*** **as in** ***chief***
allow	bloom	believe
bowl	brook	besiege
brown	broom	die
clown	cook	diet
cow	droop	grieve
crow	food	shriek
dowdy	fool	tie
growl	foot	
growth	good	
howl	hood	
now	hoof	
plow	hoop	
prowl	look	
show	loot	
shower	mood	
snow	moon	
stow	pool	
thrown	school	
tower	shook	
town	smooch	
	snooze	
	spoon	
	stood	
	stoop	
	took	

Page Speed Drills for *r*- and *l*- Controlled Vowel Patterns

Page speed drills present a page of stimuli to the student that will allow practice at recognizing and decoding any number of patterns. Page speed drills can be devised for individual letter recognition, letter pattern recognition, syllable recognition, or whole word recognition. Ask the student to use his finger to follow the line of text or to use an index card to cover all but the line he is reading. Time how quickly the student can read the stimuli. Stress accuracy. The student might read the same page drill several times to see if he can improve his speed and accuracy.

Page Speed Drills for *ir*, *ur*, *or*, and *ar*

fir	far	for	fur	far
fur	for	fur	for	fir
far	fur	for	fir	for
far	for	fir	far	for
fir	for	far	fur	fir
fur	far	fur	for	fir

tar	for	turn	turf	tarp
turf	turn	tarp	tar	for
tarp	tar	for	turn	turf
for	turf	turn	tarp	tar
turf	tarp	tar	for	turn
tar	for	turn	tarp	turf

Page Speed Drills for *a*+ *ll*

ball	bap	tall	tap	fall
tall	tap	ball	bap	mall
mall	map	tall	map	ball
tall	mall	tap	fall	bap
tap	fall	map	ball	mall
ball	fall	tall	map	bap

stall	still	mall	stick	still
stick	still	stall	mall	still
stall	mall	still	stick	stall
stick	still	stall	mall	stall
stick	stall	mall	still	stick
still	mall	stick	stall	mall

Page Speed Drills for *u*+ *ll*

full	pull	dull	hull	gull
pull	gull	dull	full	hull
full	dull	hull	gull	pull
gull	full	pull	dull	hull
pull	hull	gull	dull	full
dull	gull	full	pull	hull

Silly Stories for Other Letter Patterns/Alternate Spellings

Silly stories can be used in the same way as rhymes. Adapt as appropriate for the age of the student. Have the student highlight the target letter pattern in the passage. Then have the student read the passage aloud, paying close attention to the target letter pattern. If the student routinely misreads the pattern (e.g., usually reads *ou* as *oi*), have the student read the passage again and pronounce all the target sounds as the commonly-made error sound (e.g., read all the *ou* words as if the *ou* were really an *oi*). This further draws the student's attention to the pattern he is working on.

ph pronounced as *f*

Ralph called Phil on the phone. When Phil answered, Ralph asked, "Phil, do you have any graph paper? I need graph paper to do my homework. I am pasting photos on the graph paper." Phil said Ralph could borrow the graph paper if he would bring back the photo of the phony spaceship that he borrowed.

gh pronounced as *f*

The coach of the team is really tough. He made the players run laps on the rough road around the school. After they had run ten laps, they asked the coach if that was enough. He laughed and laughed. So they ran ten more laps on the rough road.

igh pronounced as long *i*

I had a fight with my brother about who had the right to sit by the window on the flight. We were going to be high in the sky, and I wanted to see the sights and all the bright lights. He said he might let me sit there to see the sights in the day, but he wanted to see the bright lights at night.

x pronounced as *ks*

Have you ever heard of a fox living in a box? Or paying a tax to use the fax machine? What about stirring a cake mix with an ax, or using wax to clean the windows? These things are not right. They are all mixed up!

nk pronounced as *ngk*

The soldier drove the tank up to the bank. He cashed his check and told the clerk, "Thanks." He ran over junk in the road and bumped into the trunk of a tree, but the tank kept going until he got to the skating rink. Do you think the soldier will skate at the rink?

ch pronounced as *sh*

On their anniversary, my parents decided to spend the night in a chateau. My mom wore a dress made of chiffon. Dad bought a bottle of champagne. They stopped at the Chevron station to fill the car up with gas, but the machine that takes the credit card was broken. So they never made it to the chateau.

ch pronounced as *k*

In chemistry class, the teacher keeps the chemicals on a chrome table. Right before the Christmas break, we used the chemicals in an experiment that turned into chaos. Things were spilled everywhere. After we cleaned up the mess, we went to hear the chorus sing. The dance team teacher had choreographed a number, and the team danced.

Rhyme and Silly Story for *b/d* Reversal

This rhyme and silly story provide extra practice for students who confuse the *b* and *d* graphemes. You can have the student highlight each occurrence of the letter before reading.

Did you get mad at your dad?
Did you have a bad day?
Did you cry *boo hoo*,
Or throw your games away?
Don't be mad and don't be sad.
Try to be glad, that's what I say.
Be like Bob and do your job.
Then your dad will let you stay.

I have a hobby buying old beds and painting them bright blue and dark blue. Did you ever hear of beds painted those colors? I also like to dig big holes and bury bones for the dogs to dig up. When I am digging, I see big bugs and baby bunnies in the back yard. I do like the bunnies, but I don't like the bugs.

Page Speed Drills for *b* and *d* Confusion

Page speed drills present a page of stimuli to the student that will allow practice at recognizing and decoding any number of patterns. Page speed drills can be devised for individual letter recognition, letter pattern recognition, syllable recognition, or whole word recognition. Ask the student to use his finger to follow the line of text or to use an index card to cover all but the line he is reading. Time how quickly the student can read the stimuli. Stress accuracy. The student might read the same page drill several times to see if he can improve his speed and accuracy.

Page Speed Drills for *b* and *d*

bay	day	may	lay	say
day	may	bay	say	lay
bay	may	day	say	may
day	say	may	bay	lay
bay	say	lay	day	bay
lay	bay	say	may	day
say	bay	may	day	lay

big	dig	fig	rig	big
rig	fig	dig	rig	big
dig	rig	fig	big	dig
rig	fig	dig	rig	fig
big	fig	dig	rig	big
fig	dig	big	rig	dig
big	fig	dig	rig	big

bill	dill	mill	fill	pill
mill	fill	bill	pill	dill
bill	pill	dill	mill	fill
pill	bill	fill	dill	mill
dill	fill	mill	bill	fill
bill	dill	bill	fill	mill
dill	fill	mill	bill	fill

Page Speed Drills for *b* and *d* Confusion, *continued*

bin	den	ten	men	fin
ten	men	bin	den	fin
men	den	fin	ten	bin
fin	bin	ten	den	men
den	ten	men	bin	fin
fin	men	den	bin	ten

tad	tab	tub	dub	tad
tab	tub	tad	dub	tab
dub	tub	tab	tub	tad
dub	tub	tad	tab	dub
tad	tab	dub	tub	tad
tad	tab	tud	tad	dub

bub	hub	dub	hud	hub
dub	bub	hub	hud	bub
hub	dub	bub	hub	hud
bub	hub	dub	bub	hub
hud	bub	hub	bub	dub
bub	hub	dub	hud	bub

tabby	today	tubby	today	tabby
tubby	tabby	today	tabby	today
tubby	tabby	today	tubby	today
tabby	today	tubby	tabby	today
tabby	today	tabby	tubby	tabby
tubby	tabby	today	tubby	tabby

Page Speed Drills for *b* and *d* Confusion, *continued*

bad	dub	bad	dab	bud
dad	bad	mad	dab	dub
dub	bud	mad	dub	dad
bad	dab	dab	dub	bud
bud	mad	dub	dub	bud

doo	doo	boo	bee	dee
dee	doo	dee	bee	bee
bee	boo	boo	doo	dee
boo	doo	bee	doo	boo
bee	dee	boo	dee	bee
boo	doo	boo	dee	bee

baby	buddy	bed	bud	bad
bud	baby	bubby	buddy	bad
bubby	bubby	baby	buddy	bud
bad	bed	baby	bed	bed
bud	bubby	bud	bad	buddy

abe	ade	ode	ade	obe
ade	ode	abe	abe	ade
ode	abe	ade	obe	ode
abe	ade	abe	ode	abe
obe	ode	abe	ade	obe

Onset + Rime Patterns: Nonsense Words

Use these nonsense word lists of word families to develop practice materials. The beginning of each list contains nonsense words with single consonants (e.g., *mip*, *lip*). The end of each list contains nonsense words with consonant digraphs and blends (e.g., *shap*, *trap*).

Short vowels

ab	ad	ag	am	an
bab	gad	kag	fam	gan
hab	jad	mag	gam	han
mab	kad	pag	nam	san
pab	vad	vag	tam	wan
rab	zad	chag	vam	zan
sab	shad	shag	cham	chan
chab	blad	whag	blam	shan
shab	crad	blag	flam	whan
thab	drad	clag	glam	blan
clab	flad	glag	plam	flan
glab	frad	plag	bram	glan
plab	prad	slag	dram	slan
zlab	scad	crag	fram	cran
brab	scrad	frag	smam	dran
frab	skad	prag	snam	fran
prab	slad	trag	stam	pran
smab	smad	scag	twam	tran
snab	snad	smag	spram	skan
spab	spad	spag	stram	sman
trab	sprad	twag	splam	twan
twab	stad	scrag	shram	scran
scrab	strad	sprag	thram	spran
sprab	swad	strag		stran
strab	thad	splag		splan
splab	trad	shrag		shran
shrab	twad	thrag		thran
thrab				

Onset + Rime Patterns: Nonsense Words, *continued*

Short vowels

ap	at	ack	amp	and
bap	dat	dack	bamp	cand
dap	gat	fack	famp	dand
fap	jat	gack	gamp	fand
vap	lat	vack	hamp	gand
wap	tat	chack	mamp	mand
shap	wat	glack	samp	pand
blap	zat	plack	shamp	tand
glap	quat	brack	whamp	chand
plap	blat	drack	blamp	shand
brap	clat	frack	flamp	cland
drap	glat	grack	glamp	fland
frap	plat	prack	plamp	pland
grap	smat	scack	slamp	sland
prap	snat	spack	bramp	crand
scap	scrat	swack	dramp	drand
skap	sprat	twack	framp	frand
smap	strat	scrack	pramp	prand
spap	shrat	sprack	snamp	trand
stap	thrat	strack	spamp	scand
twap		splack	twamp	skand
sprap		thrack	scramp	smand
splap			spramp	snand
thrap			stramp	spand
			splamp	swand
				twand
				scrand
				spland

Onset + Rime Patterns: Nonsense Words, *continued*

Short vowels

ang	ank	ash	ed	en
jang	dank	fash	ved	fen
kang	fank	pash	ched	sen
mang	gank	tash	cled	ven
nang	lank	vash	gled	chen
vang	mank	zash	cred	shen
zang	pank	chash	dred	blen
chang	chank	shash	gred	clen
shang	shank	blash	pred	flen
whang	whank	drash	tred	plen
blang	glank	frash	smed	slen
flang	slank	grash	sned	bren
brang	brank	prash	sted	cren
crang	grank	scash	swed	dren
drang	trank	skash	twed	fren
frang	scank	snash	spred	gren
grang	smank	spash	stred	pren
prang	twank	swash	scred	tren
trang	scrank	twash	spled	smen
scang	sprank	scrash		snen
smang	strank	sprash		spen
snang	splank	strash		sten
spang	thrank	shrash		swen
stang				twen
swang				scren
scrang				spren
strang				stren
splang				splen
shrang				shren
thrang				thren

Onset + Rime Patterns: Nonsense Words, *continued*

Short vowels

et	ell	end	ent	ess
det	kell	dend	fent	dess
fet	lell	hend	hent	fess
het	mell	jend	jent	hess
ket	nell	kend	nent	kess
ret	rell	nend	pent	ness
tet	zell	pend	zent	pess
zet	brell	zend	chent	ress
clet	crell	chend	shent	sess
flet	drell	shend	blent	tess
glet	frell	clend	clent	vess
plet	grell	flend	flent	wess
slet	prell	glend	glent	zess
cret	trell	plend	plent	shess
dret	snell	slend	slent	cless
gret	stell	brend	crent	fless
pret	twell	crend	drent	gless
tret	screll	drend	frent	pless
smet	sprell	grend	grent	sless
snet	strell	prend	prent	bress
spet	shrell	smend	skent	cress
stet	threll	snend	sment	fress
twet		stend	stent	gress
scret		swend	swent	tress
spret		twend	twent	skess
stret		scrend	scrent	smess
splet		sprend	sprent	sness
shret		strend	strent	spess
thret		splend	splent	stess
				swess
				twess
				scress
				spress
				spless

Onset + Rime Patterns: Nonsense Words, *continued*

Short vowels

est	id	ig	in	ip
dest	fid	hig	lin	bip
fest	jid	kig	nin	fip
gest	nid	lig	rin	kip
hest	pid	mig	vin	mip
kest	tid	sig	yin	pip
mest	vid	tig	zin	vip
sest	wid	vig	blin	yip
yest	yid	yig	clin	glip
shest	zid	zig	flin	plip
whest	chid	chig	glin	brip
clest	shid	shig	plin	crip
flest	blid	blig	slin	frip
glest	flid	clig	brin	prip
plest	glid	flig	crin	smip
slest	plid	glig	drin	spip
frest	brid	plig	frin	stip
grest	crid	slig	prin	swip
trest	drid	crig	trin	twip
skest	frid	drig	smin	scrip
smest	prid	frig	snin	sprip
snest	trid	grig	stin	twip
spest	smid	prig	swin	scrip
stest	snid	trig	scrin	splip
swest	spid	smig	sprin	shrip
twest	stid	snig	strin	thrip
screst	swid	spig	splin	
sprest	twid	stig	shrin	
strest	scrid	scrig	thrin	
splest	sprid	strig		
	strid	splig		
	splid	shrig		
	shrid	thrig		
	thrid			

Onset + Rime Patterns: Nonsense Words, *continued*

Short vowels

it	ick	ill	ing	ink
dit	bick	lill	bing	bink
jit	fick	rill	fing	dink
rit	jick	vill	jing	hink
vit	mick	yill	ling	jink
yit	yick	zill	ming	nink
chit	zick	brill	ning	tink
whit	shick	crill	ting	vink
blit	blick	prill	ving	yink
glit	glick	smill	ying	shink
plit	plick	snill	zing	flink
crit	crick	scrill	ching	glink
drit	drick	sprill	shing	crink
frit	frick	strill	bling	frink
prit	grick		gling	grink
trit	smick		pling	prink
smit	snick		cring	trink
stit	swick		dring	smink
swit	twick		fring	skink
scrit	scrick		gring	spink
sprit	sprick		pring	swink
strit	strick		tring	twink
shrit	splick		sking	scrink
thrit	shrick		sming	sprink
	thrick		sning	strink
			sping	splink
			twing	
			scring	
			spling	
			shring	
			thring	

Onset + Rime Patterns: Nonsense Words, *continued*

Short vowels

og	op	ot	ug	un
gog	dop	bot	kug	hun
kog	fop	fot	nug	jun
mog	gop	mot	sug	kun
rog	jop	sot	vug	lun
sog	lop	vot	wug	mun
tog	nop	wot	zug	vun
vog	rop	yot	shug	yun
wog	sop	zot	blug	chun
yog	vop	chot	clug	blun
zog	yop	flot	flug	clun
chog	zop	glot	glug	flun
shog	blop	crot	brug	glun
blog	brop	drot	crug	plun
glog	frop	grot	frug	slun
plog	grop	prot	grug	brun
slog	trop	smot	prug	crun
brog	scop	stot	trug	drun
crog	smop	swot	scug	frun
drog	snop	scrot	spug	grun
grog	spop	sprot	stug	prun
prog	twop	strot	swug	trun
trog	scrop	splot	twug	scun
scog	strop	shrot	scrug	smun
skog	splop	throt	sprug	snun
snog	shrop		strug	swun
spog	throp		splug	twun
stog			thrug	scrun
swog				sprun
twog				strun
scrog				splun
sprog				shrun
strog				thrun
splog				
shrog				
throg				

Onset + Rime Patterns: Nonsense Words, *continued*

Short vowels

ut	ump	unk	ush
dut	cump	cunk	cush
jut	fump	kunk	dush
lut	kump	lunk	fush
sut	nump	nunk	jush
vut	tump	runk	kush
yut	vump	tunk	nush
zut	wump	vunk	sush
chut	yump	wunk	vush
blut	zump	yunk	wush
clut	shump	shunk	yush
flut	blump	blunk	zush
plut	flump	glunk	chush
brut	glump	slunk	clush
crut	brump	brunk	glush
frut	crump	crunk	drush
grut	drump	frunk	frush
prut	prump	grunk	grush
trut	scump	prunk	prush
scut	skump	scunk	trush
snut	swump	smunk	skush
sput	twump	swunk	snush
stut	scrump	twunk	spush
swut	sprump	scrunk	stush
scrut	strump	sprunk	swush
sprut	splump	strunk	twush
splut	shrump	splunk	scrush
shrut	thrump	thrunk	sprush
thrut			strush
			splush
			shrush

Onset + Rime Patterns: Nonsense Words, *continued*

Long vowels

ace	ade	ake	ame	ave
dace	bade	dake	bame	bave
gace	cade	gake	hame	fave
hace	dade	hake	jame	jave
jace	gade	nake	pame	kave
nace	hade	pake	rame	lave
sace	kade	vake	vame	mave
tace	nade	yake	wame	nave
wace	tade	zake	yame	tave
yace	vade	chake	zame	vave
zace	yade	clake	chame	yave
chace	chade	glake	glame	chave
shace	clade	plake	plame	blave
blace	flade	slake	slame	clave
clace	slade	crake	brame	flave
flace	crade	frake	crame	glave
glace	drade	grake	drame	plave
slace	frade	prake	grame	drave
crace	scade	trake	prame	frave
drace	smade	scake	trame	prave
frace	snade	smake	scame	trave
prace	twade	spake	slame	scave
scace	scrade	swake	sname	skave
slace	shrade	twake	spame	smave
smace	thrade	scrake	stame	snave
snace		thrake	swame	spave
stace			twame	stave
swace			scrame	swave
twace			sprame	twave
scrace			strame	scrave
sprace			splame	sprave
strace			shrame	strave
splace			thrame	splave
shrace				shrave
thrace				thrave

Onset + Rime Patterns: Nonsense Words, *continued*

Long vowels

ate	ail	ain	eam	eat
cate	cail	bain	feam	deat
jate	dail	fain	heam	jeat
nate	lail	hain	jeam	keat
pate	zail	jain	keam	leat
tate	chail	nain	meam	reat
vate	shail	tain	neam	veat
zate	blail	wain	peam	yeat
chate	clail	yain	veam	zeat
shate	glail	zain	weam	gleat
blate	plail	shain	yeam	breat
clate	slail	blain	zeam	creat
flate	crail	clain	cheam	dreat
glate	drail	flain	sheam	freat
brate	prail	frain	bleam	preat
drate	smail	prain	cleam	smeat
prate	spail	scain	fleam	sneat
trate	swail	smain	pleam	speat
smate	twail	snain	sleam	steat
snate	scrail	spain	bream	screat
swate	sprail	swain	fream	spreat
twate	strail	twain	gream	spleat
scrate	shrail	scrain	pream	shreat
sprate	thrail	splain	tream	
splate		shrain	sneam	
shrate		thrain	speam	
thrate			sweam	
			tweam	
			spream	
			spleam	
			shream	
			thream	

Onset + Rime Patterns: Nonsense Words, *continued*

Long vowels

eed	eep	eet	ice	ide
beed	feep	deet	bice	fide
jeed	meep	jeet	fice	jide
keed	neep	keet	hice	kide
leed	teep	leet	jice	mide
meed	veep	peet	kice	nide
veed	yeep	reet	pice	pide
yeed	zeep	veet	sice	yide
cheed	cleep	yeet	tice	zide
sheed	fleep	zeet	wice	shide
cleed	breep	gleet	yice	blide
fleed	dreep	breet	zice	clide
gleed	freep	creet	chice	flide
sleed	greep	dreet	shice	plide
dreed	preep	freet	blice	cride
preed	treep	preet	flice	gride
skeed	skeep	smeet	glice	smide
smeed	smeep	sneet	plice	stide
sneed	sneep	speet	brice	swide
sweed	speep	steet	crice	twide
spreed	tweep	screet	drice	scride
streed	screep	spreet	frice	spride
spleed	spreep	spleet	grice	splide
shreed	streep	shreet	trice	shride
threed	spleep	threet	smice	thride
	shreep		snice	
	threep		stice	
			swice	
			sprice	
			strice	
			shrice	

Onset + Rime Patterns: Nonsense Words, *continued*

Long vowels

ime	ine	ite	oat	oke
bime	bine	dite	doat	boke
fime	jine	jite	foat	doke
hime	rine	pite	hoat	foke
jime	tine	vite	joat	goke
kime	yine	yite	loat	hoke
nime	zine	zite	poat	loke
pime	chine	chite	roat	moke
sime	bline	blite	soat	noke
vime	cline	clite	woat	roke
wime	fline	glite	yoat	soke
yime	gline	crite	zoat	voke
zime	pline	drite	choat	zoke
blime	sline	grite	shoat	shoke
flime	brine	prite	cloat	floke
glime	crine	snite	ploat	gloke
plime	drine	stite	sloat	ploke
brime	frine	swite	broat	sloke
drime	grine	twite	croat	droke
frime	trine	scrite	droat	froke
trime	skine	strite	froat	groke
spime	smine	splite	groat	proke
stime	scrine	shrite	proat	troke
swime	sprine	thrite	troat	scoke
twime	strine		scoat	snoke
scrime	spline		smoat	swoke
sprime	thrine		snoat	twoke
strime			spoat	scroke
splime			stoat	sproke
shrime			swoat	sploke
thrime			twoat	shroke
			sproat	throke
			stroat	
			sploat	
			shroat	

Onset + Rime Patterns: Nonsense Words, *continued*

Long vowels

ore	ose
jore	bose
nore	cose
vore	fose
zore	gose
blore	jose
clore	kose
glore	mose
plore	sose
slore	vose
skore	yose
twore	zose
	blose
	glose
	plose
	brose
	drose
	trose
	scose
	smose
	snose
	spose
	stose
	swose
	twose
	scrose
	sprose
	strose
	splose
	shrose
	throse

Appendix 4M

Onset + Rime Patterns: Real Words

Use these lists of words constructed from word families to develop practice materials. The beginning of each list contains words with single consonants (e.g., *mip*, *lip*). The end of each list contains words with consonant digraphs and blends (e.g., *shap*, *trap*).

ab	ad	ag	am	an
cab	bad	bag	bam	ban
dab	cad	gag	ham	can
gab	dad	hag	jam	fan
jab	fad	lag	ram	man
tab	had	nag	clam	pan
crab	lad	rag	cram	ran
drab	mad	sag	sham	tan
grab	pad	tag	slam	van
flab	sad	wag	swam	scan
scab	tad	brag	tram	span
slab	brad	drag	wham	
stab	glad	flag		

ap	at	ed	en	et
cap	bat	bed	den	bet
gap	cat	fed	hen	get
lap	fat	led	men	jet
map	hat	red	pen	let
nap	mat	wed	ten	met
rap	pat	bled	then	net
sap	rat	bred	when	pet
tap	vat	fled	wren	set
yap	brat	Fred		vet
zap	chat	shed		wet
clap	flat	shred		yet
flap	slat	sled		fret
scrap	spat	sped		
slap	that			
strap				
trap				
wrap				

Onset + Rime Patterns: Real Words, *continued*

ew	id	ig	in	ip
dew	bid	big	bin	dip
new	did	dig	din	hip
blew	hid	fig	fin	nip
brew	kid	jig	kin	rip
chew	lid	pig	pin	sip
crew	rid	rig	tin	tip
drew	grid	wig	chin	chip
grew	skid	brig	grin	clip
flew	slid	twig	shin	drip
knew			skin	flip
screw			spin	grip
slew			thin	ship
stew			twin	skip
threw				slip
				snip
				strip
				trip
				whip

it	og	op	ot	ug
bit	bog	cop	cot	bug
fit	cog	hop	got	dug
hit	dog	mop	hot	hug
kit	fog	pop	lot	jug
lit	hog	top	pot	lug
pit	jog	chop	rot	mug
sit	log	crop	tot	pug
flit	clog	drop	blot	rug
grit	frog	prop	plot	tug
knit	smog	shop	shot	chug
skit		stop	spot	drug
slit			trot	plug
spit				snug
split				

Onset + Rime Patterns: Real Words, *continued*

un	ut	ack	amp	and
bun	cut	back	camp	band
fun	gut	lack	damp	hand
gun	hut	pack	lamp	land
pun	nut	sack	ramp	sand
run	rut	tack	champ	bland
sun	glut	black	clamp	brand
spun	shut	crack	cramp	gland
stun	strut	shack	stamp	grand
		slack	tramp	stand
		smack		strand
		snack		
		stack		
		track		
		whack		

ang	ank	ash	ell	end
bang	bank	bash	bell	bend
fang	sank	cash	fell	lend
gang	tank	dash	sell	mend
hang	blank	gash	tell	send
rang	clank	hash	well	tend
sang	crank	mash	yell	blend
clang	drank	rash	shell	spend
slang	flank	brash	smell	trend
sprang	frank	clash	spell	
	plank	crash	swell	
	prank	flash		
	shrank	smash		
	spank	splash		
	thank	stash		
	yank	trash		

Onset + Rime Patterns: Real Words, *continued*

ent	ess	est	ick	ill
bent	less	best	kick	bill
cent	mess	nest	lick	dill
dent	bless	pest	pick	fill
lent	chess	rest	sick	hill
rent	dress	test	wick	mill
sent	press	vest	brick	pill
tent	stress	west	chick	sill
went		chest	click	till
scent		crest	flick	will
spent			slick	chill
			stick	drill
			thick	grill
			trick	skill
				spill
				still
				thrill

ing	ink	ump	unk	ush
king	link	bump	bunk	gush
ring	mink	dump	dunk	hush
sing	pink	hump	hunk	mush
wing	sink	jump	junk	rush
bring	wink	chump	punk	blush
fling	blink	clump	sunk	brush
sling	drink	grump	chunk	crush
spring	shrink	plump	flunk	flush
sting	stink	slump	shrunk	plush
string	think	stump	skunk	slush
swing		thump	slunk	thrush
thing			spunk	
			stunk	

Onset + Rime Patterns: Real Words, *continued*

ace	ade	ake	ame	ave
face	fade	bake	came	cave
lace	jade	cake	dame	gave
mace	made	fake	fame	pave
pace	wade	lake	game	rave
race	blade	make	lame	save
brace	glade	rake	name	wave
grace	grade	sake	same	brave
place	shade	take	tame	crave
space	spade	wake	blame	grave
trace	trade	brake	flame	shave
		flake	frame	slave
		shake	shame	
		snake		
		stake		

ate	ail	eam	eat	ain
date	bail	beam	beat	gain
gate	fail	seam	heat	main
hate	hail	team	meat	pain
late	jail	cream	neat	rain
mate	mail	dream	seat	vain
rate	nail	gleam	bleat	brain
crate	pail	scream	cheat	chain
plate	rail	steam	cleat	drain
skate	sail	stream	pleat	grain
slate	tail		treat	sprain
state	wail		wheat	stain
	frail			strain
	snail			train
	trail			

Onset + Rime Patterns: Real Words, *continued*

eed	eep	eet	ice	ide
deed	deep	beet	dice	hide
feed	jeep	feet	lice	ride
need	keep	meet	mice	side
seed	peep	fleet	nice	tide
weed	weep	greet	rice	wide
bleed	bleep	sheet	vice	bride
breed	cheep	sleet	price	glide
creed	creep	street	slice	pride
freed	sheep	sweet	spice	slide
greed	sleep		splice	stride
speed	steep		twice	
steed	sweep			
tweed				

ime	ine	ite	oat	oke	ore	ose
dime	dine	bite	boat	joke	bore	hose
lime	fine	kite	coat	poke	core	nose
time	line	site	goat	woke	fore	pose
chime	mine	spite	bloat	yoke	lore	rose
crime	nine	white	float	broke	more	chose
grime	pine	write	gloat	choke	pore	close
prime	vine		throat	smoke	tore	prose
slime	wine			spoke	wore	those
	prine			stroke	chore	
	shine				score	
	shrine				shore	
	spine				snore	
	swine				spore	
	twine				store	
	whine				swore	

Onset + Rime Nonsense and Real Words—Card Games

Any of the lists from Appendix 4L and 4M (pages 81-99) can be written on index cards and used in card games. Some suggestions for games include:

- **Flash cards**
  Tell the student he is going to see a nonsense word or a real word that ends with a silent e (long vowel) or does not end in a silent e (short vowel). He is to read it as soon as he sees it.

- **Word Sort**
  Write several of the rime types (e.g., *ipe*, *at*, *ike*) on signs and place them on the table. Shuffle the word cards. The student draws a card, reads it, and sorts it into the right category. You could also do this with the two word types: short vowel and long vowel (V, C, + silent e)

- **Flip It**
  Shuffle the word cards. You may want to write the two types of words on the board for reference. Divide the cards into two stacks, one for each player. Each player turns over a card from the top of his stack, reads the word, and says the word type. For example, if the student turns over the word *cape*, he says, "*Cape*, that's *a* + silent e = long vowel." The other player reads his syllable. For example, "*Tip*, that's a short vowel word." If the two word types are the same, the first player to say, "Two long vowels + silent e" or "Two short vowels" gets both cards. If the word types don't match, the cards go into a discard pile. The game ends when the stacks are empty. The winner is the player with the most cards.

- **Go Fish**
  Create a deck of cards comprised of two of each rime type (e.g., *-ime*, *-ike*, *-ip*, *-at*, *-ill*). Shuffle the cards and deal five to each player. The rest of the cards remain in the draw pile which is placed facedown on the table. Players remove any pairs (e.g., two *-ime* words: *lime/time*) from their hands and place them on the table.

  The game is played according to the rules of *Go Fish*, with each player asking the other for a card to try to find a match to a card in his hand. For example, "Do you have a word that ends in *-am*?" If the other player has a match, she must give it to the first player, who places the match on the table. The first player then gets another turn. If no match is found, the asker must "fish" by choosing a card from the draw pile. If a match is made when choosing a card from the draw pile, the player places the card from his hand and the card from the draw pile on the table. If no match is made, the player puts the card from the draw pile in his hand and that is the end of his turn. Play then moves to the next player. The game ends when one player gets rid of all his cards.

Page Speed Drills for Letter Patterns

Page speed drills present a page of stimuli to the student that will allow practice at recognizing and decoding any number of patterns. Page speed drills can be devised for individual letter recognition, letter pattern recognition, syllable recognition, or whole word recognition. Ask the student to use his finger to follow the line of text or to use an index card to cover all but the line he is reading. Time how quickly the student can read the stimuli. Stress accuracy. The student might read the same page drill several times to see if he can improve his speed and accuracy.

Example of drill for student who doesn't attend to blends

say	say	stay	sop	stop
sop	say	stop	say	stay
stay	sop	stay	say	sop
stay	say	stay	sop	say
sop	say	sop	stay	say
stay	sop	stay	say	sop

fist	fit	loss	mit	miss
mist	fist	miss	mit	lost
loss	fit	lost	fist	fit
mist	mit	lost	miss	fist
floss	mist	fit	fist	mist
lost	loss	mit	miss	fist

Example of drill for student who has trouble with two-letter vowel sounds

feet	fit	feed	seed	deep
dip	feet	fit	sad	seed
sad	dip	deep	feed	fit
fit	feet	deep	feed	seed
seed	feed	seed	feet	fit
sad	deep	feet	feed	sad

daup	houp	loup	paut	toup
tout	lout	daup	laut	taup
loup	houp	paut	daup	toup
toup	tout	loup	toup	paut
laut	daup	tout	loup	laut
paut	tout	houp	toup	loup

Appendix 4P

Computer Games

The chart reflects computer games that address letter pattern recognition. Some of these same games may have been listed in Appendix 3A in Chapter 3 (pages 46-47) because they also address phonological awareness.

Games	Blends	Digraphs	Vowel patterns	*r* & *l* patterns	*ph, gh, igh, nk, ch*	*b/d*	Onset+ rime	Timed
Earobics #2								
Hippo				X				
Duck Luck	X	X		X				X
Lexia PB—Level 1								
Consonant Castle							X	
Sort *b, d, p*						X		
Lexia PB—Level 2								
Change							X	
Spin It	X	X						
Lexia PB—Level 3								
Pirate Ship			X					X
Super Change							X	
Word Stairs				X				
Lexia SOS—Level 1								
Consonant Blast	X	X						
Master *b, d, p*						X		X
Lexia SOS—Level 2								
Letter Switch	X	X						
Lexia SOS—Level 3								
At the Mall				X				
Sea Hunt			X					
Reading Blaster-Ages 6-7								
Socks		X						

Chart continued on next page.

Computer Games, *continued*

Games	Blends	Digraphs	Vowel patterns	*r & l* patterns	*ph, gh, igh, nk, ch*	*b/d*	Onset+ rime	Timed
Reader Rabbit								
Dandy's Tree House	X							
Decorator Crab		X						
Falling Peacenuts	X							
Kelp Forest							X	
Reader's Basement							X	
Rules, Rules, Rules								
Groups 7, 8, 9			X					
Groups 12-15			X					
Groups 27, 28, 29, 33	X							
Groups 31, 32	X							
Group 34				X				
Groups 27, 38			X					
Sound Reading Solutions								
PA 11			X					
PA 12			X					
Word Workout—Level 1								
Lesson 4				X				
Word Workout—Level 2								
Lesson 12				X				
Lesson 16					X			

For information on where to obtain these materials, see the Resources list on pages 260-262.

Other Materials

This chart contains a list of other games and materials that can be used to increase the speed of reading letter patterns.

Materials	Blends	Digraphs	Vowel patterns	*r & l* patterns	*ph, gh, igh, nk, ch*	Onset+ rime	Timed
Blend It, End It	X	X		X		X	
Dog Bones Long & Short Vowels						X	
Lakeshore Word Family Activity Program						X	
Lakeshore Word Family Flips						X	
Lakeshore Word Family Sliders						X	
Making Big Words	X	X	X	X	X		
Making Words	X	X	X	X	X		
Pharaoh's Phonics	X						
Quizmo	X	X					
Snap It Up						X	X
Wacky Wahoo Word Lab	X	X	X	X	X	X	
Write & Wipe						X	

For information on where to obtain these materials, see the Resources list on pages 260-262.

Using PowerPoint for Timed Presentation of Stimuli

Improving reading fluency is largely about increasing speed. PowerPoint is an excellent tool that allows you to control the rate of presentation and force automaticity. Whether you are helping the student recognize letter patterns, multi-syllabic words, or connected text, you can structure the activities so that the student is forced to speed up a little bit.

PowerPoint allows you to control the rate at which the student is expected to read one stimuli (whether that is a syllable, word, or sentence) before the next appears on the screen. You can type in any stimuli that you want the student to read. You could accomplish the same thing by writing the stimuli on cards and only allowing the student so many seconds to read the card before presenting the next. However, students don't find that nearly as much fun as seeing the stimuli on the screen with the special effects that can be created.

Here are instructions for using PowerPoint to teach letter patterns, but it can be used in any of the subsequent chapters.

Instructions for using PowerPoint

1. Open PowerPoint.
2. Choose to *Open* a blank presentation.
3. Choose the second slide layout.
4. Select a font size that is easy for the student to read.
5. Type the stimuli (word, phrase, or sentence) with the desired number of words on each line in text box (not the title box).
6. Click *Slide Show* from the bar on top of the screen.
7. Click *Custom Animations*.
8. Click the animate sign objects.
9. Choose *Text 2*.
10. Under the *Effect* tab, select whatever effects you want. This determines how the text will appear.
11. Under the *Order* and *Timing* tab, you can choose *Mouse Click* or *Automatically*. *Automatically* means that you can select the number of seconds you want the stimuli to stay on the screen before the next line of text appears. This will help to force speed.
12. Click *OK*.
13. Click *Slide Show*.
14. Click *View Show*.

Chapter 5

Increasing Speed of Reading Syllable and Word Patterns

Quickly recognizing letter patterns, as discussed in Chapter 4, will certainly improve the speed of the student's reading. However, students need to continue to improve their skills along the continuum, recognizing larger and larger portions of a word. The next step in the continuum is to help the student increase speed in recognizing and reading frequently occurring simple and complex syllable patterns. This chapter addresses syllable patterns as well as some simple one-syllable word patterns. You may want to combine the work in this chapter with the activities in Chapter 6 (pages 145-152) on multi-syllabic words.

Recognizing basic syllable shapes

To help your student increase speed of reading, you must first make sure that she understands the eight basic syllable shapes:

Eight basic syllable shapes	
• VC	• CCV
• CV	• CCVC
• CVC	• CVCC
• VCC	• CCVCC

Remind the student that each syllable must contain a vowel. Providing her with practice in recognizing these patterns, or shapes, will lay the groundwork for her to decode and read multi-syllabic words more quickly. (See Appendices 5A and 5B, pages 117-126.) If she can easily recognize where the syllable boundaries occur, she will more quickly be able to read the multi-syllabic words.

See Appendices 5A and 5B.

Open versus closed syllable types

In addition to the syllable shapes described above, there are different types of syllables. These syllable types are controlled by the kinds of consonant and vowel patterns within the syllable. One of the basic distinctions of syllable types is open versus closed. Open syllables are those that end with a vowel. Closed syllables end with a consonant.

See Appendix 5C.

Of the eight basic syllable shapes listed above, the second (CV) and fifth (CCV) are open. All others are closed. Open syllables ending in the vowels *a*, *e*, *i*, *o*, or *u* are pronounced with a long vowel. Closed syllables are typically pronounced with a short vowel. For example, in the word *ta ble*, the first syllable has a long vowel, whereas in the word *bab ble*, the first syllable has a short vowel. (Note: Vowels *oo*, *ou*, *ow*, *au*, *aw*, *oi*, and *oy* do not follow this long/short rule.) For practice, have the student read the nonsense syllables in Appendix 5C, page 127. However, these syllables are most easily taught and practiced in the context of multi-syllabic words and will be addressed again in Chapter 6.

Simple syllables with short-long vowel markers

One of the patterns students learn early in their education is the short vowel/long vowel contrast. When a silent e appears at the end of a word, the vowel "says its name, not its sound." Words that have C + *a*, *i*, *o*, or *u* + C + *e* are pronounced with the alphabet name of the vowel in the middle (e.g., *time*, *line*, *mane*). When the vowel in the middle is another *e*, the silent *e* does not go at the end of the word. We tell the students "those two *e* sounds like to sit together" (e.g., *beet*, *feet*, *peep*). Students with fluency problems need lots of practice reading these words (syllables), especially when they appear in different forms (e.g., verb tenses as in *dine*/*dining*). Appendix 5D (page 128) provides a list of simple syllable C + *e* marker words for practice.

See Appendix 5D.

Other spelling rules that affect one-syllable words

Other predictable patterns should be practiced so that the student can more quickly process and read one-syllable words. Some of these patterns were addressed in Chapter 4. They are briefly explained here. Practice activities are provided in Appendices 5E, 5F, 5G, 5H, and 5I (pages 129-137).

c followed by *i*, *e*, or *y*

When *c* is followed by an *i*, *e*, or *y*, it is pronounced as *s* and not *k*. When *c* is followed by any other vowel, it is pronounced as *k*.

See Appendix 5E.

g followed by *i*, *e*, or *y*

The *g* rule is not as clear cut as the *c* rule. If *g* is followed by an *i*, *e*, or *y*, it might be pronounced as a *j*. Students need to practice trying these words with each sound (hard *g* or soft *j*) and then determine which is the real word. When the *g* is followed by any other vowel, it is pronounced as the hard *g*.

See Appendix 5F.

Doubling consonants

The consonants *l*, *f*, *s*, and *z* are usually doubled at the end of a one-syllable word immediately following a short vowel, as in *bell*, *cuff*, *mess*, and *fuzz*. There are exceptions to this and most other rules. For example, the *s* is not doubled in *gas*. When students encounter these exceptions, tell them, "That word just doesn't play by the rules," or "That word doesn't play fair." At the one-syllable word level, this rule has little impact on reading (i.e., whether a word is spelled *pas* or *pass*, the student is likely to recognize and read this as containing a short vowel). It has more impact on spelling than reading. Therefore, practice activities for this rule are not provided in appendices for this chapter.

-*ck* is used for the -*k* sound if it comes after a short vowel

Tell the students the job of the *c* is to make the vowel say its sound and not its name. The vowel is a short vowel in words like *luck*, *peck*, and *back*. In words with long vowels (e.g., *like*, *take*), a *k* is used at the end of the word with the silent *e*. Tell the students that you can't put an *e* after a *ck*. The *c* stands in the way and won't let the *e* tell the vowel to say its name. Also show them how odd it looks if they tried to spell a word with a long vowel, a *ck*, and an *e*, as in *licke* or *tacke*. The exception to short vowel words needing the *ck* is if another consonant stands in for the *c* (e.g., the *r* in *park*, the

See Appendix 5G.

l in *talk*, the *n* in *think)*. These extra consonants "keep the vowel short." (Note: Students may think there are only two categories of vowels: long and short. But vowels such as *au*, *aw*, and *oo* are neither long nor short. These are followed by *-k*.)

-tch is used after a short vowel

This rule (and the next) makes sense to students after they have learned the *-ck*/*-k* rule because the pattern is the same. If the word ends in *-tch*, the vowel sound will be short. Tell the students that the job of the *t* is to tell the vowel to be short. All other vowel sounds will have a *-ch* at the end, as in *peach*, *couch*, *poach*. The exception is that if an *l* or *r* or *n* appears before the *-ch*, then the *t* is not needed. The vowel will still be short, as in *mulch* or *torch*. There are, of course, words that break the rule. They have a short vowel but end in *-ch* (e.g., *attach*, *rich*, *such*, and *which*).

See Appendix 5H.

-dge is used after a short vowel and *-ge* is used with long vowels

Students will expect the vowel to always be long when there is a silent *e* at the end of the word. However, this rule works best with one-syllable words. In a two-syllable word, if the *-ge* is in an unstressed syllable (e.g., *passage*), the vowel will sound like the schwa instead of the expected long vowel. Tell students that the job of the *d* is to stand guard and not let the *e* get his message to the vowel. Therefore, the vowel is short in words like *judge*, *badge*, and *edge* and long in words like *page*, *huge*, and *age*. The exception to short vowel words needing the *d* is if another consonant stands in for the *d* (e.g., the *r* in *large*, the *l* in *bulge*, the *n* in *hinge*). These other consonants serve the same purpose and keep the vowel short.

See Appendices 5I and 5J.

Card games to practice the spelling rules for one-syllable words are described in Appendix 5J, pages 138-139.

C + *-le* pattern at end of words

Many two-syllable words end with a consonant followed by *-le*. The *e* is silent. Students may want to pronounce these syllables as if they were an open syllable with a long vowel. They may try to say *plee* instead of *pul* or *flee* instead of *ful*. This chart shows the typical C + *-le* endings. Words with these endings are found in Chapter 6, Appendix 6J, page 169.

-ble	-dle
-fle	-gle
-kle	-ple
-sle	-stle (the *t* is silent)
-tle	-zle

Morpheme patterns

Adams and Henry (1997) discussed the skills needed to move beginning readers along the developmental continuum of word recognition. In addition to recognition of syllable shapes and types, they also pointed out the importance of recognizing morpheme patterns borrowed from different languages that evolved into English.

There are two types of morphemes: free and bound. Free morphemes can stand alone as a whole word and cannot be divided without losing their meaning. Bound morphemes cannot stand alone but can be combined with the free morpheme to modify its meaning. Prefixes and suffixes are good examples of bound morphemes. For example, *pre* cannot stand alone but is combined with other morphemes to modify their meaning (e.g., *prenatal*, *prearrange, prepaste*).

Adams (1990) found it helpful for spelling and understanding the meaning of words to teach students to look at morphological cues. Henry (1990) found that teaching children morpheme patterns helped them to improve not only morphological knowledge but also helped them to improve their decoding and spelling abilities. Elbro's study (1990) suggested that if the student can analyze and synthesize morphemes, then the student has one more tool in his toolbox for reading in addition to whole word recognition and letter level decoding.

A brief introduction to morphemes is provided in this chapter, as you may want to do some work on helping students recognize the single syllable morpheme. However, most of the work on morphemes will need to be done in the context of multi-syllables and is covered in more detail in Chapter 6.

Morphemes in English have evolved from three basic languages:

- Anglo-Saxon
- Latin (also called Romance)
- Greek

Henry (1990) summarizes the types of words typical to each of these old languages:

Anglo-Saxon	Common, everyday words used frequently and in many books. Often consist of compound words, prefixes, and suffixes.
Latin/Romance	Technical, sophisticated words used in more formal settings and in literature. Consist of roots (e.g., *vis*, *tract*, *ped*), prefixes, and suffixes.
Greek	Specialized words often used in science and technology (though some are common, like *television*). Consist of two equally important parts.

Learning morpheme patterns can help a student with vocabulary acquisition and fluency because it helps her become more familiar with word parts and enhances her associations of lexical and semantic information.

Adams and Henry provide excellent information about the derivation of morphemes. Morphemes may compound or affix. Morphemes that compound have meaning when standing alone (free) in words such as *flashlight*, *railroad*, and *sailboat*. Morphemes may also affix either as a prefix or a suffix. Some words have both a prefix and a suffix, as in ***un**likely*, ***for**get**ful***, ***dis**order**ly***, and ***un**mistak**able***.

Anglo-Saxon morphemes

Anglo-Saxons used a simple vocabulary comprised mainly of short words describing activities that took place in their daily lives (Steere et al. 1998). Many of our commonly used verbs are Anglo-Saxon. Students might find it interesting to know that they can recognize Anglo-Saxon words by the following patterns, described by Steere et al.

- prefixes and suffixes (see chart below and on the following pages)
- consonant combinations (e.g., *-ck*, *-tch*, *-dge*)
- *wr* and *wh* at the beginning of words
- *gh* in words
- *ow* in words
- many words with double consonants
- groups of short words with stems that rhyme (e.g., *big*, *dig*, *fig*) and those that end in the same Anglo-Saxon suffix (e.g., *blanket*, *trinket*, and *bucket*)
- *k* in words

Anglo-Saxon words typically compound or affix (prefix and suffix). Some words compound and have an affix (e.g., *understat**ing***, ***mid**shipman*, *overcook**ed***). Adams and Henry indicate that common affixes can be introduced as early as mid-second grade. Many Anglo-Saxon morphemes are prepositions (e.g., *under*, *in*, *by*).

The following are common Anglo-Saxon prefixes that can be taught early, along with their meanings:

a- on, in, from, without	*be-* about, around	*by-* beside, around
de- away from	*for-* in front of	*fore-* before
in- not (most frequent meaning)	*mis-* wrong	*out-* outward, external
over- too much	*un-* not	*under-* place, situation, below, beneath

Suffixes may hold certain meaning, but they're often grammatical markers. The chart below lists some early Anglo-Saxon suffixes:

-able tending to	*-ed* forms past tense	*-en* to put into or on
-er comparative degree of adjectives or adverbs	*-est* superlative degree of adjective	*-et* small
-ful full of	*-hood* state, condition	*-ing* action, process
-ish of or belonging to	*-less* without	*-like* characterized by or like
-ly specified manner	*-ness* state, quality	*-s (-es)* plural
-ship state, quality	*-some* like	*-th* act, action
-ward in, toward	*-y* characterized by, like	

Practice with words that have these suffixes is found in Chapter 6, Appendix 6J, pages 167-169.

Adding suffixes to many base words requires knowing these basic suffix addition rules. Some of these have been described already and are reiterated here in the context of suffixes. Practice applying these rules is included in Chapter 6, Appendices 6H through 6J, pages 162-169. The basic suffix addition rules follow:

- the one-syllable doubling rule
  Words of one syllable which end in one consonant preceded by one vowel must double the final consonant when getting a suffix beginning with a vowel (e.g., *tip* becomes *tipped*).
- silent *e* rule
  - Base words ending in a silent *e* drop the final *e* when adding suffixes beginning with a vowel (e.g., *time* becomes *timing*).
  - Base words ending in silent *e* keep the *e* when adding suffixes beginning with a consonant (e.g., *time* becomes *timely*).
- the final *y* rule
  Change the *y* to an *i* when the *y* is preceded by a consonant and the suffix begins with any letter except *i* (e.g., *dry* becomes *dried*, but *dry* becomes *drying*).

Latin morphemes

Steere et al. (1998) indicate that Latin words can be recognized by:

- prefixes and suffixes (see below)
- consonant combinations *ct* and *pt* at the end of the stem
- connectives *i*, *u*, *ul*, *ol*
- doubling consonants at the beginning of words when prefix is added (e.g., *arrive*)
- Latin *sh* combinations *ti*, *si*, *ci*, *xi*

This chart includes Latin prefixes.

ab- away from	*ad-* to, toward, at	*ambi-* both
ante- before	*bi-* two	*circum-* around
co-/com- together	*con-* with	*contra-* against
de- down from, concerning	*dis-/di-* opposite, apart from, not	*en-/em-* make
ex-/e- out of	*extra-* beyond	*in-* in, into, not
inter- among, between	*intra-* within	*mid-* middle
mis- wrong	*ne-* not	*non-* not
ob- against	*per-* through	*post-* after
pre- before	*re-* again, back	*se-* apart from
sub- under	*super-* over	*trans-* across

These usually affix to bound roots. Bound roots are meaningless when they stand alone (e.g., *rupt* in *interrupt*). In this example, neither the root nor the affix can stand alone. The root generally gets the primary accent. Bound roots remain constant as prefixes and suffixes are added (e.g., ***vis**ionary*, ***vis**ual*, *tele**vis**ion*, *re**vis**e*).

Knowing that the bound root remains constant will help students understand why words are spelled as they are in unaccented syllables with the schwa patterns:

compete/**compet**ition **confid**e/**confid**ential (Henderson 1990)

Information on the use of the schwa and accent is found in Chapter 6, pages 149-150.

Some roots hold specific meaning, and this helps with vocabulary building. Latin roots are found in the following chart:

aud hear	*bene* well, good	*cred* to believe	*dic/dict* to say, tell
duc/duce/duct to lead	*fac/fact* to make, do	*flec/flex* to bend	*form* to shape
fract to break	*jac/jec/ject* to throw, lie	*jud* judge	*junct* to join
mit/miss to send	*pel/puls* to drive/push	*pend* to hang	*port* to carry
rupt to break	*scrib/script* to write	*spec/spect* to see, watch	*spir* to breathe
st/sta/stat to stand	*stru/struct* to build	*tang/tact* to touch	*tract* to pull
vert/vers to turn	*voc* voice, to call	*vor* to eat	

Latin also provides us with common suffixes. They typically do not have a specific meaning, but do make the word a particular part of speech (Henry 1990). For example, you would find *-ous* in adjectives and *-ity* in nouns. Many suffixes can be used in several parts of speech (e.g., *-age* can be in a noun such as *package* or in a verb like *damage*). The chart below includes Latin suffixes:

-age action, process	*-ant* one who performs or promotes	*-ent* one who performs or promotes
-ible able to be	*-ist* one who makes or produces	*-ive* tending to
-or condition, quality	*-tion* action, result	*-ure* action, result

Greek morphemes

Greek words are often made up of two parts, pronounced with almost equal stress. Greek words are often found in scientific texts. Greek words typically compound two roots rather than use affix, although sometimes the word parts are called prefixes and suffixes. Sometimes this is also called *combining forms*, since the two parts have equal importance. This makes them similar to Anglo-Saxon compound words. Some of the parts can be used only at the beginning of a word, and others can only be used at the end (Henry 1990). Examples of Greek words include *tele* + *graph*, *phon* + *ology*, and *anthro* + *pod.*

Greek words also have certain letter combinations that frequently occur. These are alternate spellings that may not be familiar to the students. These include:

- *ph* alternate spelling for *f*
- *ch* alternate spelling for *ck*
- *y* alternate spelling for *i* in the middle of words
- *p* silent *p* as in *psychology*

The following charts list typical Greek morphemes that occur at the beginning and end of words and their meanings. Greek morphemes commonly occurring at the beginning of words are below:

a-/an- of, belonging to	*anti-* against	*arch-* extreme, ultimate	*astro-* stars, outer space
auto- self	*biblio-* book	*bio-* life	*chron-* time
deca- ten	*derma-* skin	*duo-* two, twice	*en-* in
geo- earth, ground	*hemi-* half	*hydro-* water, wet	*hyper-* over, above, beyond
hypo- under, beneath	*macro-* large	*mega-* big	*meta-* with, after
micro- small	*mono-* one, single	*neo-* new, recent, revived	*peri-* around, near
philos- the love of	*phon-* sound	*photo-* light	*poly-* much, many
pro- before, in front of	*psych-* mind	*pyro-* fire	*semi-* half
syn-/sym- with, together	*tech-* art, skill, craft	*tele-* distant	*theo-* god
therm- heat	*tri-* three		

Greek morphemes commonly occurring at the end of words are below:

-cracy government rule	*-crat* supporters of government	*-gram* things written
-graph writing	*-meter* measure	*-ology* study
-phile love of	*-phobia* fear	*-polis* city
-scope instrument for viewing	*-sphere* three-dimensional	

As mentioned previously, most of the work with morphemes will need to be in the context of multi-syllabic words (see Chapter 6). However, materials are provided in the appendices in this chapter to allow for some drill work to increase speed of recognition and understanding of various morphemes. (See Appendices 5K, 5L, and 5M, pages 140-142.) Introduce only the syllable shapes and patterns that are appropriate to the age of the child with whom you are working. Adams and Henry (1997) suggest that students in second grade should be exposed to VC/CV patterns (e.g., closed syllable with short vowel as in *rabbit*), and third graders need to understand V/CV (e.g., open syllable with long vowel as in *hobo* and *vacation*), VC/V (e.g., closed syllable as in *solid* and *limit*), and C + *-le* (e.g., *bubble* and *wiggle*). They indicate that only older students need to be exposed to more complex patterns with digraphs.

See Appendices 5K, 5L, and 5M.

How to use the appendices in this chapter

Any of the appendices in this chapter can be used to help a child improve phonological awareness and decoding. To improve fluency and to achieve a level of automaticity, remember the following:

- Have the child read the stimuli multiple times.
- If the student reads something incorrectly, correct the error.
- Have the student pre-read the stimuli (e.g., word list) to make sure she can read all the words (or nonsense stimuli) before beginning the activity.
- Introduce an element of time. Use a stopwatch or timer and see if the student improves the time it takes to complete the activity on successive trials.
- Copy the stimuli onto index cards to make flash cards so the timing of presentation of the stimuli can be controlled. This works best with stimuli that are word length (e.g., onset + rime) or two words (e.g., two contrasting pronunciations of a word or nonsense syllable) rather than sentence or story level stimuli.
- Use commercially-available computer games and materials for practice (Appendices 5N and 5O, pages 143-144).
- PowerPoint software can be used for any length stimuli to control the speed of presentation (Appendix 4R, page 105).

See Appendices 5N and 5O.

See Appendix 4R.

Note: Not all of the appendices will be appropriate for all ages of children because of the level of vocabulary and concepts included.

List of Appendices for Chapter 5

Word Lists for Basic Syllable Shapes

Use these lists of nonsense syllables for students to read and practice recognizing each of the basic syllable shapes.

VC

ap	ig	uf	im	eb
ut	en	ak	ep	id
ab	et	ug	um	ik
ef	ek	ob	ot	im

CV

bu	ko	fa	mu	ni
re	la	wo	ge	lu
si	ta	su	bi	ga
po	ki	ba	ma	tu

CVC

baf	kep	tup	mif	sor
hiv	lod	mav	wuk	nog
bif	til	fup	bik	cas
min	naf	tif	wap	paf

VCC

alt	elb	olg	ist	ugs
ild	olk	ack	imp	emp
ast	iks	ups	est	ims
ets	elp	alm	oft	ifs

CCV

dro	fra	ste	pli	gru
tra	cru	tre	cro	pla
blo	stu	spi	tru	dre
cri	sku	smi	fli	sta

CCVC

drap	kled	fris	proz	flup
stin	skup	flad	tred	drod
drot	frap	stet	plip	gruk
blop	stut	spem	trun	drep

CVCC

laft	wefs	fost	sigs	buld
posp	sont	nump	tant	wilp
bilk	simp	bemp	tifs	tups
balt	koft	sims	tups	bolk

CCVCC

stist	plats	skump	trant	plon
klemp	frump	drist	plost	smant
draps	kleds	frist	prosp	flups
flaft	swefs	frisp	stant	swilp

Switch-a-letter Practice for Basic Syllable Shapes

This game is designed to help students quickly and accurately recognize common syllable shapes and be able to manipulate sounds and letters to change the syllable, still maintaining the same syllable shape.

Materials needed: write and wipe board
markers
word lists for each of the eight basic syllable shapes (See Appendix 5A, page 117).

To play Switch-a-letter, write the syllable shape at the top of the board (e.g., CVC, CCVCC). Then use any of the three variations of the game below.

- **Write and Wipe**
  Pronounce the first syllable or word and have the student write the syllable in the first row on a write and wipe board. Then give the student a direction to change one of the letters or letter patterns by pronouncing them as sounds, but not telling the letter. For example, in a chain changing a syllable from *let* to *bet*, you would say, "Change /*l*/ to /*b*/, rather than saying "Change the *l* to a *b*." The student erases the sound(s) you requested and writes a letter to represent that sound. She then tells what word or syllables she has created. Remind the student that the syllable shape stays the same as changes are made to the vowel or consonants. Depending on the student's expertise with spelling, you may have to guide the student in spelling some of the words correctly (e.g., spelling *loaf* rather than *lofe*).
- **Make a Chain**
  Pronounce the first syllable or word and have the student write the syllable in the first row on a write and wipe board. Then give the student a direction to change one of the letters or letter patterns by pronouncing them as sounds (not the letter). Have the student write the new syllable or word under the first, so she can see all the changes that have been made. The student then tells what word or syllable she has created. Remind the student that the syllable pattern or shape is staying the same as changes are made to the vowel or consonants.
- **Invisible Write and Wipe**
  To make this a more difficult task, have the student "write" the word on the table with her finger. Give the student a direction to "change" one of the letters or letter patterns by pronouncing them as sounds (not the letter). Ask her to try to "see" what she has written and to make the "changes" on the table. The student then tells what word or syllable she has created by pronouncing it. Remind her that the syllable pattern or shape is staying the same as changes are made to the vowel or consonants.
- **Syllable and Word Lists for Switch-a-letter Games** (pages 118 through 126)

Syllable Shape: VC

Student writes:	Tell student to make this change:
in	Change *n* to *t*
it	Change *t* to *f*
if	Change *f* to *s*
is	Change *i* to *u*
us	Change *u* to *a*
as	Change *s* to *t*
at	Change *t* to *m*
am	Change *m* to *n*
an	

Switch-a-letter Practice for Basic Syllable Shapes, *continued*

Syllable Shape: VC

Student writes:	Tell student to make this change:
on	Change *o* to *i*
in	Change *i* to a
an	Change *n* to *t*
at	Change *a* to *ea*
eat	Change *ea* to *ou*
out	Change *ou* to *i*
it	Change *t* to *s*
is	Change *i* to *u*
us	Change *s* to *p*
up	

Syllable Shape: CV

Student writes:	Tell student to make this change:
tie	Change *t* to *p*
pie	Change *p* to *l*
lie	Change *ie* to *aw*
law	Change *l* to *p*
paw	Change *p* to *r*
raw	Change *aw* to *ow*
row	Change *ow* to *ay*
ray	Change *r* to *p*
pay	Change *p* to *m*
may	

Switch-a-letter Practice for Basic Syllable Shapes, *continued*

Syllable Shape: CV

Student writes:	Tell student to make this change:
too	Change *t* to *b*
boo	Change *oo* to e
be	Change e to *ay*
bay	Change *b* to *d*
day	Change *ay* to *ie*
die	Change *d* to *t*
tie	Change *ie* to *oo*
too	Change *oo* to *oe*
toe	

Syllable Shape: CVC

Student writes:	Tell student to make this change:
sip	Change *s* to *t*
tip	Change *t* to *d*
dip	Change *d* to *l*
lip	Change *p* to *t*
lit	Change *i* to e
let	Change e to *o*
lot	Change *l* to *t*
tot	Change both *t's* to *p's*
pop	Change *o* to e
pep	Change the last *p* to *t*
pet	

Switch-a-letter Practice for Basic Syllable Shapes, *continued*

Syllable Shape: CVC

Student writes:	Tell student to make this change:
leaf	Change *ea* to *oa*
loaf	Change *f* to *d*
load	Change *oa* to e
led	Change *l* to *b*
bed	Change *d* to *t*
bet	Change e to *i*
bit	Change *b* to *f*
fit	Change *i* to *a*
fat	Change *t* to *n*
fan	

Syllable Shape: VCC

Student writes:	Tell student to make this change:
ilk	Change *i* to e
elk	

Student writes:	Tell student to make this change:
eels	Change ee to *ai*
ails	Change *ai* to *oi*
oils	

Student writes:	Tell student to make this change:
amp	Change *a* to *i*
imp	

Switch-a-letter Practice for Basic Syllable Shapes, *continued*

Syllable Shape: VCC

Student writes*:	Tell student to make this change:
arm	Change *m* to *t*
art	Change *t* to *f*
arf	

Student writes:	Tell student to make this change:
end	Change e to *a*
and	Change *d* to *t*
ant	

Student writes*:	Tell student to make this change:
irk	Change *i* to *a*
ark	Change *k* to *c*
arc	Change *c* to *t*
art	

Student writes:	Tell student to make this change:
airs	Change *ai* to *ea*
ears	Change *ea* to *oa*
oars	Change *oa* to *ou*
ours	

Student writes:	Tell student to make this change:
eats	Change *ea* to *ou*
outs	Change *out* to *i*
its	Change *i* to *oa*
oats	

*If the student has been taught that *ar*, *or*, and *ur/er/ir* are considered vowels, then do not use these chains, as they actually represent VC rather than VCC.

Switch-a-letter Practice for Basic Syllable Shapes, *continued*

Syllable Shape: CCV

Student writes:	Tell student to make this change:
stay	Change *ay* to *ow*
stow	Change *t* to *n*
snow	Change *n* to *l*
slow	Change *ow* to *aw*
slaw	Change *s* to *c*
claw	Change *c* to *f*
flaw	Change *aw* to *ee*
flee	Change *l* to *r*
free	Change *f* to *t*
tree	Change *ee* to *ue*
true	

Student writes:	Tell student to make this change:
try	Change *y* to *ay*
tray	Change *t* to *g*
gray	Change *ay* to *ew*
grew	Change *g* to *b*
brew	Change *r* to *l*
blew	Change *b* to *f*
flew	Change *ew* to *ee*
flee	Change *f* to *g*
glee	Change *ee* to *ow*
glow	

Switch-a-letter Practice for Basic Syllable Shapes, *continued*

Syllable Shape: CCVC

Student writes:	Tell student to make this change:
stem	Change *m* to *p*
step	Change *e* to *o*
stop	Change *t* to *l*
slop	Change *s* to *f*
flop	Change *f* to *c*
clop	Change *o* to *i*
clip	Change *c* to *s*
slip	Change *p* to *m*
slim	Change *i* to *a*
slam	Change *m* to *p*
slap	

Student writes:	Tell student to make this change:
trap	Change *a* to *i*
trip	Change *p* to *m*
trim	Change *t* to *b*
brim	Change *i* to *oo*
broom	Change *b* to *g*
groom	Change *oo* to *i*
grim	Change *i* to *a*
gram	Change *g* to *t*
tram	Change *m* to *sh*
trash	Change *t* to *c*
crash	Change *a* to *u*
crush	Change *c* to *b*
brush	

Switch-a-letter Practice for Basic Syllable Shapes, *continued*

Syllable Shape: CVCC

Student writes:	Tell student to make this change:
boats	Change *b* to *c*
coats	Change *oa* to *a*
cats	Change *t* to *p*
caps	Change *c* to *t*
taps	Change *a* to *i*
tips	Change *i* to *o*
tops	Change *p* to *t*
tots	Change first *t* to *l*
lots	Change *o* to *e*
lets	Change *l* to *g*
gets	

Syllable Shape: CCVCC

Student writes:	Tell student to make this change:
steps	Change *e* to *o*
stops	Change *t* to *l*
slops	Change *o* to *a*
slaps	Change first *s* to *f*
flaps	Change *a* to *o*
flops	Change *o* to *i*
flips	Change *f* to *s*
slips	Change *p* to *t*
slits	Change *l* to *p*
spits	Change *i* to *o*
spots	Change *o* to *a*
spats	Change *p* to *l*
slats	

Switch-a-letter Practice for Basic Syllable Shapes, *continued*

Syllable Shape: CCVCC

Student writes:	Tell student to make this change:
traps	Change *a* to *i*
trips	Change *p* to *m*
trims	Change *i* to *a*
trams	Change *t* to *c*
crams	Change *a* to *ea*
creams	Change *c* to *d*
dreams	Change *ea* to *u*
drums	

Appendix 5C

Open and Closed Nonsense Syllables

Have the student read these nonsense syllables. Instruct him that if the syllable is open (ends with a vowel), he should pronounce it with a long vowel. If the syllable is closed (ends with consonant), he should pronounce it with a short vowel.

tap	pap
tul	te
su	tab
bab	ka
tek	sas
fum	ko
tin	fud
po	pe
tup	kav
seg	bek
ta	Tim
tus	fod
ba	fi
kem	taf
se	si
fip	ke
siv	tep
bif	ku
to	puk
feb	tek
pi	ki
tom	sop
so	bom
kip	po
bu	fal
sut	tat
fo	ti
pif	kog
buk	pu
pa	bi
kud	tu
sa	tep
tip	tell
tot	bo
fa	ti
pem	fe

Simple Nonsense Syllables and Real Words: VC + silent e Marker Contrasted with Short Vowels in Similar Syllables

These lists give the student extra practice in quickly recognizing and decoding simple syllable VC + silent e marker words.

C+V+C	C+V+C+e
sip	sipe
map	mape
lap	lape
dat	date
fat	fate
gat	gate
hat	hate
lat	late
mat	mate
rat	rate
bat	bate
mop	mope
hop	hope
dat	date
lip	lipe
rip	ripe
gal	gale
mal	male
pal	pale
sal	sale
pal	pale
tal	tale
cap	cape
tap	tape
lip	lipe
rik	rike
bin	bine
cam	came
lam	lame
tam	tame
min	mine

Words in Which *c* is Followed by *i, e,* or *y*

The lists on pages 129 through 131 give the student extra practice in quickly recognizing and decoding syllables with *c* followed by *i*, *e*, or *y*.

In this list, the student has to decide if the *c* is pronounced as a *k* or *s*.

Nonsense syllables with c at the beginning that have a variety of vowels following		
cack	cem	cet
cal	cyp	ces
ceb	caz	cez
cec	cim	com
ceg	cib	cen
caz	cip	cac
cig	cyn	cep
ces	cul	cag
cir	cos	cys
cuh	cel	cer
cyp	cek	cor
cus	ciz	cil
cas	ced	cid
cif	cuf	cis

Words in Which *c* is Followed by *i, e,* or *y*, *continued*

Words with *c* at the beginning followed by *i, e,* or *y*

ci, ce, cy
central
circle
center
cider
ceiling
circus
censor
civil
cymbal
cell
cent
city
cereal
cite
certain

This list provides the student with practice pronouncing the *c* as an *s*.

Words with *c* at the end or in the middle followed by *i, e,* or *y*	
brace	dance
racy	nice
France	juicy
ice	twice
notice	practice
Nancy	Lucy
sentences	dancing
prance	race
sentence	face
space	fence
Quincy	rice
surface	voice
icy	dancer
lacy	fancy

Words in Which *c* is Followed by *i*, *e*, or *y*, *continued*

This list provides the student with practice in deciding if the *c* is pronounced as a *k* or *s*.

Words with *c* at the beginning that have a variety of vowels following	
come	cup
central	cereal
cube	cite
calf	cab
coin	certain
circle	coal
center	center
cow	cane
cider	cub
cake	cap
cord	circle
ceiling	corn
circus	cider
censor	car
can	cut
civil	civil
curb	central
cage	card
cute	cite
cymbal	corn
cell	care
call	comb
cent	cent
camp	cuff
cone	coat
city	cell
came	code
cook	cold

Words in Which *g* is Pronounced as *g* or *j*

The lists on pages 132-133 are for students to read and practice. Have the student try pronouncing each syllable with a *g* and a *j*.

Nonsense syllables

try with a *j* sound	try with a *g* sound
gep	gep
gis	gis
git	git
gys	gys
gim	gim
gen	gen
gib	gib
gyt	gyt
gif	gif
gif	gif
gik	gik
gid	gid
gek	gek
gyb	gyb
ges	ges
ged	ged
gik	gik

When the student encounters a word with *e*, *i*, or *y* following the *g*, the student may need to try pronouncing it both ways if he doesn't recognize the word.

Real words

g with a variety of vowels following		
gap	gem	guide
gem	goop	gift
gene	gate	giant
gent	golf	gin
girl	gave	get
good	gear	gape
gym	gypsy	gene
gold	gill	gas
guard	give	gel
game	gone	go

Words in Which *g* is Pronounced as *g* or *j*, *continued*

Ask the student to try pronouncing it both ways to see which is the real word.

One-syllable real words with initial *g*

try with a *j* sound	try with a *g* sound
gem	gem
giving	giving
gene	gene
give	give
gent	gent
girl	girl
gym	gym
gem	gem
gear	gear
gill	gill
give	give
gentle	gentle
gift	gift
gerbil	gerbil
giant	giant
geese	geese
gin	gin
get	get
gyp	gyp
gene	gene
gibe	gibe
gel	gel
getting	getting

Words Ending in *-ck, -ke,* or *-k*

These lists give the student extra practice in quickly recognizing and decoding syllables ending in *-ck, -ke*, or *-k*.

short vowel words ending in *-ck*	
back	neck
block	pack
brick	pick
check	rock
chick	sack
dock	sick
duck	sock
flick	stack
kick	tack
lack	tick
lick	tuck
lock	wick

long vowel words ending in *-ke*	
bake	like
bike	make
brake	Mike
broke	quake
cake	sake
choke	smoke
fake	stake
flake	strike
hike	stroke
joke	take
lake	wake

Words Ending in -*ck*, -*ke*, or -*k*, *continued*

Double ee words and words with other alternate long vowel spellings (*oa*) that end in plain -*k*

Words that have the vowel oo (/u, U/, or *au*/*aw* or in which the -*k* is preceded by an *r*, *l*, or *n* (e.g., *park*, *bulk*, *thank*)

-ee, -ea, -oa, rk, lk, nk, and -k	
bark	milk
beak	nook
bleak	oak
book	park
break	peek
bulk	pink
cheek	shook
creak	sneak
creek	soak
croak	spook
hawk	spunk
hook	squawk
jerk	talk
junk	thank
lark	think
look	took
lurk	walk
meek	week

Words Ending in *-tch* or *-ch*

These lists give students extra practice in quickly recognizing and decoding words ending in *-tch* or *-ch*.

Words with short vowels ending in *-tch*

-tch
batch
blotch
catch
clutch
ditch
fetch
hatch
hitch
itch
latch
match
patch
scratch
sketch
switch
watch
witch

Words ending in *-ch* (long vowels and other vowels such as *oo* and *ou*) and those that end in *-rch*, *-nch*, and *-lch*

-ch	
beach	mulch
bench	peach
branch	pooch
brunch	porch
bunch	pouch
coach	preach
couch	punch
drench	ranch
each	reach
flinch	roach
French	smooch
grouch	speech
gulch	teach
lunch	torch
march	touch

Words Ending in -ge or -*dge*

These lists give students extra practice in quickly recognizing and decoding words ending in -*ge* or -*dge*.

Words ending in -*ge* (long vowel) and words ending in -*rge*, -*nge*, and -*lge*

-ge	
age	lunge
barge	outrage
bilge	page
bulge	purge
cage	rage
change	refuge
charge	sage
engage	stage
forge	surge
gage	urge
hinge	wage
huge	

Words with short vowel ending in -*dge*

-dge	
badge	knowledge
bridge	ledge
dodge	lodge
dredge	misjudge
edge	nudge
fridge	pledge
fudge	porridge
grudge	ridge
judge	wedge

Card Games for Syllable Shapes, Syllable Types, and Word Types

Any of the words or syllables from this chapter or the appendices in this chapter can be used in card games. Write syllable shapes, syllable types (e.g., open/closed), or word types (e.g., words ending in *-ge* or *-dge*) on index cards. Some game suggestions follow:

- **Flash cards**
  Show the student the flash cards one at a time and have the student read the syllable shape, syllable, or word as soon as you show it to her.

  - **Syllable Shapes**: Write the shape of the syllable (e.g., CV, CCVC) on the board before showing the flash card to the student.
  - **Open and Closed Syllables**: Explain that the syllables may be real words. Remind students to pronounce the open syllables with long vowels and the closed syllables with short vowels.

- **Word Sort**
  Write syllable shapes, syllable types, or word types on sheets of paper and place them on the table in front of the student. Then shuffle the flash cards. Have the student draw a card, read it, and sort it into the right category (e.g., words where *c* is pronounced as *k* vs. words where *c* is pronounced as *s*, words where *g* is pronounced as *j* vs. words where *g* is pronounced as *g*).

- **Flip It**
  You may want to write the syllable shapes, syllable types, or word types on the board for reference. Shuffle the cards and divide them into two stacks, one stack for each player. Each player turns over a card from the top of her stack to see if the syllables or word types match. When a player turns over a card, she needs to say the syllable shape, syllable type, or word type on the card and identify it. For example:

  > The student turns over the syllable shape *stimp* and says, "*Stimp*. That's a CCVCC." Then the other player turns over his card and says, "*Jamp*. That's a CVCC." The cards do not match.
  >
  > The student turns over the word *lake* and says "*Lake*. That's a long vowel with *-ke* at the end." Then you turn over your card and say, "*Make*. That's a long vowel with *-ke* at the end." The cards match.

  When the two syllable shapes, syllable types, or word types match (e.g., both players have CVC words, both players have words ending in *-ch*), the first player to say "same syllable shape (syllable type/word type)" gets both cards and puts them in a separate pile. If the cards don't match, they go into a discard pile. The game ends when the original stacks are gone. The winner is the player with the most cards.

  To extend play, split the discard pile when the stacks are gone and continue playing until the cards are gone once again.

Card Games for Syllable Shapes, Syllable Types, and Word Types, *continued*

Syllable and Word Types	Responses when the cards are a match
Syllable Shapes	same syllable shape or two CVC syllable shapes
Open and Closed Syllables	two opens/two closed
Simple Syllables VC + silent e Marker Words	two long vowels + silent e/two short vowels
Words in Which *c* is Followed by *i*, *e*, or *y*	c followed by *i*, e, or *y*/c not followed by *i*, e, or *y*
Words in Which *g* is Pronounced as *g* or *j*	both sound like *g*/both sound like *j*
Words Ending in -*ck*, -*ke*, or -*k*	both end in -*ck*/both end in -*ke*/both end in -*k*
Words Ending in -*ch* or -*tch*	both end in -*ch*/both end in -*tch*
Words Ending in -*ge* or -*dge*	both end in -*ge*/both end in -*dge*

- **Go Fish**
  Create a deck of cards comprised of two of each syllable shape, syllable type, or word type. Use a limited set of word (e.g., 10-12 pairs). Shuffle the cards and deal five to each player. The rest of the cards remain in the draw pile which is placed facedown on the table. Players remove any pairs (e.g., two CCVC syllable shapes, two words ending in -*ck*) from their hands and place them on the table.

  The game is played according the rules of *Go Fish*, with each player asking the other for a card to try to find a match to a card in her hand. For example, "Do you have a word that has CCVCC syllable shape?" If the other player has a match, she must give it to the first player, who places the match on the table. The first player then gets another turn. If no match is found, the asker must "fish" by choosing a card from the draw pile. If a match is made when choosing a card from the draw pile, the player places the card from her hand and the card from the draw pile on the table. If no match is made, the player puts the card from draw pile in her hand and that is the end of her turn. Play then moves to the next player. The game ends when one player gets rid of all her cards.

  - **Syllable Shapes**: You may need to write the syllable shape in small letters in the upper corners of the cards for some students.
  - **Open and Closed Syllables**: No *Go Fish* game is recommended because with only open or closed syllables as choices, you'd get a match 50% of the time. The game would be over very quickly.
  - **Simple Syllables VC + silent e Marker Words**: No *Go Fish* game is recommended as it would be very easy and fast to get matches plus you would have to include foil words (i.e., words that don't end in VC + silent e).

Anglo-Saxon Prefixes and Suffixes

These lists will help students become familiar with Anglo-Saxon morphemes. Put the morphemes on flash cards or have students read the list. Students will learn more effectively when you work with these in the context of multi-syllabic words in Chapter 6.

Anglo-Saxon prefixes
a-
be-
by-
de-
for-
fore-
in-
mis-
out-
over-
un-
under-

Anglo-Saxon suffixes
-able
-ed
-en
-er
-est
-et
-ful
-hood
-ing
-ish
-less
-like
-ly
-ns
-s/-es
-ship
-some
-th
-ward
-y

Latin Prefixes and Suffixes

These lists will help students become familiar with Latin morphemes. Put the morphemes on flash cards or have students read the list. Students will learn more effectively when you work with these in the context of multi-syllabic words in Chapter 6.

Latin prefixes
ab-
ad-
ambi-
anti-
bi-
circum-
co-
com-
con-
contra-
de-
di-
dis-
en-
em-
ex-/e-
extra-
in-
inter-
inter-
intra-
mid-
mis-
ne-
non-
ob-
per-
post-
pre-
re-
se-
sub-
super-
trans-

Latin suffixes	
-aud	-mit/-miss
-age	-or
-ant	-pal/-puls
-ar	-pend
-bene	-port
-cred	-rupt
-dic/-dict	-scrib/-script
-duc/-duce/-duct	-spec/-spect
-ent	-spir
-fac/-fact	-st/-sta/-stat
-flec/-flex	-stru/-struct
-form	-tang
-fract	-tion
-ible	-tract
-ist	-ure
-ive	-vert/-vers
-jac/-jec/-jeck	-voc
-jud	-vor
-junct	

Greek Prefixes and Suffixes

These lists will help students become familiar with Greek morphemes. Put the morphemes on flash cards or have the student read the lists. Students will learn more effectively when you work with these in the context of multi-syllabic words in Chapter 6.

Greek prefixes	
derma-	mega-
a-/an-	meta-
anti-	micro-
arch-	mono-
astro-	neo-
auto-	peri-
biblio-	philos-
bio-	phon-
chron-	photo-
deca-	poly-
duo-	pro-
en-	psych-
geo-	pyro-
hemi-	syn-/sym-
hier-	tech-
hydro-	tele-
hyper-	theo-
hypo-	therm-
macro-	tri-

Greek suffixes
-cracy
-crat
-gram
-graph
-meter
-ology
-phile
-phobia
-polis
-scope
-scope
-sphere

Computer Games

The chart reflects computer games that address simple and complex syllable and word patterns.

Computer game	Syllable shapes VC, CV, CVC, etc.	Silent e rule syllables	Two vowels go walking	*r* - controlled syllables	One-syllable doubling rule	Prefixes/ suffixes	Other morphemes added to syllables (e.g., past tense, *-ing*, plurals)	Timed
Lexia PB—Level 1								
Change	X							
Consonant Castle	X							
Lexia PB—Level 2								
Balloons	X	X						
Score	X	X						
Lexia PB—Level 3								
Pirate Ship			X					
Super Change	X	X						
Train	X	X						
Word Stairs				X				
Lexia SOS—Level 1								
Consonant Blast	X							X
Lexia SOS—Level 2								
E-maze		X						
Letter Switch	X							
Search & Spell	X							
Lexia SOS—Level 3								
Add It							X	
At the Mall				X				
Sea Hunt	X		X					X
Reading Blaster—Ages 7-8								
Level 3—Geyser							X	
Level 5—Geyser							X	
Rules, Rules, Rules	X	X		X	X	X	X	
Word Workout						X		

For information on where to obtain these materials, see the Resources list on pages 260-262.

Other Materials

The chart reflects games that address simple and complex syllable and word patterns.

Materials	Syllable types VC, CV, CVC, etc.	Silent e rule syllables	Two vowels go walking	r-controlled syllables	Prefixes/ suffixes	Other morphemes added to syllables (e.g., past tense, *-ing*, plurals)	Timed
Dog Bones	X	X	X				
Pharaoh's Phonics		X	X				
Snap It Up	X	X	X	X			X
Syllabification					X	X	
Wacky Wahoo	X	X	X	X			

For information on where to obtain these materials, see the Resources list on pages 260-262.

Chapter 6

Decoding Multi-syllabic Words

Chapter 5 addressed improving the efficiency of the student's use of structural analysis (i.e., the analysis of the internal structure of a word that permits decoding). Structural analysis requires that the student draws on his knowledge of syllables and morphemes. The application of this skill is most apparent as the student deals with multi-syllabic words. Abbott and Berninger (1999) summarized how to teach students structural analysis, and most of those steps were addressed in Chapter 5. Many steps will be reviewed again in this chapter as students learn to apply their knowledge for reading multi-syllabic words.

Henry (1998) found that third, fourth, and fifth graders who received instruction in both decoding and structural analysis improved more in reading and spelling than those who received only a basal approach. Abbott and Berninger (1999) demonstrated that children in the fourth through seventh grades improved their word recognition when given explicit structural analysis instruction, especially in the alphabetic principle.

Direct instruction in the following skills help students learn to quickly and efficiently decode words containing more than one syllable:

- understanding concept of syllables
- counting the number of syllables heard (segmentation)
- counting the number of syllables in the printed word
- knowing where stress occurs
- understanding schwa in unstressed syllables
- applying morpheme analysis to multi-syllabic words
- dividing a word into its syllable parts
- applying stress to the printed word

These skills can then be applied to help the student read both real and nonsense multi-syllabic words more efficiently and automatically.

Understanding the concept of syllables

The first step in syllabification is to ensure that the student has a concept of syllables. One of the easiest ways to help a student understand the concept of syllables is to use proper names (first and last), including his own. Students enjoy saying the names of students they know and listening to the different parts of the names. You can also use the names of characters in movies or books which with they are familiar. Say the first name and help the student decide how many syllables are in the first name. Repeat with the last name.

For added fun, write first names and last names on separate index cards. Cut the index cards into pieces to divide the names into syllables. Be sure to use curved and angled cuts so they can be put together as puzzle pieces. Mix all the pieces together on the table. Have the student find the pieces that fit together and say each syllable as he places the pieces together.

See Appendix 6A.

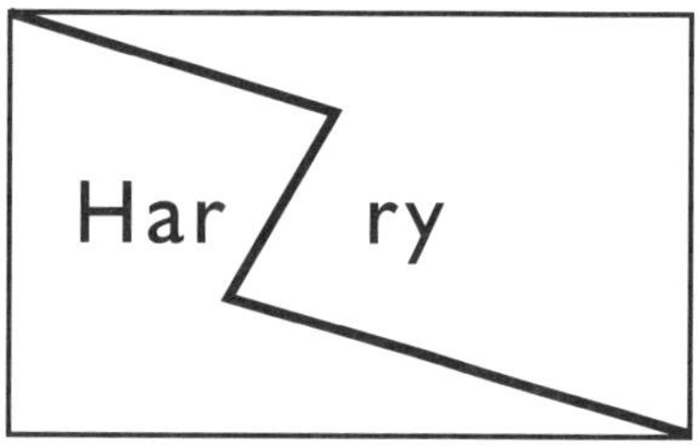

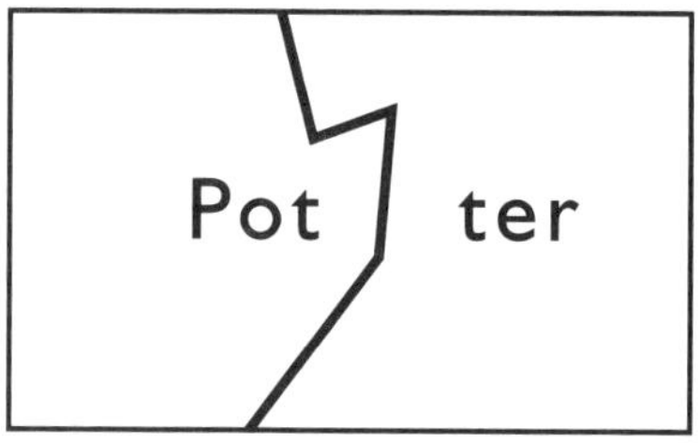

Another easy way to teach the concept of syllables is through the use of compound words, words in which each syllable carries meaning. (See Appendix 6A, page 154 for a list of compound words.) Teaching the concept of syllables leads very quickly to counting syllables.

Counting the number of syllables heard (segmentation)

Students may have been taught different strategies by their classroom teachers to break a word into syllables. They may tap the desk or count on their fingers for each part of the word. Some may have been taught to feel their jaw move, representing the different vowel shapes for each syllable. This phonological awareness skill (i.e., listening to a word and repeating it syllable by syllable) is a necessary precursor to being able to divide a printed word into syllables. A list of multi-syllabic words for practice can be found in Appendix 6B, page 155.

See Appendix 6B.

Counting the number of syllables in the printed word

A student may have adequate segmentation skills that allow him to hear a multi-syllabic word and tell where the syllables break down. However, this does not mean that he will be able to do the same thing when he reads a multi-syllabic word. At this level, you simply want the student to read the word aloud and tell how many syllables he hears. Actually dividing the word into syllables is described later in this chapter. For extra practice counting syllables, use the list in Appendix 6C, page 156. If those words are too hard, try the words in Appendix 6A, page 154.

See Appendix 6C.

Understanding where stress occurs

Stress at the word level means that one syllable is perceived as more prominent than the others. Stress can be achieved with a louder volume, higher pitch, or lengthened vowel segment. Often, more than one of these markers is used by the speaker to indicate stress. In English, syllables have primary, secondary, or weak stress. For the purposes of understanding where stress occurs, we will not expect the student to differentiate secondary from weak stress. For reading success, it is most important for the student to be able to perceive where the primary stress occurs. Students need to understand that stress can change the meaning of what is being read. Many students have no concept of stress or word level accent. Using the same technique for teaching the concept of syllables (see page 145), use the student's name and friends' names to teach the concept of stress. You can also use the activities described in Appendix 6D (page 157) for additional practice.

See Appendix 6D.

There are eight basic word level patterns of stress in the English language, and they are described below. The marks for the three types of syllable stress: primary stress (also called strong stress), secondary stress, and weak stress are explained on page 148. Note: When pronouncing a word, it is difficult to hear any difference in the weak stress and secondary stress.

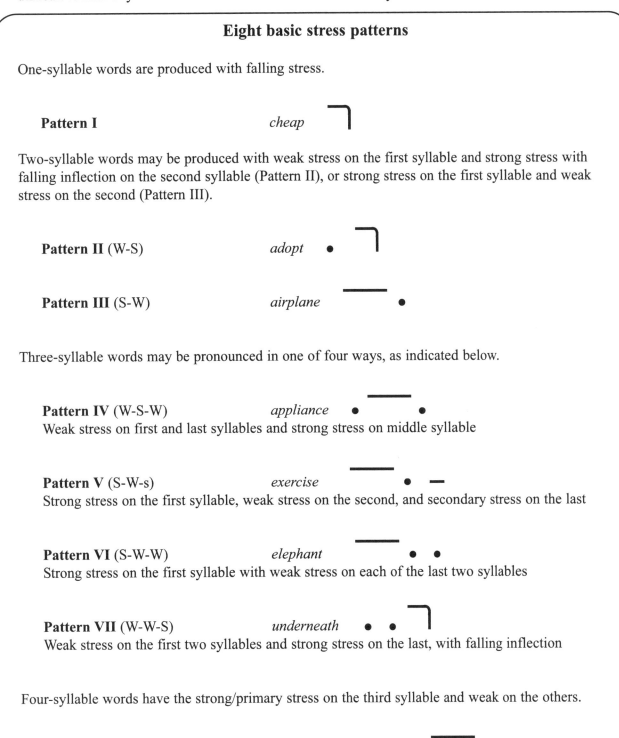

Eight basic stress patterns

One-syllable words are produced with falling stress.

Pattern I *cheap*

Two-syllable words may be produced with weak stress on the first syllable and strong stress with falling inflection on the second syllable (Pattern II), or strong stress on the first syllable and weak stress on the second (Pattern III).

Pattern II (W-S) *adopt*

Pattern III (S-W) *airplane*

Three-syllable words may be pronounced in one of four ways, as indicated below.

Pattern IV (W-S-W) *appliance*
Weak stress on first and last syllables and strong stress on middle syllable

Pattern V (S-W-s) *exercise*
Strong stress on the first syllable, weak stress on the second, and secondary stress on the last

Pattern VI (S-W-W) *elephant*
Strong stress on the first syllable with weak stress on each of the last two syllables

Pattern VII (W-W-S) *underneath*
Weak stress on the first two syllables and strong stress on the last, with falling inflection

Four-syllable words have the strong/primary stress on the third syllable and weak on the others.

Pattern VIII (W-W-S-W) *transportation*

Understanding stress marks

A long line means that the syllable has primary stress. (S)

A short line means secondary stress. (s)

A ● means weak stress. (W)

A means the stress is falling at the end of the word.

As stated on the preceding page, it is hard to hear the difference in weak stress and secondary stress. For example, Pattern V (as in *exercise*) has strong stress on the first syllable, weak stress on the second syllable, and secondary stress on the third. Pattern VI (as in *elephant*) is almost the same, but has strong stress on the first and weak stress on the second and third syllables. Say the words *exercise* and *elephant*. The last syllable in *elephant* is a little shorter (i.e., less stress) than the last syllable in *exercise*.

Since Patterns V (strong-weak-secondary) and VI (strong-weak-weak) are so similar, it may be easier to teach the students seven patterns combining these two patterns. Therefore, the seven basic patterns of stress to teach students are these:

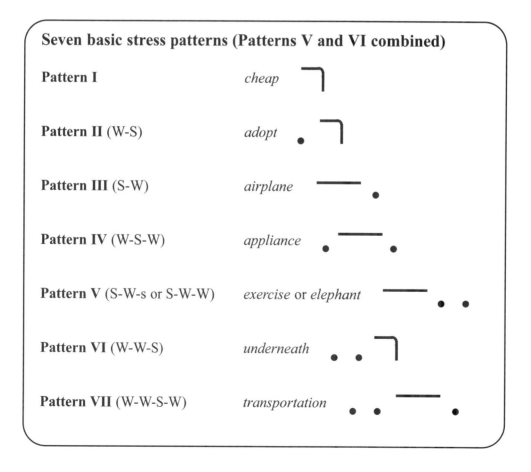

Seven basic stress patterns (Patterns V and VI combined)

Pattern I	*cheap*
Pattern II (W-S)	*adopt*
Pattern III (S-W)	*airplane*
Pattern IV (W-S-W)	*appliance*
Pattern V (S-W-s or S-W-W)	*exercise* or *elephant*
Pattern VI (W-W-S)	*underneath*
Pattern VII (W-W-S-W)	*transportation*

There are many other combinations of word level intonation as prefixes and suffixes are added to words. However, understanding these seven basic patterns will greatly improve the student's ability to pronounce words correctly as he reads.

Different methods can be used to help students visualize these patterns. The *Lindamood Phoneme Sequencing Program for Reading, Spelling, and Speech* (LiPS) teaches students to listen to multi-syllabic words and represent the number of syllables they have heard using felt squares. Small felt squares are used for the unstressed syllables and a large felt square is used for the syllable containing primary stress. For example, the diagram below shows the word *appliance.*

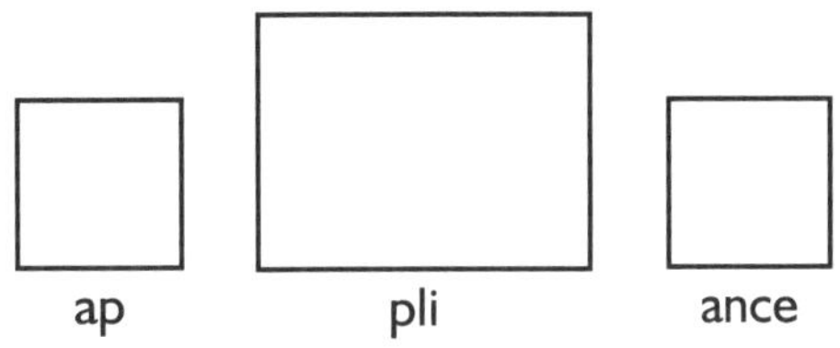

Students might be taught to clap softly for each weak stressed syllable and loudly for each stressed syllable. They can use blocks or other manipulatives and move them above or below a line drawn on a table, with the stressed syllable above the line. For example, the diagram below shows the word *dalmation.*

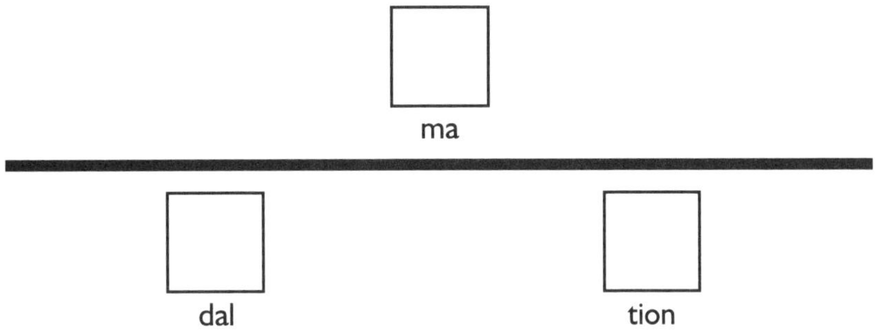

The activities in Appendix 6E (page 158) will also help students recognize stress patterns.

See Appendix 6E.

Understanding schwa in weak syllables

After the student demonstrates understanding of syllables, how to break a word into its syllable parts, and where the stress occurs, it will be necessary to teach the student about the schwa /ə/. The schwa, or unstressed vowel, is often confusing to students in decoding and, especially in encoding.

Some students may have been exposed to the concept of the vowel circle in their early phonics instruction. If not, you can briefly explain that when we say vowel sounds, some are produced with the tongue high in the mouth and some with the tongue low in the mouth. Tell the students the /ə/ is made with the tongue low in the mouth and that the jaw is lax when producing it. Discuss the tension used to increase the volume and pitch on stressed syllables. Help the student understand a schwa will not occur in a stressed syllable because the mouth is being very careful to get everything right in the most important, or stressed, syllable. Then contrast this with how the mouth gets a little lazy on the weak syllables and often, although not always, lets the jaw relax and produce the schwa. Teach the students to be flexible in their attempted pronunciations. First, they should try pronouncing a word with the vowels as they should be pronounced. If they don't recognize the word, they should find the unstressed syllable(s) and try it with a schwa. Then they can see if the word sounds right.

Multi-syllabic words with schwa, such as those in Appendix 6F (pages 159-160), can be written on index cards and cut apart between the syllables.

See Appendix 6F.

Have the student arrange the parts of the card on a table with the syllable with primary stress moved above the line and the syllable with the schwa moved below the line. The other weak syllables that retain their vowel pronunciation should rest on the line.

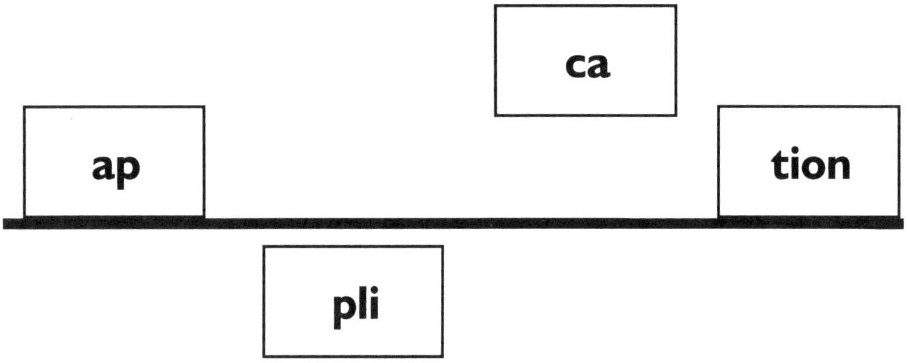

Applying morpheme analysis to multi-syllabic words

Information about morpheme types was provided in Chapter 5, but a caution was given that most practice with morphemes needs to be done in the context of multi-syllabic words. Moats and Smith (1992) suggest an order for teaching morphemes:

Anglo-Saxon morphemes

1. Compounds (Appendix 6G, page 161)
2. Inflected and derivational endings with no spelling changes (Appendix 6H, pages 162-163)
3. Inflected and common derivational morphemes with spelling changes (Appendix 6I, pages 164-166)
4. Prefixes and suffixes (Appendix 6J, pages 167-169)

See Appendices 6G through 6N.

Latin (Romance) morphemes

5. Roots (Appendix 6K, page 170)
6. Prefixes (Appendix 6L, pages 171-172)
7. Suffixes (Appendix 6M, page 173)
8. Assimilated prefixes that change form to match the root (not addressed in the appendices)

Greek morphemes

9. Combining forms (Appendix 6N, pages 174-176)

Dividing a word into its syllable parts

Many of the activities discussed regarding segmentation have been from a phonological awareness perspective (i.e., listening to what the word sounds like and determining how many syllables are heard). After the student begins to demonstrate competence and quickness in the ability to identify the number of syllables in a word heard or read (see Appendices 6A through 6C, pages 154-156), the student must learn to look at a word and divide it into syllables.

Even though a student has adequate segmentation skills, he may not be able to divide a printed word into syllables (Balmuth 1982). This is partly due to the fact that segmenting the written word does not always correspond with segmenting the spoken word. For example, when you hear the word *funny*, you would say that the first syllable was *fun* and the second syllable was *ee*. However, the written word would need to be divided between the two *n* letters. Teaching syllabification can help students decode longer, unfamiliar words. Adams and Henry (1997) suggest this may be particularly helpful in words that do not contain an affix and a root.

Lindamood (LiPs) teaches "breaking rules," which are tips for dividing a word into syllables. The "breaking rules" are listed below. A student handout with the same information is in Appendix 6O (page 177).

See Appendix 6O.

1. Estimate the number of syllables by putting a dot under each vowel sound. There has to be a vowel sound in each syllable.
   - Sometimes a vowel "sound" is represented by two letters (e.g., *reason* has only two vowel sounds, the long e and the schwa. But these two vowel "sounds" are represented by three "letters": the e and *a*, and the *o*. Put a dot under the *o* and only one dot under the *ea*.
   - Remember that sometimes the two letters representing one vowel sound are divided by a consonant(s). For example, in the word *pine,* there are two vowel letters but just one vowel sound, the long *i* with the silent e. When the two letters representing the vowel sound are separated by a consonant, it is helpful to put a dot under each vowel letter, but connect them with a scoop mark (e.g., *pineapple*).
2. Look for any beginnings or endings that you recognize. Use a highlighter to mark them, or draw a line under them.
   - Break syllables in front of any endings.
   - Break syllables at the end of any beginnings.
3. Start at the end of the word and work your way back to the beginning of the word.
   - Find the last vowel and let it partner with the consonant in front of it (syllables like to start with a consonant when possible).
   - Then find the next vowel and see if there is a consonant to go with it.
4. Break syllables between double consonants.
5. Remember the open/closed syllable rule.
   - In an open syllable, the vowel says its name (*ca per*).
   - In a closed syllable, the vowel says its sound (*cap per*).

As the student gains skill in breaking a word into syllables with a pencil or marker, he must transfer this ability to "breaking with his eyes." If he is to read connected text smoothly and efficiently, he must be able to see the syllables as he looks at the word. The lists in Appendices 6P and 6Q (pages 178-179) provide multi-syllabic nonsense words and real words for the student to practice breaking into syllables.

See Appendices 6P and 6Q.

Applying stress to the printed word

Thus far we have had the students listen to multi-syllabic words as you read them and determine where they hear the stress and what stress pattern is represented. As students try to read multi-syllabic words, they may encounter difficulty if they don't know how to "flex" their pronunciation. They need to understand how to pronounce the word by:

- trying the stress on different syllables
- using a schwa in weak syllables if it still doesn't "sound right" (See Appendix 6F, pages 159-160)

If they don't do this, they will become frustrated when they read a long word but don't recognize it. The word lists in Appendix 6R (pages 180-183) provide multi-syllabic words for your students to practice.

See Appendix 6R.

All of these strategies will help students more easily handle words of more than one syllable in length. The more practice a student gets, the more confident and competent he will become when encountering a long word in text. Increased confidence and competence will yield more fluent reading. Encourage speed as well as accuracy in all the practice activities. Completing the activities multiple times will help increase efficiency. Computer games and other materials for practice are listed in Appendices 6S and 6T (pages 184-185).

See Appendices 6S and 6T.

List of Appendices for Chapter 6

Two-syllable Compound Words for Concept of Syllables

Read this list of two-syllable compound words to students or ask students to read it. Have students tell what the two parts of the word (i.e., syllables) are.

airplane
baseball
bathroom
birdhouse
birthday
blackbird
bluebird
bookstore
boyfriend
campfire
carefree
chalkboard
countdown
crosswalk
crossword
downstairs
earthquake
fireworks
freeway
girlfriend
greenhouse
homemade
jaywalk
lighthouse
notebook
playground
rainbow
sailboat
snowflake
touchdown

Multi-syllabic Words for Syllable Segmentation

Select a word from one of the columns and read the word to the student. Ask the student to repeat the word and determine how many syllables he hears. Teach the student to put his hand under his chin to feel his jaw move for each syllable. Remind him that every syllable has to have a vowel.

2 syllables	3 syllables	4 syllables	5 syllables
across	absolute	altogether	accidentally
action	accurate	American	administration
almost	advantage	bacteria	artificially
beside	approval	calculator	association
borrow	carpenter	celebrated	cafeteria
center	charity	constitution	determination
chamber	conclusion	conversation	developmental
dessert	condition	digestible	educational
favor	daffodil	elevator	elaboration
finger	dangerous	experience	interchangeable
harvest	deposit	jubilation	justification
lettuce	difficult	legendary	laboratory
meadow	education	misdemeanor	Louisiana
monkey	entertain	negotiate	metropolitan
pretend	envelope	perishable	necessarily
pretty	eventful	petroleum	occupational
puzzle	magazine	political	realization
raisin	mineral	secretary	recommendation
session	monument	television	refrigerator
severe	operate	unexpected	satisfactory
teacher	pajamas	violation	university
volume	president	zoology	unreliable

Mixed List of Multi-syllabic Words for Students to Read

Use this list to provide students with extra practice in reading words with two, three, four, and five syllables. Have the student read each word aloud. Ask him to tell you how many syllables he hears in the word.

festival	handle	heavy	accident
beverage	never	carpet	laterality
journey	geranium	academy	Friday
family	metal	invent	interior
baby	anticipation	battery	ready
tangibility	master	material	nickel
investigation	even	curtain	liberalism
abandon	judiciary	accidental	hobby
happy	into	number	indigestion
body	champion	finger	department
barbecue	intelligent	consequently	bigger
lady	paper	appetite	magic
uncomfortable	ferry	other	artificially
depart	tomorrow	comparatively	fellow
understanding	local	admit	bibliography
omit	agreeable	capital	ketchup
indefinitely	fasten	limit	community
color	inform	theater	human
university	already	defeat	genealogy
offer	recover	navy	automobile
minute	arrive	skeleton	lemon
enemy	testimony	expect	television
comfortable	buffalo	movie	adopted
eastern	improve	flammable	closet
relative	citizen	basement	telescope

Teaching Stress on Names

These activities will help students learn about stress in multi-syllabic words.

- Select a first or last name with at least two syllables and ask the student to pronounce it. After he does so, you pronounce it with the stress on an incorrect syllable. Ask the student if that "sounds funny." Students can easily recognize that something is wrong with the word pronunciation. This leads to a discussion of stress.

- Use the name cards explained in Chapter 6 (pages 145-146). Read the name aloud and have the student decide which syllable is accented. Use a highlighter to mark the stressed syllable.

- Read the lists of character names below to the student. Stress the syllable in bold as you read. Read them three ways, one way with correct stress and two ways without. The correct pronunciation is indicated by an asterisk (*). Have the student listen to all three pronunciations and then tell which had the correct stress.

Bilbo Bag**gins**	Bilbo **Bag**gins *	Bil**bo** Baggins
Bugs Bunny	Bugs Bun**ny**	Bugs **Bun**ny *
Captain **Hook** *	**Cap**tain Hook	Cap**tain** Hook
Cinderella	Cin**der**ella	Cinder**ell**a *
Count Olaf	Count **O**laf *	Count O**laf**
Dumbledore*	Dumble**dore**	Dum**ble**dore
Fred Flintstone	Fred **Flint**stone *	Fred Flint**stone**
Gryffindor *	Gryffin**dor**	Gryf**fin**dor
Harry Potter	Harry **Pot**ter*	Har**ry** Potter
Mickey Mouse	Mic**key** Mouse	Mickey **Mouse** *
Peter **Pan** *	**Pe**ter Pan	**P**eter Pan
Porky Pig	Por**ky** Pig	Porky **Pig** *
Road Runner *	Road **Run**ner	Road Run**ner**
Rumplestiltskin	Rumple**stilt**skin*	Rum**ple**stiltskin
Scooby Doo	Scoo**by** Doo	Scooby **Doo** *
Spi**der**man	**Spi**derman *	Spider**man**
Super**man**	Su**per**man	**Su**perman *
Terminator *	Ter**min**ator	Termina**tor**
Vol**de**mar	Volde**mar**	**Vol**demar *
Winnie the Pooh	Winnie the **Pooh** *	Winnie **the** Pooh
Wonder Woman *	Won**der** Woman	Wonder Wo**man**

Recognizing Stress Patterns

These activities will help students learn to hear stress in multi-syllabic words.

- Read each of the words below to the student. Have him listen to the word and tell what syllable the stress is on. He might use one of the techniques described in Chapter 6 to represent the stress (e.g., felts or blocks).

- Make word cards from these words. Read each word to the student and have him sort it according to the seven basic types of stress.

- Make signs demonstrating each of the stress patterns and place them on the table (see below). Then make word cards from the words. Hold up a word card and read it to the student. Have him sort the word cards into the correct piles. Note: This is a good time to reinforce the concept of open and closed syllables (see Chapter 5). Point out to the student that when a stressed syllable ends in a vowel, the vowel will say its name. See pages 149-150 for information on what happens in unstressed syllables with a schwa.

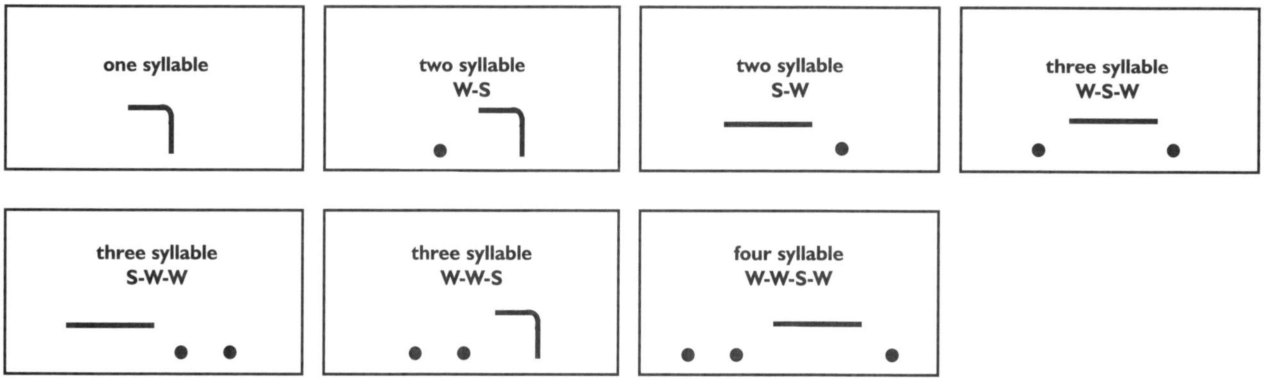

One syllable	W-S	S-W	W-S-W	S-W-W	W-W-S	W-W-S-W
boost	acute	airplane	accepting	articles	disappoint	artificial
bound	adapt	baby	adapted	benefit	engineer	cultivation
breed	advance	carpet	agenda	carefully	introduce	education
brief	affirm	enter	apparel	continent	overcome	execution
chair	afloat	fewer	belated	elephant	overhead	illustration
cheap	befall	hairy	conclusive	emphasis	overtake	independent
cope	decline	napkin	concerning	general	overthrow	recreation
fact	delete	often	elated	hospital	referee	regulation
peer	morale	rider	forsaken	opposite	underneath	transportation
pitched	recruit	scary	solutions	usual	understand	universal
talked	surmise	woman	united	wonderful	undertake	violation

Words with a Schwa

This page has the vowels that are pronounced as a schwa marked in bold. Have the student read a word on the student copy (page 160) in which the schwa is not marked and select the syllable with primary stress. Then have the student tell where he hears the schwa in one of the unstressed syllables.

Teacher

Words with schwa marked	
abs**o**lute	dipl**o**mat
absurd	el**e**vate
acquire	emph**a**size
acr**o**bat	guar**a**ntee
across	inv**i**tation
ago	just**i**fy
agree	m**a**chine
ahead	mag**a**zine
an**i**mal	m**a**rine
appl**i**cation	marv**e**lous
appreciate	m**o**rale
arrange	**o**pinion
attach	opp**o**site
b**a**lloon	prop**a**ganda
b**a**ton	rel**a**tive
b**e**nign	r**e**spond
cap**i**tal	simpl**i**fy
c**o**llect	tel**e**phone
comp**e**tition	terr**i**ble
c**o**ncur	test**i**fy
d**e**lete	**u**pon

Words with a Schwa, *continued*

Student

Words with schwa unmarked	
absolute	diplomat
absurd	elevate
acquire	emphasize
acrobat	guarantee
across	invitation
ago	justify
agree	machine
ahead	magazine
animal	marine
application	marvelous
appreciate	morale
arrange	opinion
attach	opposite
balloon	propaganda
baton	relative
benign	respond
capital	simplify
collect	telephone
competition	terrible
concur	testify
delete	upon

Anglo-Saxon Compound Words

As described in Chapter 5, many Anglo-Saxon words are compound words (i.e., words made up of two smaller words). The list on this page contains prefixes that can compound with more than one second syllable to make compound words. Use the list in the following ways to help students learn to read multisyllabic words:

- **Mix and Match a Word**: Write each syllable on an index card. Use one color of index cards for the first syllables and a different color for the second syllables. Shuffle these two decks and place them facedown on the table. Take turns drawing a card from each pile. If a player turns over two cards that make a real compound word (e.g., *forget*, *outside*, *overwork*), that player keeps those two cards. If the two cards do not make a real compound word (e.g., *overside*, *underdoor*), the two words are returned to the bottom of the respective pile. The game is over when no more compound words can be made. The winner is the player with the most cards in his pile.
- **Unreal Compound Words**: Use the cards described above and set up the two stacks of cards as indicated. However, this time the goal is to find the words that aren't real. If the two cards turned over make a real compound word, they are discarded. If the word is not real, the player may keep them if he can use the invented compound word in a sentence to indicate what its meaning might be. For example, if the cards turned over are *lady* + *head* and the player gives a sentence such as, "The ladyhead was too small for the hat," the player can keep the cards. Or if the cards were *be* + *thing*, the silly sentence might be, "The bething made so much noise that the dogs woke up."
- **Read Aloud Compounds**: Write the real compound words on flash cards. Have the student read them as fast as he can when you show them to him.
- **How Many Can We Make?:** Write one of the first syllables on a write and wipe board. Have players take turns writing or calling out a second syllable to make a compound word. Players earn a point for each real compound word and lose a point for a word that is not a real compound word.

Prefix	Second syllable
air-	line, plane, brush, pressure, ship, tight, mail, line, craft, port, strip
any-	thing, where, body, more, one, place, time, way, where
be-	hold, side, came, fall, fore, friend, half, long, low, witch
black-	bird, board, berry, mail, out, smith, top
blue-	berry, bell, jay, grass, print
by-	gone, line, pass, product, stander
cross-	word, stitch, bow, eye, road, walk
cup-	cake, board
for-	get, bid, give, age, sake
in-	side, tend, vent, come, complete, correct, dent, deed
lady-	bug, bird
out-	law, side, door, break, cast, come, field, fit, going, grow, line, patient, ran, rage, smart, standing
over-	all, coat, head, weight, come, pass, board, cast, dress, eat, due, grow, lap, night, seas
shoe-	maker, string, lace, box, horn
under-	ground, stand, wear, paid, go, hand, line, pants, pass, sea, stood, take, world

Anglo-Saxon Inflected and Derivational Word Endings with No Spelling Changes

Use the lists on pages 162-163 to help students learn to recognize morphemic endings.

Verbs that have endings applied (-*ed*, -*s*/-*es*, -*ing*) without a spelling change

verb	-ed	-s/-es	-ing
back	backed	backs	backing
bash	bashed	bashes	bashing
borrow	borrowed	borrows	borrowing
brief	briefed	briefs	briefing
bump	bumped	bumps	bumping
burn	burned	burns	burning
call	called	calls	calling
chart	charted	charts	charting
check	checked	checks	checking
cheer	cheered	cheers	cheering
cook	cooked	cooks	cooking
crack	cracked	cracks	cracking
delight	delighted	delights	delighting
dress	dressed	dresses	dressing
fear	feared	fears	fearing
flex	flexed	flexes	flexing
hand	handed	hands	handing
help	helped	helps	helping
jump	jumped	jumps	jumping
kick	kicked	kicks	kicking
learn	learned	learns	learning
lick	licked	licks	licking
list	listed	lists	listing
mix	mixed	mixes	mixing
mouth	mouthed	mouths	mouthing
need	needed	needs	needing
neglect	neglected	neglects	neglecting
pass	passed	passes	passing
play	played	plays	playing
print	printed	prints	printing
prompt	prompted	prompts	prompting

Chart continued on next page.

Anglo-Saxon Inflected and Derivational Word Endings with No Spelling Changes, *continued*

verb	-ed	-s/-es	-ing
push	pushed	pushes	pushing
reach	reached	reaches	reaching
remain	remained	remains	remaining
report	reported	reports	reporting
rest	rested	rests	resting
snicker	snickered	snickers	snickering
stump	stumped	stumps	stumping
talk	talked	talks	talking
treat	treated	treats	treating
wait	waited	waits	waiting
walk	walked	walks	walking
watch	watched	watches	watching
wonder	wondered	wonders	wondering
work	worked	works	working

Other words that have endings applied (-*er*, -*ful*, -*less*, -*ly*) without a spelling change

-er	-ful	-less	-ly
catcher	cheerful	backless	bashfully
charter	delightful	careless	briefly
greater	faithful	faceless	cowardly
neater	forgetful	fearless	directly
northerner	helpful	flightless	friendly
printer	hopeful	heartless	gladly
prisoner	joyful	helpless	gradually
reader	mouthful	homeless	grimly
reporter	neglectful	hopeless	lively
singer	peaceful	listless	madly
talker	tactful	meaningless	obviously
teacher	thoughtful	meatless	promptly
tougher	useful	reckless	quickly
walker	wonderful	restless	rapidly
		senseless	really
		sleepless	sadly
		spineless	slowly
		tactless	suddenly
		tasteless	timely
		tearless	

Anglo-Saxon Inflected and Derivational Morphemes with Spelling Changes

Use the lists on pages 164-166 to demonstrate three common spelling rules.

Verbs that double the final consonant in single syllable words before adding endings

verb	-ed	-ing
bug	bugged	bugging
clap	clapped	clapping
drug	drugged	drugging
hop	hopped	hopping
jog	jogged	jogging
pop	popped	popping
rip	ripped	ripping
shop	shopped	shopping
slip	slipped	slipping
snag	snagged	snagging
snap	snapped	snapping
wrap	wrapped	wrapping

Verbs that drop the final e on a word before adding endings

verb	-ed	-ing
bake	baked	baking
change	changed	changing
dance	danced	dancing
date	dated	dating
hope	hoped	hoping
like	liked	liking
love	loved	loving
move	moved	moving
receive	received	receiving
scrape	scraped	scraping
shape	shaped	shaping
skate	skated	skating
smile	smiled	smiling
wrestle	wrestled	wrestling
write	n/a	writing

Anglo-Saxon Inflected and Derivational Morphemes with Spelling Changes, *continued*

Verbs that change the final y to i before added endings

verb	-ed	-s/-es	-ing*
ally	allied	allies	allying
apply	applied	applies	applying
baby	babied	babies	babying
comply	complied	complies	complying
cry	cried	cries	crying
disqualify	disqualified	disqualifies	disqualifying
diversify	diversified	diversifies	diversifying
dry	dried	dries	drying
fly	n/a	flies	flying
fry	fried	fries	frying
hurry	hurried	hurries	hurrying
intensify	intensified	intensifies	intensifying
justify	justified	justifies	justifying
multiply	multiplied	multiplies	multiplying
notify	notified	notifies	notifying
nullify	nullified	nullifies	nullifying
pacify	pacified	pacifies	pacifying
party	partied	parties	partying
pry	pried	pries	prying
qualify	qualified	qualifies	qualifying
ratify	ratified	ratifies	ratifying
reply	replied	replies	replying
satisfy	satisfied	satisfies	satisfying
supply	supplied	supplies	supplying
tally	tallied	tallies	tallying
testify	testified	testifies	testifying
try	tried	tries	trying

*Explain to the student that the *y* must stay in this context or there would be two *i*'s.

Anglo-Saxon Inflected and Derivational Morphemes with Spelling Changes, *continued*

Other words that change the final *y* to *i* before adding endings

-er	-ful	-less	-ly
chillier	beautiful	merciless	dizzily
classier	bountiful	penniless	happily
dizzier	fanciful		hastily
fancier	pitiful		
fattier			
giddier			
hillier			
moldier			
smellier			

Appendix 6J

Anglo-Saxon Prefixes and Suffixes

Use these lists for more practice reading Anglo-Saxon words with prefixes and suffixes (some of these may be compound words and may have appeared on the list in Appendix 6G, page 161). The goal is to try to have the student quickly and accurately recognize the prefix or suffix. This will make reading the long word less intimidating.

Anglo-Saxon prefixes

be-	de-	dis-	in- (not)	mis-	re-	un- (not)
became	debate	disable	inability	misbehave	react	unable
become	debug	disadvantage	inaccurate	miscalculate	reappear	unaware
before	decamp	disagree	inappropriate	miscount	rearrange	unbelievable
befriend	decay	disappear	inaudible	misfortunate	reassure	uncertain
behalf	deceived	disapprove	incapable	misguided	rebate	unclear
behave	decent	discharge	incite	misinterpret	recall	uncomfortable
beheld	declare	discount	incline	misplace	recline	uncommon
behind	decode	discover	income	misprint	recollect	undecided
belated	decompose	disdain	incompatible	misrepresent	recover	undo
belittle	decoy	disgrace	incomplete	misshapen	recruit	uneasy
belong	decrease	disguise	inconclusive	misspell	redeem	unemployed
beloved	deface	disgust	incorporate	mistake	reelect	unequal
below	default	dishonest	incorrect	mistreat	refill	uneven
beneath	defect	disinfect	incurable	mistrust	reflex	unfamiliar
beset	defend	dislocate	indeed	misunderstood	reform	unfasten
beside	define	dismiss	indent	misuse	refresh	unhappy
betray	deflate	dismount	independent		refuse	unhealthy
betroth	defrost	disobey	indirect		rehearse	unheard
beware	degrade	dispatch	indoor		relate	unimportant
bewilder	dehydrate	display	indulge		relay	uninterested
bewitch	delay	dispute	inedible		remark	unkind
	delight	disregard	inexpensive		remind	unlikely
	demand	disrespect	inflammable		remodel	unload
	demerit	distemper	inflate		renew	unnatural
	demolish	distort	inform		repay	unnecessary
	denote	distress	inhabited		replace	unpack
	denounce	distrust	inland		reproduce	unpopular
	depart		insane		reside	unravel
	deposit		insecure		resort	unreasonable
	despair		inside		respond	unstable
	destroy		intake		restrain	untie
	detail		intrude		retreat	untrue
	detect		invade		return	unusual
	detour		invert		reveal	
	devote		inward		revise	
					reword	
					rewrite	

Anglo-Saxon Prefixes and Suffixes, *continued*

Anglo-Saxon suffixes

-able	-ful	-hood	-ish	-like
capable	bashful	boyhood	boyish	catlike
exchangeable	beautiful	childhood	childish	childlike
knowledgeable	careful	likelihood	foolish	
laughable	cheerful	manhood	girlish	
likeable	delightful	neighborhood	outlandish	
lovable	forgetful		roguish	
movable	graceful		selfish	
questionable	hateful			
trainable	helpful			
usable	hopeful			
workable	joyful			
	mouthful			
	neglectful			
	peaceful			
	playful			
	plentiful			
	resourceful			
	skillful			
	tactful			
	thoughtful			
	useful			
	wonderful			

-ness	-ship	-some	-ward
happiness	craftsmanship	bothersome	backward
kindness	friendship	foursome	downward
sadness	hardship	handsome	forward
	penmanship	lonesome	inward
		threesome	outward
		troublesome	upward
		twosome	
		worrisome	

Anglo-Saxon Prefixes and Suffixes, *continued*

C + -*le* words

As noted in Chapter 5, many two-syllable words end with a consonant followed by -*le*. The e is silent (e.g., *apple*, *giggle*). The student may try to pronounce these endings as *plee* and *glee* instead of as *pul* and *gul*. These activities will help students practice C + -*le* syllables.

- Make signs demonstrating each of the C + *le* endings listed in the chart and place them on the table. Then make word cards from the list below. Have the student sort the word cards into the appropriate piles. He must read the word aloud before placing it in the pile.

-ple	**-gle**	**-zle**	**-fle**	**-kle**
-ble	**-tle**	**-stle**	**-dle**	**-sle**

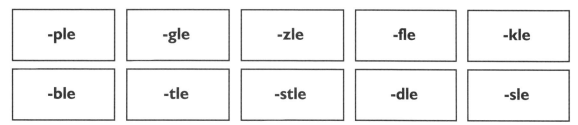

- Write the beginning syllable of words from the chart on index cards (e.g., *ap*- from *apple*, *ta* from *table*, *whis* from *whistle*, and *an* from *ankle*). Shuffle the cards and place them facedown on the table. Place the C + -*le* signs on the table. Have the student take a card from the deck and place it in front of each ending. Have him read it aloud until he gets to a real word. For example, if he draws the beginning *waf*, he has to read *waf ple*, then *waf gle*, then *waf zle*, and finally *waffle* before finding the real word.

  This is also an excellent time to practice the concept of open and closed syllables (see Chapter 5). As the student turns over a beginning syllable, ask if it is open (ends in a vowel) or closed (ends in a consonant). Remind him that in open syllables, the vowel will say its name, and in closed syllables it will say its sound.

C+ -*le* words

-ble	-dle	-fle	-gle	-kle	-ple	-sle	-stle	-tle	-zle
able	boodle	baffle	bangle	ankle	apple	hassle	bristle	battle	dazzle
babble	bridle	muffle	beagle	buckle	maple	tussle	bustle	beetle	drizzle
bubble	candle	piffle	bugle	crackle	nipple		castle	bottle	fizzle
bumble	cradle	raffle	dangle	fickle	people		hustle	cattle	frazzle
cable	curdle	rifle	eagle	heckle	ripple		nestle	gentle	muzzle
dabble	fondle	ruffle	gargle	pickle	sample		rustle	hustle	puzzle
double	fuddle	scuffle	giggle	rankle	simple		whistle	kettle	razzle
durable	handle	shuffle	goggle	sickle	staple		wrestle	little	swizzle
fable	idle	sniffle	jingle	sparkle	supple			mettle	twizzle
fumble	ladle	trifle	tangle	tackle				rattle	
gable	middle	truffle	wiggle	tickle				settle	
gamble	needle	waffle	wrangle	trickle				spittle	
marble	paddle							subtle	
rubble	saddle							tattle	
								whittle	

Latin Roots

This list supplies the Latin root and a number of words that contain the root. Use this list in the following ways:

- **Discuss**: Discuss the meaning of the root with your student. Then have the student try to generate words containing that root. Write the words on the board.
- **Read Aloud**: Write the words made from Latin roots on index cards. Have the student practice reading the words as quickly as he can.
- **Word Sort**: Use the word cards for a word sort activity. Have the student read the words and sort them into piles according to the root (e.g., a pile for *bene*, one for *cred*, one for *junct*).

Root	Meaning	Words with root
aud	hear	audible, audience, audio, audition, auditorium
bene	well, good	benefit, beneficial, benefactor, benediction
cred	to believe	credit, credible, discredit, incredible
dict	to say, tell	dictate, diction, dictionary, contradiction
duc(t)	to lead	deduce, introduce, produce, reduce
fac	to make, do	fact, factual, factory, manufacture
flec/flex	to bend	reflection, deflect, flexible, inflect, inflection
form	to shape	formation, deform, formula, inform, reform
fract	to break	fracture, refract, fraction
ject	to throw, lie	reject, eject, inject, project, interject
jud	judge	judgment, prejudice, judicial
junct	to join	junction, conjunction, injunction
mit/miss	to send	missile, mission, missionary, missive, mitigate
pels/puls	to drive/push	propel, compel, pulsate, pulsar
pend	to hang	suspend, impending, depend
port	to carry	transport, support, export, import
rupt	to break	corrupt, interrupt, bankrupt
scrib/script	to write	inscribe, transcribe, prescription, prescribe, describe, description
spect	to see, watch	inspect, suspect, spectacle, spectator
spir	to breathe	respiration, inspire, expire, inspiration, expiration
st/sta/stat	to stand	stable, station, statue, obstacle, static
struct	to build	construct, destruct, construction, destruction, instruct, instruction
tang/tact	to touch	tangle, contact, intact
trac/tract	to pull	tractor, distract, traction, intractable
vert/vers	to turn	revert, vertical, convert, invert, conversion
voc	voice, call	vocal, vocalize, vocalization
vor	to eat	carnivore, herbivore, omnivore, voracious

Latin Prefixes

This list supplies the Latin prefix and a number of words that contain the prefix. Use this list in the following ways:

- **Discuss**: Discuss the meaning of the prefix with your student. Then have the student try to generate words containing that prefix. Write the words on the board.
- **Read Aloud**: Write the words on index cards. Have the student practice reading the words as quickly as he can.
- **Word Sort**: Use the word cards for a word sort activity. Have the student read the words and sort them into piles according to the prefix (e.g., a pile for *pre*-, one for *mid*-, one for *bi*-).

Prefix	Meaning	Words with prefix
ab-	away from	absentee, absolve, abduct, absence, abstract, abnormal
ad-	to, toward, at	adhesive, adduct, addition, adhere, adjacent, adjunct, adjoin, adjustment
ambi-	both	ambidextrous, ambiguous, ambivalence
ante-	before	antecedent, antebellum
bi-	bi	biceps, bicycle, bipolar, biped, bifocals, binary
circum-	around	circumference, circumstance, circumscribe
co-/com-	together	combine, complex, complete, compute, copay, coordinate, cooperate
contra-	against	contrary, contrast, contradict, contraindicate
de-	down from, concerning	decrease, defrost, defraud, deflate, decompose, declassify, debug, decode, decentralize, decapitate, decelerate, decongestant, debilitate
dis-/di-	opposite, apart	disable, disagree, dismember, disrespect, disoblige, disorderly, disorganized, disorient, disinformation, displace, displeasure, disprove, disqualify
en-/em-	make	entitle, engrave, enjoy, enrage, enrich, enforce, endanger, enable, enclose, encode, endear, engender, engulf, enlighten, embattle, embrace
ex-/e-	out of	expel, expand, exhaust, exhale, excrete, exchange, exclaim, excavate, exfoliate, export, external, extract
extra-	beyond	extraordinary, extraterrestrial, extravagant, extraneous, extrapolate
in-	in, into, not	incline, increase, indeed, inhuman, inside, inlet, indwell, induct, indistinct, inevitable, indifferent
inter-	among, between	interact, intercept, intersection, interrupt, interface, international, intercostals, intercontinental
intra-	within	intravenous, intramural, intrastate, intranet

Latin Prefixes, *continued*

Prefix	Meaning	Words with prefix
mid-	middle	midday, middle, midwife, midnight, midway, midweek, midsection, midtown, midwinter, midyear
mis-	wrong	misbehave, misuse, misfortune, mislead, misread, mistake, misspell, mistreat, misstep, misspend
ne-	not	never, negate, negligent, negative
non-	not	nonfiction, nonsense, nonstop, nonentity, noncommittal, nonconformist, nondescript, nonevent, nonmetal, nonpartisan, nonprofit, nonstick, nonstop, nonviolence, nonperson
ob-	against	object, obstacle, obscure, obstruct
per-	through	perambulate, perforate, periscope, permeable, persevere, peruse, pervade
post-	after	postscript, postnatal, postgraduate, posthypnotic, postlude, postnasal, postwar, postgame, postrace
pre-	before	prefix, premature, preamble, prepare, preface, preempt, preteen, prefabricate, prefigure, prehistoric, preliminary, preliterate, premiere, premonition, prepackage, prejudge, predict, preview
re-	again, back	recover, refer, remind, refund, replay, repaint, restate, resell, refurbish, refinish, rewind, reconsider, reclaim, return
se-	apart from	separate, secede, sedate, select, senile, sequester, sever
sub-	under	submit, subordinate, subset, subside, subway, submarine, subdivide, subcategory, subatomic, submerge, subcontract, sublease, submission, substrate, subsidiary, subsoil
super-	over	superior, superlative, supermarket, supernatural, superman, superwomen, superintendent, supervisor, superficial, supercharge, superhighway, superhuman, supernatural, superpower, supersonic, superimpose
trans-	across	transaction, transform, translate, transmit, transparent, transcontinental, transatlantic, transport, transfer, transition, transworld

Latin Suffixes

This list supplies the Latin suffix and a number of words that contain the suffix. Use this list in the following ways:

- **Discuss**: Discuss the meaning of the suffix, if it has one. Have the student try to generate words containing that root. Write the words on the board.
- **Read Aloud**: Write the words on index cards. Have the student practice reading the words as quickly as he can.
- **Word Sort**: Use the word cards for a word sort activity. Have the student read the words and sort them into piles according to the suffix (e.g., a pile for *-tion*, a pile for *-ant*, and a pile for *-ive*).

Suffix	Meaning	Words with suffix
-age	action or process	manage, damage, bandage, voyage, engage
-ant	one who performs or promotes	supplicant, accountant, commandant, complainant applicant, aspirant
-ar	of, relating to	familiar, polar, circular, triangular, muscular, jugular, popular
-ent	one who performs or promotes	president, dependent
-ible	able to be	edible, sensible, compatible, responsible, possible, impossible, irresponsible, legible, flexible
-ist	one who makes or produces	psychiatrist, cyclist, jurist, apologist, dentist, psychologist, pathologist, novelist, colonist, pianist
-ive	tending to	excessive, compulsive, massive, passive, sensitive, possessive, decisive, effective, objective, restrictive, expensive
-or	condition or quality	stupor, senior, junior, humor
-tion	action or result	generation, position, location, station, situation, direction, formation, production, invention, creation, destination, caution, hesitation, execution
-ure	action or result	gesture, posture, temperature, venture, capture, rapture, adventure

Greek Combining Forms

The lists on pages 175 and 176 contain Greek morphemes that typically occur at the beginning or end of a word and words that contain these morphemes. Use the lists to help students learn to read multi-syllabic words.

- **Read Aloud**
  Write the words on cards and have the student practice reading them as quickly as possible.

- **How Many Can We Make?**
  Write the beginning morphemes on one color index card and the ending morphemes on another color. Discuss the meaning of each morpheme. Have the student try to generate as many words as possible containing that morpheme.

- **Mix and Match a Word**
  Use both colored decks of morpheme cards described above (beginning morphemes on one color of card and ending morphemes on another). Shuffle each of these two decks and place them facedown on the table. Take turns drawing a card from each pile. If the two cards turned over make a real Greek combined form word (e.g., *program*, *democrat*, *theology*), the player keeps the cards. If the two cards do not make a real Greek combined form (e.g., *telecrat*, *pyroscope*), the two words are returned to the bottom of the pile. The game is over when no more compound words can be made. The winner is the player with the most cards in his pile.

- **Unreal Greek Combined Form Words**
  Use the cards described above and set up the two stacks of cards as indicated. However, this time the goal is to find the words that aren't real. If the two cards turned over make a real Greek combined form word, they are discarded. If the word is not real, the player may keep the cards if he can use the invented word in a sentence to indicate what its meaning might be. For example, if the cards turned over are *pyro* + *meter*, and the player gives a sentence such as, "The fire ranked a seven on the pyrometer," he can keep the cards. Or if the cards are *duo* + *phobia*, the silly sentence might be, "The third grader suffered from a bad case of duophobia whenever he had to do his times tables."

Greek Combining Forms, *continued*

Greek morphemes at the beginning of words

Prefix	Meaning	Words with prefix
anti-	against	antisocial, antibacterial, anticipate, antidote, antifreeze, antiestablishment
arch-	extreme or ultimate	archangel, archenemy, archbishop
aster-/astro-	stars or outer space	astronomy, asterisk, astronomer, asteroid, astronomical, astronaut
auto-	self	autograph, autobiography, automatic, automated, automobile
biblio-	book	bibliography, bibliophile
bio-	life	biology, biography, biofeedback, biosphere, bionic, biodegradable
chron-	time	chronic, chronology, chronological, chronograph
deca-	ten	decameter, decathlon, decade, decagon
derm-	skin	dermatologist, epidermis, dermatitis
en-	in	enclose, endanger, enter, entrance, encapsulate, enrapture, entrap, enrich, entomb, entrust, envelope
geo-	earth	geology, geologist, geography, geometric, geothermal
hemi-	half	hemisphere, hemiplegia
hydr-	water, wet	hydrant, hydroplane, hydrate, dehydrate
hyper-	over, above, beyond	hypercritical, hyperactive, hypernasal, hyperthermia
hypo-	under or beneath	hypothermia, hyponasal, hypodermic
macro-	large	macroeconomics, macrocosm, macroscopic, macrobiotics
mega-	big	megabyte, megaphone, megahertz
meta-	with, after	metamorphic, metaphor, metalinguistics, metamorphosis, metaphysical, metatarsus
micro-	small	microwave, microscope, microfilm, microchip, microphone, microcosm
mono-	one, single	monotone, monopoly, monologue, monocle, monomania, monograph, monorail
neo-	new, recent	neonatal, neology, neoplasm
peri-	around, near	perimeter, periodic, periscope, periodontal, peripheral
phon-	sound	phonograph, phonics, phonology
photo-/phos-	light	photograph, photographer, photosynthesis, photocopy
poly-	many, much	polygon, polyhedron, Polynesia, polysyllabic
pro-	before, in front of	program, promote, propose, propel, profession, prognosis, progressive, prohibit, prologue
psych-	mind	psychology, psychiatrist, psychosis, psychosomatic

Chart continued on next page.

Greek Combining Forms, *continued*

Greek morphemes at the beginning of words, *continued*

Prefix	Meaning	Words with prefix
pyro-	fire	pyrotechnic, pyromania
syn-/sym-	with or together	synonym, synthetic, symphony, sympathy, synapse, synchronize, syndicate, syndrome, synthesis
techn-	art, skill, craft	technology, technical, technique, technician
tele-	distant	telephone, telegraph, telegram, telecast, television, telescope, telephoto, telepathic
theo-	God	theology, theologian, theocracy, theosophy
therm-	heat	thermometer, thermal, thermostat, thermodynamics
tri-	three	triangle, triplet, trifecta, trisect, triage, triad, triangular

Greek morphemes at the end of words

Suffix	Meaning	Words with suffix
-cracy	government rule	democracy, plutocracy
-crat	supporters of government	democrat, aristocrat, plutocrat
-gram	things written	telegram, monogram, grammatical
-graph	writing	autograph, biography, graphic, telegraph, autobiography
-meter/-metr	measure	metric, diameter, geometry, kilometer, centimeter, millimeter
-ology	study	sociology, biology, physiology, pathology, ideology, ecology, zoology, anthropology, astrology, psychology
-phile	love of	bibliophile
-phobia	fear	arachnophobia, hydrophobia, claustrophobia, agoraphobia
-pol/-polis	city	metropolis, metropolitan, Annapolis, Indianapolis, Minneapolis
-scope	watch, see	microscope, telescope, endoscope, periscope
-sphere	three-dimensional	hemisphere, stratosphere

Tips for Breaking a Word into Syllables

Use these strategies to know where to insert syllable breaks in words.

1. Estimate the number of syllables by putting a dot under each vowel sound. There has to be a vowel sound in each syllable.
   - Sometimes a vowel "sound" is represented by two letters (e.g., *reason* has only two vowel sounds, the long e and the schwa. But these two vowel "sounds" are represented by three "letters": the e and *a*, and the *o*. Put a dot under the *o* and only one dot under the *ea*.
   - Remember that sometimes the two letters representing one vowel sound are divided by a consonant(s). For example, in the word *pine,* there are two vowel letters but just one vowel sound, the long *i* with the silent e. When the two letters representing the vowel sound are separated by a consonant, it is helpful to put a dot under each vowel letter, but connect them with a scoop mark (e.g., *pineapple*).

2. Look for any beginnings or endings that you recognize. Use a highlighter to mark them, or draw a line under them.
   - Break syllables in front of any endings.
   - Break syllables at the end of any beginnings.

3. Start at the end of the word and work your way back to the beginning of the word.
   - Find the last vowel and let it partner with the consonant in front of it (syllables like to start with a consonant when possible).
   - Then find the next vowel and see if there is a consonant to go with it.

4. Break syllables between double consonants.

5. Remember the open/closed syllable rule.
   - In an open syllable, the vowel says its name (*ca per*).
   - In a closed syllable, the vowel says its sound (*cap per*).

Multi-syllabic Nonsense Words for Breaking into Syllables

These lists provide two-, three-, four-, and five-syllable nonsense words for the student to practice breaking into syllables.

flesp
brunfer
benesten
imflication
simtoplastify

brount
stockness
enpender
libricosting
cochemfistation

starks
timming
strimpumel
jasterpature
ambiflistetude

smake
steaker
jagapine
bactesdatience
beneficiate

glot
bricken
unwaster
trigratable
metrononymous

blurge
hardex
spectension
avapitude
denomitacial

stilp
apank
mepinish
comteniate
obweshtapience

clant
bapent
taplensky
blortastuption
dumikifier

flast
capfunse
binegat
affompany
deparitively

courts
janny
depelop
fertunstantial
intestitable

crast
fundrad
finician
goysenflarry
constabufistion

frain
baufty
intesty
graptistature
restiflunator

desp
stenful
fonpucher
addiptioning
pergonpacity

floup
cosper
trination
unspellisture
capaciflator

tresp
trinless
haptaken
trimastitune
jaspertunity

carsh
stanfess
demasted
entrunker
reflibucation

barsh
temmus
ecrustion
pronasticate
extrapensulate

trints
abgost
megatude
seminesting
copumastery

woin
pretine
telehood
captinascope
abnorsurnation

brout
edcant
wapingless
trimatory
precreditable

quorn
soptive
anlagram
steptoptiture
vegibarian

Multi-syllabic Words for Breaking into Syllables

Use this list of two- to five-syllable words for the student to practice breaking into syllables.

civilization
middle
definition
holly
governor
circulation
borrow
orientation
independent
apparently
furnish
vocabulary
departure
personality
society
company
prevention
negotiation
organize
observation
penny
differentiate
especially
describe

confident
objection
contain
inspection
medication
congratulations
discover
additional
program
gymnasium
decoration
flexible
substitution
pencil
anniversary
benediction
energy
reasonable
angle
individual
development
navigation
convention
pineapple

Words with Stress Marked to Flex Pronunciation

This list and the lists on pages 181-183 provide two-, three-, four-, and five-syllable words for the student to practice applying stress to. Each word is provided with the stress marked on different syllables. Only one pronunciation for each word is correct. Have the student read the words, stressing the syllable in bold. Point out how funny the word sounds when the stress is on the wrong syllable. Remind the student that when he is reading a word he doesn't know, he may have to try the stress on different syllables until the word sounds like a word he knows. (Note: Some of these words are divided by pronunciation. They may not match the syllable division in your dictionary.)

Two-syllable words	
al most	al **most**
base ment	base **ment**
af ford	af **ford**
a float	a **float**
can dle	can **dle**
chick en	chick **en**
cof fee	cof **fee**
dan ger	dan **ger**
ex plore	ex **plore**
fe ver	fe **ver**
ap plaud	ap **plaud**
fold er	fold **er**
gal lon	gal **lon**
grav el	grav **el**
him self	him **self**
home sick	home **sick**
in vite	in **vite**
jack et	jack **et**
ba ton	ba **ton**
jour nal	jour **nal**
de cline	de **cline**
lad der	lad **der**

Two-syllable words	
mark er	mark **er**
moun tain	moun **tain**
de lete	de **lete**
nick el	nick **el**
nor mal	nor **mal**
num ber	num **ber**
a cute	a **cute**
a dapt	a **dapt**
of fice	of **fice**
pa per	pa **per**
a dopt	a **dopt**
par ty	par **ty**
ad vance	ad **vance**
pic ture	pic **ture**
rea son	rea **son**
rob in	rob **in**
ad just	ad **just**
ad vice	ad **vice**
scis sors	scis **sors**
sig nal	sig **nal**
to night	to **night**
vol ume	vol **ume**

Words with Stress Marked to Flex Pronunciation, *continued*

Three-syllable words		
am bu lance	am bu **lance**	am **bu** lance
bas **ket** ball	**bas** ket ball	bas ket **ball**
cal en **dar**	cal **en** dar	**cal** en dar
cast **a** way	**cast** a way	cast a **way**
col lec tion	col **lec** tion	col lec **tion**
com e **dy**	com **e** dy	**com** e dy
de part ment	de part **ment**	de **part** ment
din o **saur**	**din** o saur	din **o** saur
dis **tur** bance	**dis** tur bance	dis tur **bance**
e lec tric	e **lec** tric	e lec **tric**
es ti mate	es **ti** mate	es ti **mate**
ex **am** ple	ex am **ple**	**ex** am ple
fam **i** ly	**fam** i ly	fam i **ly**
for got **ten**	for **got** ten	**for** got ten
gro cer y	gro **cer** y	gro cer **y**
Hal **lo** ween	Hal lo **ween**	**Hal** lo ween
in cor rect	in cor **rect**	in **cor** rect
o ver throw	o **ver** throw	o ver **throw**
in **stru** ment	**in** stru ment	in stru **ment**
in ter **view**	in **ter** view	**in** ter view
li **brar** y	li brar **y**	**li** brar y
mul ti ply	mul ti **ply**	mul **ti** ply
news **pa** per	**news** pa per	news pa **per**
op er ate	op **er** ate	op er **ate**
un der stand	un **der** stand	un der **stand**
o ver come	o **ver** come	o ver **come**
pa **ja** mas	**pa** ja mas	pa ja **mas**
pine ap ple	pine **ap** ple	pine ap **ple**
re **cov** er	**re** cov er	re cov **er**
Sat ur **day**	Sat **ur** day	**Sat** ur day
syl la ble	syl la **ble**	syl **la** ble
o ver come	o **ver** come	o ver **come**
tal **en** ted	**tal** en ted	tal en **ted**
to geth **er**	to **geth** er	**to** geth er
un **der** shirt	un der **shirt**	**un** der shirt
un der wear	un der **wear**	un **der** wear
un der neath	un **der** neath	un der **neath**
o ver look	o **ver** look	o ver **look**
va **ca** tion	va ca **tion**	**va** ca tion
won der ful	won **der** ful	won der **ful**

Words with Stress Marked to Flex Pronunciation, *continued*

Four-syllable words			
a **vai** la ble	a vai **la** ble	a vai la **ble**	**a** vai lable
ac ci den tal	ac **ci** den tal	ac ci **den** tal	ac ci den **tal**
al li ga tor	al li ga **tor**	al li **ga** tor	al **li** ga tor
bac ter i a	bac ter **i** a	bac ter i **a**	bac **ter** i a
bi o gra **phy**	bi o **gra** phy	bi **o** gra phy	**bi** o gra phy
cal cu la tor	cal cu **la** tor	cal **cu** la tor	cal cu la **tor**
com mun i **ty**	com **mun** i ty	**com** mun i ty	com mun **i** ty
de fi ni tion	de fi ni **tion**	de fi **ni** tion	de **fi** ni tion
de vel op **ment**	de **vel** op ment	de vel **op** ment	**de** vel op ment
e le va tor	e le va **tor**	e **le** va tor	e le **va** tor
en ter **tain** ment	en **ter** tain ment	**en** ter tain ment	en ter tain **ment**
Feb ru ar **y**	Feb ru **ar** y	Feb **ru** ar y	**Feb** ru ar y
fun da men tal	fun da **men** tal	fun **da** men tal	fun da men **tal**
gen er a tion	gen **er** a tion	gen er **a** tion	gen er a **tion**
gra du **a** ted	gra **du** a ted	gra du a **ted**	**gra** du a ted
his **tor** i cal	his tor **i** cal	**his** tor i cal	his tor i **cal**
im **pos** si ble	im pos si **ble**	im pos **si** ble	**im** pos si ble
in vi ta **tion**	**in** vi ta tion	in vi **ta** tion	in **vi** ta tion
kin der gar ten	kin der **gar** ten	kin der gar **ten**	kin **der** gar ten
lo co **mo** tive	lo co mo **tive**	lo **co** mo tive	**lo** co mo tive
ma ter i **al**	ma **ter** i al	ma ter **i** al	**ma** ter i al
min i a ture	min **i** a ture	min i a **ture**	min i **a** ture
nat u **ral** ly	nat **u** ral ly	**nat** u ral ly	nat u ral **ly**
or **di** nar y	or di **nar** y	**or** di nar y	or di nar **y**
pho to gra phy	pho to **gra** phy	pho **to** gra phy	pho to gra **phy**
pop u la **tion**	pop u **la** tion	pop **u** la tion	**pop** u la tion
rea son a ble	rea **son** a ble	rea son **a** ble	rea son a **ble**
sec **re** tar y	sec re **tar** y	**sec** re tar y	sec re tar **y**
sig **ni** fi cant	sig ni fi **cant**	sig ni **fi** cant	**sig** ni fi cant
te le vi **sion**	te **le** vi sion	te le **vi** sion	**te** le vi sion
tem per a ture	tem per a **ture**	tem **per** a ture	tem per **a** ture
un u su al	un **u** su al	un u **su** al	un u su **al**
vi o la **tion**	vi **o** la tion	vi o **la** tion	**vi** o la tion

Words with Stress Marked to Flex Pronunciation, *continued*

Five-syllable words				
ap pre ci a tion	ap pre **ci** a tion	ap pre ci a **tion**	ap **pre** ci a tion	ap pre ci **a** tion
al **pha** bet i cal	al pha bet **i** cal	al pha bet i **cal**	al pha **bet** i cal	**al** pha bet i cal
as so ci a **tion**	**as** so ci a tion	as so **ci** a tion	as **so** ci a tion	as so ci **a** tion
bib li **o** gra phy	bib li o **gra** phy	**bib** li o gra phy	bib li o gra **phy**	bib **li** o gra phy
caf e ter i a	caf **e** ter i a	caf e **ter** i a	caf e ter **i** a	caf e ter i **a**
co op **er** a tion	co op er a **tion**	**co** op er a tion	co **op** er a tion	co op er **a** tion
com mun i ca **tion**	com mun **i** ca tion	com mun i **ca** tion	com **mun** i ca tion	**com** mun i ca tion
con **grat** u la tions	con grat u la **tions**	con grat **u** la tions	**con** grat u la tions	con grat u **la** tions
de vel op **men** tal	de **vel** op men tal	de vel **op** men tal	de vel op men **tal**	**de** vel op men tal
dis ci pli nar **y**	dis ci pli **nar** y	dis ci **pli** nar y	dis **ci** pli nar y	**dis** ci pli nar y
ed u ca tion al	ed **u** ca tion al	ed u **ca** tion al	ed u ca **tion** al	ed u ca tion **al**
ex am **i** na tion	ex am i **na** tion	ex **am** i na tion	**ex** am i na tion	ex am i na **tion**
hip **po** pot a mus	hip po pot a **mus**	**hip** po pot a mus	hip po **pot** a mus	hip po pot **a** mus
in tel lec tu **al**	**in** tel lec tu al	in tel lec **tu** al	in **tel** lec tu al	in tel **lec** tu al
in di vid u al	in **di** vid u al	in di **vid** u al	in di vid **u** al	in di vid u **al**
long **i** tud i nal	long i tud **i** nal	long i **tud** i nal	**long** i tud i nal	long i tud i **nal**
mac a dam i **a**	mac a dam **i** a	mac a **dam** i a	mac **a** dam i a	**mac** a dam i a
ne ces sar i **ly**	**ne** ces sar i ly	ne ces sar **i** ly	ne ces **sar** i ly	ne **ces** sar i ly
o **bit** u ar y	o bit u **ar** y	**o** bit u ar y	o bit u ar **y**	o bit **u** ar y
or gan i za **tion**	or gan i **za** tion	or gan **i** za tion	or **gan** i za tion	**or** gan i za tion
re cov er **a** ble	re **cov** er a ble	**re** cov er a ble	re cov **er** a ble	re cov er a **ble**
re frig er a tor	re **frig** er a tor	re frig **er** a tor	re frig er **a** tor	re frig er a **tor**
sat is fac tor **y**	sat is fac **tor** y	sat is **fac** tor y	sat **is** fac tor y	**sat** is fac tor y
ser **en** dip i ty	**ser** en dip i ty	ser en dip i **ty**	ser en dip **i** ty	ser en **dip** i ty
soc i ol o **gy**	soc i **ol** o gy	**soc** i ol o gy	soc **i** ol o gy	soc i ol o **gy**
tes ti mon i al	tes **ti** mon i al	tes ti **mon** i al	tes ti mon **i** al	tes ti mon i **al**
un **com** for ta ble	un com for ta **ble**	un com for **ta** ble	un com **for** ta ble	**un** com for ta ble
vo cab u lar **y**	vo **cab** u lar y	**vo** cab u lar y	vo cab u **lar** y	vo cab **u** lar y

Computer Games

This chart reflects computer games that address reading multi-syllabic words.

Computer game	Syllable counting	Affixes	Open/closed syllables	Compound words	Syllable combining	Timed
Lexia PB—Level 3						
Elevator				X		
Lexia SOS—Level 2						
Find & Combine					X	
Lexia SOS—Level 3						
Add it					X	
Quick Link					X	X
Syllable Puzzler					X	
Lexia SOS—Level 4						
Detect & File			X		X	
Syllable Puzzler					X	
Lexia SOS—Level 5						
Anglo Saxon		X		X	X	
Greek		X				
Latin		X			X	
Meaning Structure	X				X	
Special Accents		X				
Reading Blaster—Ages 7-8						
Geyser Level 1	X					
Geyser Level 2				X		
Volcano Climb 4				X		
Volcano Climb 5		X				
Reading Blaster —Ages 6-7						
Marbles				X		
Rules, Rules, Rules		X	X			
Word Workout		X			X	

For information on where to obtain these materials, see the Resources list on pages 260-262.

Other Materials

This chart reflects products and games that address reading multi-syllabic words.

Materials	Syllable counting	Affixes	Open/closed syllables	Compound words	Syllable combining
100% Reading: Decoding & Word Recognition		X			X
125 Vocabulary Builders		X			
Compound Words Puzzles				X	X
COMPOUNDS Gr. 3-8				X	X
Just for Me! Phonological Awareness				X	
No-Glamour Reading: Syllables	X		X		X
SYLLABLES Gr. 3-8	X	X			X
Tic-Tac-Language & Match		X			
Tic-Tac-Read & Match					X

For information on where to obtain these materials, see the Resources list on pages 260-262.

Chapter 7

Recognizing Sight Words

What are sight words? Ehri (1992) indicates that sight words are those that are recognized at a single glance. These are words the reader has read accurately on previous occasions, and the sight of the word activates the memory of how that word was read before. The sight activates the pronunciation and meaning immediately, without requiring that the word be sounded out. The reader is able to recognize the word as a whole unit. Ehri indicates that this is a connection forming process between the printed word and the meaning in oral language.

Ehri suggests that there are two routes to word recognition: either the student locates the word as a unit or she continues to use a blend of phonemes. Finding the word as a unit is what we mean by sight word reading. Sight word reading occurs when the visual orthographic image is accessed directly. Speed of reading familiar words is one measure that indicates the child is using an orthographic, rather than phonological, route to reading.

Why do we work on sight word recognition? Most experts agree that improving sight word vocabulary is key to developing accurate and fluent reading.

- Speed of word recognition is generally acknowledged as an important marker for reading skill (Perfetti 1985).
- The development of rapid word recognition skills is the primary factor which distinguishes skilled from less skilled reading performance (Chabot et al. 1984).
- Sight word inefficiency is the primary reason for decreased reading fluency (Torgesen 2002).

Torgesen points out that intervention is often effective in improving reading accuracy, but that reading fluency remains substantially impaired. He states the students remain non-fluent because there are too many words at their grade level of reading. They cannot acquire them all in their sight vocabulary. He describes fluency as a moving target.

Abbott and Berninger (1999) indicate that learning to read typically takes place in the primary grades, but by the time the children reach intermediate grades, they're expected to read to learn. They state, "The timing of this developmental shift in focus of instruction may work well for many children who master basic word skills such as accurate and fluent word recognition in the primary grades. However, this developmental timing does not effectively accommodate those children who are still learning to read when the instructional shift occurs." Clark (1988) also acknowledges this developmental shift at ages 8 to 10, during which typically developing children switch from recognizing words using a phonological process to a rapid recognition of words. This shift helps to promote the child's rate and fluency of reading.

Initially, an individual may read a word by decoding it. The next several times the individual sees the word, there may be some recoding needed. However, this need soon ends. The individual develops a link between what the word looks like, what it says, and what it means, and retains this information as an orthographic image. Ehri and Wilce (1983) describe this as "unitizing a word" (i.e., recognizing a complex letter string as a word as quickly as identifying a single digit).

Samuels et al. (1978) found that second graders were still using some composite letter processing in recognizing words. Each additional letter in a word added about 55 milliseconds to the time the student needed to recognize the word. By fourth grade, students were transitioning between holistic and component letter processing. By sixth grade, they were doing holistic processing, recognizing words in the same amount of time despite the length of the word.

Acquiring orthographic representation of sight words

How does a student acquire an orthographic representation of the word? This is typically thought to involve memory for the visual and spelling patterns of these words or word parts (Torgesen et al. 1997). These representations then allow rapid identification of the word as a whole unit, or at least a unit composed of patterns rather than of individual letters.

These orthographic representations are acquired when the student is exposed to repeated associations between the word's correct pronunciation and its visual representation. Torgesen (2002) describes the pronunciation as the anchor for the word. The letters in the word indicate how the word sounds, and this is matched with a word in the oral vocabulary. Obviously, saying the word aloud helps to cement the pronunciation, or anchor, of the word for the child. How can you help to improve the memory for the visual/spelling pattern, or what the word looks like?

For some students, simply exposing them to the word multiple times will result in a mental picture of the orthography of the word. For other students, a more multi-sensory approach might be needed. You might use techniques that have been described in the spelling literature, such as writing the word multiple times on paper or in the air. If you have the student write it in the air, be sure she keeps her eyes fixed on the letters hanging in the air. This technique is described by Bell in the *Seeing Stars* program. Other techniques described by Bell include asking the student questions about the hanging word, such as "What is the second letter?" or "Can you spell it back to front?" You do not want the student to write the word backwards, as that changes the visual image you are trying to preserve. Instead, you want her to look at the letters hanging in the air and read them from the back to the front for you. For example, if the word the student wrote in the air is *with*, she would spell it back to front by saying, "*h - t - i -* w." If the student can perform that action, she is probably visualizing the word well and holding it in short term memory.

You can also draw a line on the board or on paper for each letter of the word, fill in some of the letters (e.g., *w h* ___ ___ *h* for *which*), and have the student fill in the missing letters. It is wise for the student to then rewrite the whole word so that motor learning for the whole sequence of letters takes place.

Because written words are processed as phonemic maps, the student has to have good phonemic awareness skills to develop sight word vocabulary. Ehri (1992) and Perfetti (1992) agree that the reason some children do not establish good sight word vocabularies is that they have a deficit in phonological codes. If that is the case, add work on phonological processing to the student's treatment plan.

Bowers et al. (1994) suggest that there is another stumbling block to obtaining a visual orthographic image, and that is the process indexed by naming speed. They point out that early naming speed is most predictive of later word recognition (e.g., regular words, irregular words, nonsense words). Interestingly, they state that the sustained deficit in general word retrieval (i.e., confrontation naming and semantic fluency) that appears among all readers with impairment may appear for different reasons between dyslexics and "garden variety" poor reader groups. Dyslexics appear to have depressed naming performance because of faulty retrieval of known words. "Garden variety" poor readers have the same poor naming performance, but this is based on less vocabulary knowledge (Wolf and Obregon 1992). Severe word retrieval problems often continue to be a major characteristic of the most impaired readers with dyslexia in adulthood.

Sight word drills

Reitsma (1983) found that six exposures to unfamiliar printed words were sufficient to give good first grade readers an advantage in naming these words, compared to unfamiliar spellings with the same pronunciation. Six exposures were not sufficient to familiarize older, poor readers with the spellings, even though highly familiar words learned in the past could be distinguished from unfamiliar spellings with the same pronunciation. Poor readers can learn to recognize the difference in words, but not in the same number of exposures as good readers.

How many exposures does it take? Poor readers take much longer to recognize individual words. They also require many more exposures to the word before they can begin to recognize it automatically (Ehri and Wilce 1983, Reitsma 1983). Poor readers may be slow to identify targets that they have practiced up to 18 times (Ehri and Wilce 1983, Manis 1985).

Remembering Torgesen's caution that fluency is a moving target because the number of sight words continues to grow, it is important to build substantial time into the treatment plan for activities designed to improve sight word recognition. Meyer and Felton (1999) suggest spending about 20 minutes per session on flash card drills.

What is important when working on sight word recognition?

- Drill, drill, drill.
- Drill on error words is probably more effective than drill on new words.
- Correct any errors.
- Drill practice transfers to reading in connected text.
- A time limit is needed when reading flash cards.
- Drill can be done with lists, but the timing is better controlled with flash cards.

Should you drill new sight words, or should the drill be on words that the student has missed when reading a passage? Hansen and Eaton (1978) summarized some of the studies that have been done to analyze the effectiveness of these activities. They concluded that word drills are an effective intervention approach for improving oral reading and that drilling on error words may be more effective than drilling on new words. However, they agreed that new word drill is "better development than no drill." They postulated that error word drill may be superior to new word drill because it focuses on specific words the child cannot decode.

Word drill appears to improve subsequent recognition of the original error words. This is typically done by massing practice on the words in error at the end of the reading session (Jenkins and Larson 1979). During contextual reading, the instructor makes note of any words the student is not able to read automatically. These words then comprise the drill at the end of the session.

Flash cards can be used for developing sight word vocabulary. You want the child to practice enough until she has achieved a level of automaticity. Bell (*Seeing Stars*) describes a particular method for developing sight word recognition. She "captures" words from the Fry 1000 Most Common Words List. (The Fry 1000 Most Common Words List and Dolch list are readily available on the Internet. Complete a *Google* search with the word *Fry* or *Dolch*.) The student is told that any words that give her trouble will be captured for practice.

If the student cannot read the word quickly and accurately on the pre-test, the word is printed on an index card and placed in the "slow" pile. The word stays in the "slow" pile until the student can accurately and quickly identify it at least five times. The word then moves into the "fast" pile and stays there until a student has five more accurate and speedy identifications. That word can then be "retired." Students may enjoy drawing a picture of something to represent "slow," "fast," and "retired" on a card for the respective piles. You can record daily sight word practice on the tracking sheet in Appendix 7B (page 193). A sample tracking sheet can be found in Appendix 7A (page 192).

See Appendices 7A and 7B.

A periodic recheck of retired words is necessary. Randomly select words from the retired pile (e.g., 10-25 cards) and assure that the student can still read these quickly. Put the cards on the floor face up about 12" apart to form a "road." Have the student read each word. If she says the word quickly and accurately, have her step on the card and advance to the next word. If not, pick up the card and return it to the "slow" pile for more practice. You can record these periodic rechecks using the tracking sheet on Appendix 7D (page 195) or the "road" on *Take the Sight Road* (Appendix 7F, page 197). A sample tracking sheet can be found in Appendix 7C (page 194) and a sample "road" can be found in Appendix 7E (page 196).

See Appendices 7C, 7D, 7E and 7F.

Some school systems provide parents with lists of sight words that the child is expected to master by the end of each of the primary grades. Appendix 7G (page 198) provides an example of how one school system adapted the Dolch list by dividing it into words that should be mastered at each primary grade level.

See Appendix 7G.

With any list of words being drilled, the speed of presentation is important. The words should be flashed at the student every one to two seconds. Accuracy and rate should be recorded. Rate can be recorded by "counting up" or "counting down." In the counting up methodology, a pre-determined number of cards are selected (e.g., 25 cards). The cards are presented one per every one or two seconds, and the student is timed to see how long it takes to name the words on the cards. Only the correct responses are counted, and any errors are corrected as they occur. In addition, when the student finishes reading the 25 words, any error words should be discussed and practiced.

In the counting down methodology, the timer is set, and cards are flashed at the student at the speed of one per second. Those words read correctly before the next card is shown are counted. Errors are quickly corrected by the instructor before the next card is shown. A total of the number of words read in the time limit set (usually one minute) is obtained. You can keep track of progress using the tracking sheet in Appendix 7I (page 200) for the counting up method or in Appendix 7K (page 202) for the counting down method. Sample tracking sheets can be found in Appendix 7H (page 199) and Appendix 7J (page 201).

See Appendices 7H, 7I, 7J, and 7K.

After practicing with flash cards, the student should be able to read the words she has practiced from a list of words on a page. Fleisher et al. (1979) suggest a goal of 90 WPM with 95 percent accuracy. Page speed drills, such as those used in Chapter 4, can also be used to develop increased automaticity of reading single words. Fischer (1995) had students read pages of alternating word sequences as fast as possible in one minute. For younger students, there may be only three or four words repeated randomly on the page. For older students, more variety of words can be presented. Fischer recommends a goal of

See Appendices 7L, 7M, and 7N.

reading correctly 30 WPM and gradually increasing to 60 WPM by the middle of third grade. Sample page speed drills for sight words can be found in Appendix 7L (page 203). You can track progress on the tracking sheet in Appendix 7N (page 205). A sample tracking sheet is in Appendix 7M (page 204).

These flash card drills do transfer to improved fluency in text reading. In order for this to be effective, however, the students have to read words or phrases on flash cards within strict time limits as described previously. Time limits are generally defined as one or two seconds per word. This drill results in improved speed and accuracy of text containing those words (Tan and Nicholson 1997, Levy et al. 1997). It also results in improved reading rates of non-practiced lists of similar words (van den Bosch et al. 1995).

Practice stories can be designed containing error words (see Appendix 7O, page 206.) Heibert (2003) has written 60 expository passages with frequently occurring words for reading grade levels 2, 3, and 4. These "QuickReads" are described as a research-based fluency program that features short, high interest nonfiction texts. Each level contains high-frequency words and phonic patterns and a read-along CD. In addition, little stories can be written specifically for a student with her frequently missed words.

See Appendix 7O.

Using a variety of activities to help the student improve accuracy and speed with sight word reading will keep the sessions interesting. Drill on words the student has missed from a list you have tested or from contextual reading. A significant portion of each session should be devoted to sight word development, if the student is to improve reading fluency. Computer games and other materials for practice are listed in Appendices 7P (page 207) and 7Q (page 208).

See Appendices 7P and 7Q.

List of Appendices for Chapter 7

Appendix 7A

Sample Tracking Sheet for Daily Sight Word Practice

Name: Alex

This is a sample completed tracking sheet to keep cumulative totals of the sight words the student is practicing. This can be used with any list of sight words, but this example is based on use of the Fry 1000 Most Common Words List.

Date	Practiced, but no words changed categories	# of words tested (*where on list)	# of words captured to "slow"	# of words moved to "fast"	# of words "retired"	Total in "slow"	Total in "fast"	Total in "retired"
5-1		50 (1-50)	12	N/A	N/A	12	N/A	N/A
5-3	X							
5-5	X							
5-8				8	0	4	8	0
5-10	X							
5-12				2	2	2	8	2
5-12		50 (50-100)	9			11	8	2
5-15	X							
5-17	X							
5-19				5	3	6	10	5
5-22				4	0	2	14	5
5-25	X							
5-26				1	3	1	12	8
5-26		25 (100-125)	7			8	12	8

* "where on list" indicates what columns of words in the Fry List were tested

Appendix 7B

Tracking Sheet for Daily Sight Word Practice

Name: ______________________________

Date	Practiced, but no words changed categories	# of words tested	# of words captured to "slow"	# of words moved to "fast"	# of words "retired"	Total in "slow"	Total in "fast"	Total in "retired"

Sample Tracking Sheet for Retired Sight Words

Name: Enrique

Use this form to track the number of sight words the student has "retired."

Date	Total in "retired" at beginning of session	# checked	# returned to work	# in "retired" now
6-2	8			8
6-12	13			13
6-21	22			22
7-1	34			34
7-12	52			52
7-15	56	15	4	52
8-20	77	10	1	76
9-18	85	20	4	81
11-1	110	20	5	105

Appendix 7D

Tracking Sheet for Retired Sight Words

Name: ______________________________

Date	Total in "retired" at beginning of session	# checked	# returned to work	# in "retired" now

Sample Tracking Sheet for Younger Students: Take the Sight Road

This student accumulated 51 sight words on 11/15. On that date, 20 words were randomly chosen and retested. Of those 20, the student missed (i.e., took too long to read or read incorrectly) three. Those three were "detoured" and placed back into the "slow" pile for more practice. There were 48 words left in the retired pile. Another random check was done was on 12/15. This time, 15 words were randomly selected for a check and four were detoured (71 words remained in the retired pile). On 1/30, when the student had 102 words in her retired pile, 20 words were randomly selected for recheck. None were detoured, so all were left in the retired pile.

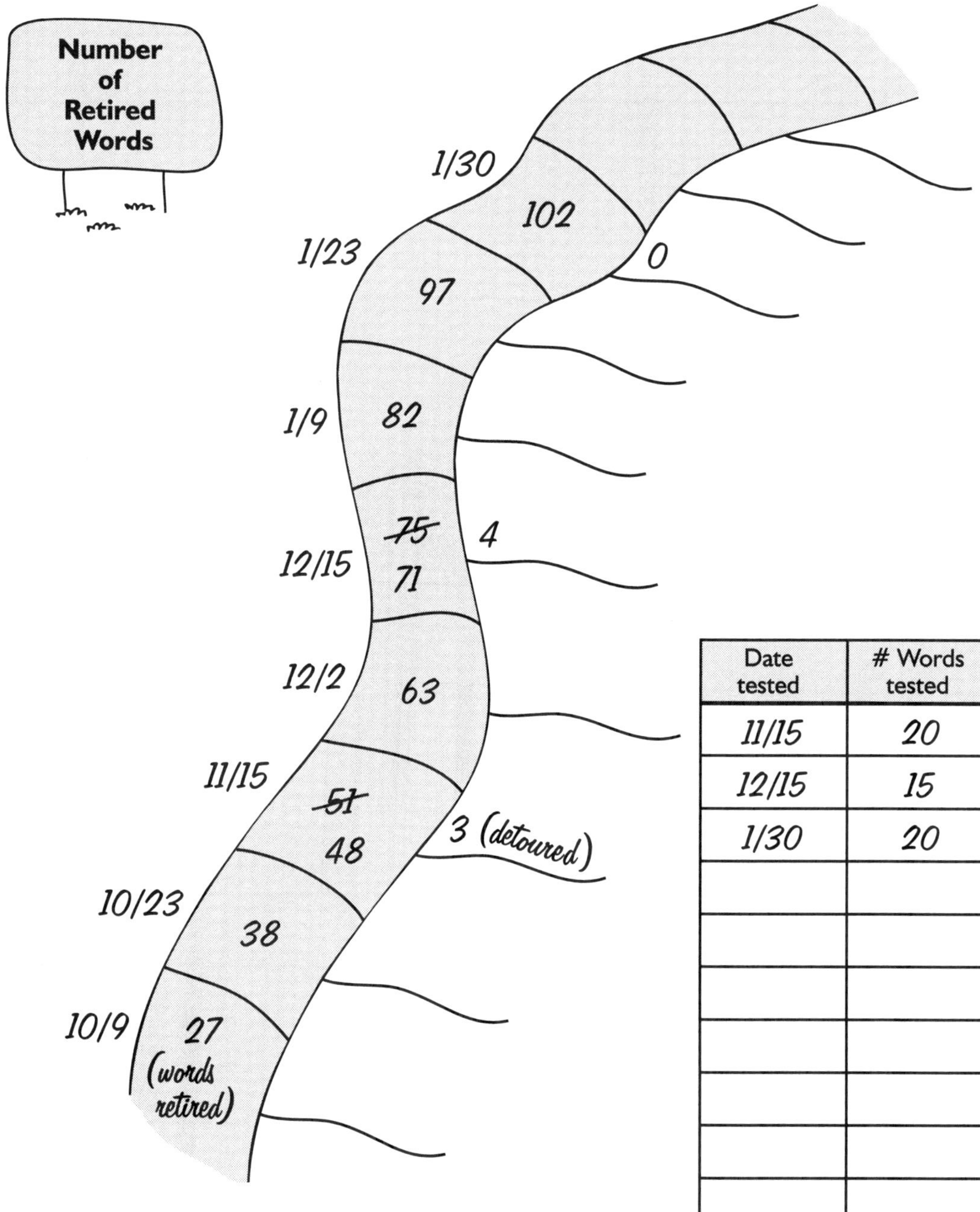

Date tested	# Words tested	# Detoured for practice
11/15	20	3
12/15	15	4
1/30	20	0

Take the Sight Road

Use this form to track the student's progress of sight word recognition.

Name ______________________________

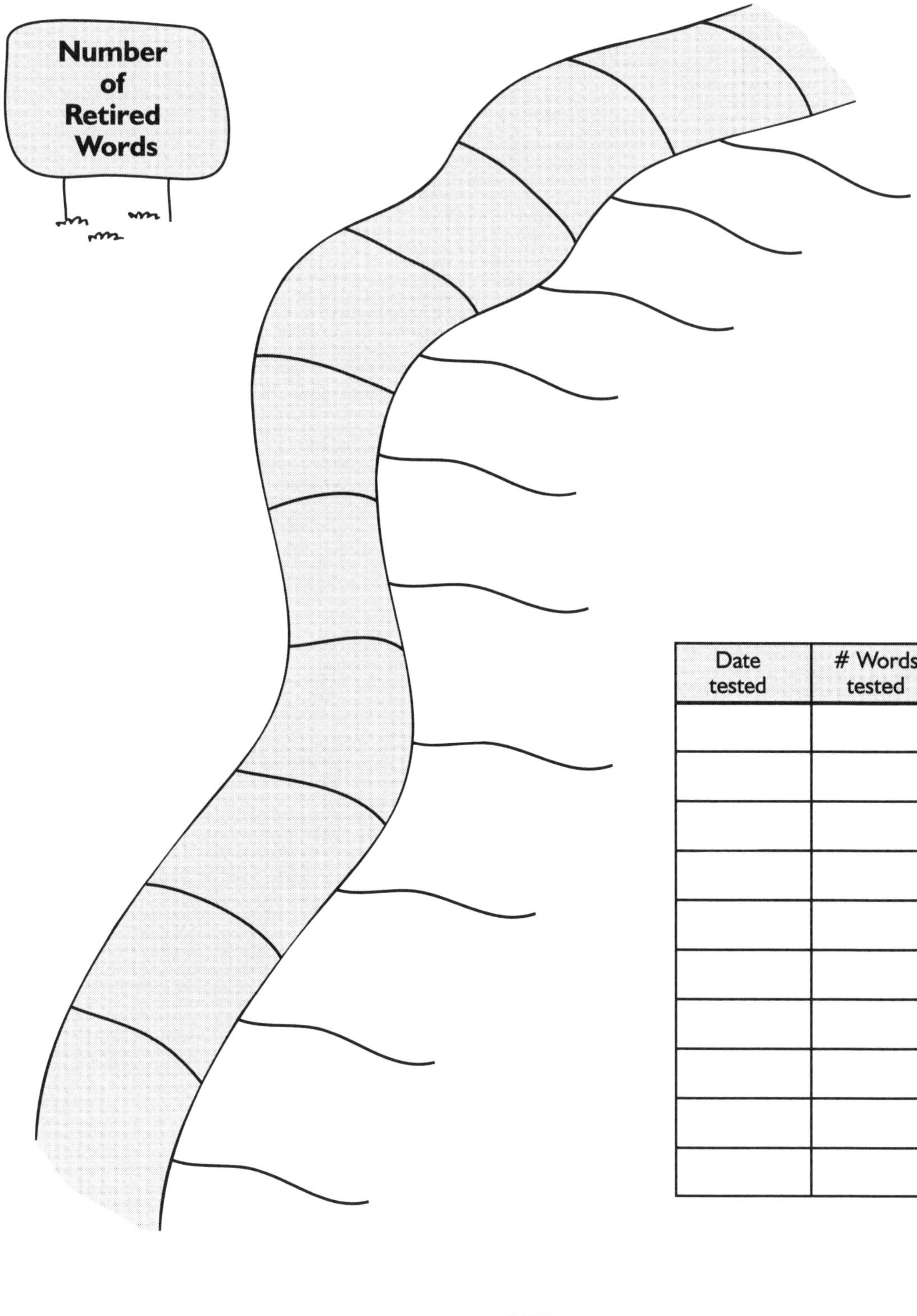

Date tested	# Words tested	# Detoured for practice

Appendix 7G

Graded Sight Word List Adapted from Dolch

Level A	Level B	Level C	Level D	Level E		Level F	Level G	Level H
a	big	and	all	about	live	as	always	cone
can	but	are	am	after	long	ate	away	drink
go	come	at	any	again	made	been	because	full
going	did	be	best	an	many	before	black	green
help	do	fly	bring	around	myself	better	buy	round
I	find	for	don't	ask	new	blue	carry	wash
not	funny	little	he	both	of	fast	clean	
to	get	make	how	brown	once	first	cold	
we	good	may	jump	by	only	from	done	
will	have	me	much	call	or	grow	eight	
you	here	my	on	came	our	hold	fall	
	in	no	one	could	over	just	far	
	into	red	play	cut	ran	must	hurt	
	is	some	please	does	say	never	light	
	it	tell	put	down	sleep	off	own	
	its	that	read	draw	so	old	pick	
	like	this	run	eat	soon	open	ride	
	look	where	she	every	start	pretty	seven	
	now	with	show	five	their	pull	shall	
	out	work	sing	found	them	right	sit	
	see	yes	stop	four	then	under	six	
	take	your	thank	gave	these	use	small	
	the		there	give	three	warm	ten	
	think		they	goes	two	wish	those	
	too		today	got	up	yellow	together	
	want		try	had	upon		white	
	what		why	has	us			
	would			her	very			
				him	walk			
				his	was			
				hot	well			
				if	went			
				keep	were			
				kind	when			
				know	which			
				laugh	who			
				let				

Appendix 7H

Sample Tracking Sheet for Sight Word Drills Using Counting Up Method

Name: *Juanita*

Source for words practiced: *words missed in reading last two weeks*

Date	Trial	# of flash cards drilled	How long it took to read them all	# correct
10-3	1	22	:65	18
	2	22	:60	20
	3	22	:50	22
10-8	1	22	:52	21
	2	22	:50	22
10-10	1	22	:45	20
	2	22	:45	22
	3	22	:40	22
	4	22	:38	22
10-14	1	22	:40	20
	2	22	:40	22
	3	22	:37	22
	4	22	:35	22

Tracking Sheet for Sight Word Drills Using Counting Up Method

Name: ________________________________

Source for words practiced: ____

Date	Trial	# of flash cards drilled	How long it took to read them all	# correct

Sample Tracking Sheet for Sight Word Drills Using Counting Down Method

Name: *Stefan*

Source for words practiced: *the list classroom teacher provided*

Date	Trial	Time limit	How many flash cards read	# correct
11-4	1	1:00	30	27
	2	1:00	33	30
	3	1:00	34	34
	4	1:00	35	34
11-6	1	1:00	35	35
	2	1:00	40	39
	3	1:00	40	40
11-9	1	1:00	43	40
	2	1:00	44	43
	3	1:00	45	44
	4	1:00	42	42

Tracking Sheet for Sight Word Drills Using Counting Down Method

Name: ____________________________________

Source for words practiced: ____

Date	Trial	Time limit	How many flash cards read	# correct

Sample Page Speed Drills for Sight Words

Ask the student to use her finger to follow the line of text or to use an index card to cover all but the line he is reading. Time how quickly the student can read the stimuli. Stress accuracy. The student might read the same page drill several times to see if she can improve his speed and accuracy.

the, of, and, a, to

the	of	and	a	to
and	a	the	to	of
a	to	of	and	the
to	the	a	of	and
to	and	of	a	the
the	a	to	and	of
of	to	the	a	and

in, is, you, that, it

in	is	you	that	it
is	you	that	in	it
that	in	it	you	is
in	it	is	that	you
it	is	you	that	in
you	in	it	is	that
that	is	it	in	you

he, was, for, on, are

he	was	for	on	are
for	on	are	he	was
are	was	for	on	he
was	for	he	are	on
on	he	are	was	for
are	for	was	on	he
for	on	are	he	was

how, word, said, their, but

how	word	said	their	but
word	their	but	how	said
but	said	how	word	their
but	how	word	said	their
said	word	their	but	how
their	but	how	word	said
how	said	word	their	but

Appendix 7M

Sample Tracking Sheet for Page Speed Drills for Sight Words

Name: Robert

Select the page you want the student to practice based on words commonly in error (see Appendix 7L, page 203). It is more effective if you design a page speed drill specifically for the student with error words from contextual reading or words the student has missed on sight word testing. Practice until the student achieves 90 words correct per minute on a specific set (or less stringent requirement set by you).

Date	Trial	Page speed drill for words	# of words read in one minute	# errors	# correct
12-2	1	their, there, when, how, it, some	58	4	54
	2		59	3	56
	3		63	1	62
	4		66	1	65
	5		67	0	67
12-9	1	their, there, when, how, it, some	65	3	62
	2		68	2	66
	3		72	1	71
	1	send, not, use, do, by	68	6	62
	2		70	2	68
	3		75	2	73
12-18	1	their, there, when, how, it, some	78	3	75
	2		83	3	80
	3		87	0	87
	1	send, not, use, do, by	70	4	66
	2		75	2	73
	3		77	1	76

Appendix 7N

Tracking Sheet for Page Speed Drills for Sight Words

Name: ________________________________

Date	Trial	Page speed drill for words	# of words read in one minute	# errors	# correct

Creating Sample Stories Containing Target Sight Words

Construct simple stories to provide repetitive practice of target sight words. Have the student read a story several times. See Chapter 9 for an explanation of repeat reading as a technique. Highlight the target words. Use the examples below to help you structure simple stories for your students.

During the reading lesson over the last four to five days, Student A missed the following words (either by reading them incorrectly altogether, or taking too long to recognize the word).

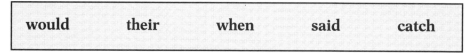

would	**their**	**when**	**said**	**catch**

The following simple story was constructed to drill on the student's error words. The missed words have been highlighted so the student is on alert for them when reading the passage.

Their mother **said**, "**When** you are done with your work, **would** you like to play **catch?**" Dan and Sam **said** they **would** like to play **catch**, but they didn't want to wait until **their** work was done. They asked **their** mother, "**Would** you let us play **catch** now instead of later?" **Their** mother **would** not let them play **catch** now and **said** they had to **wait** until they were finished.

Student B missed the following words.

instead	**correct**	**then**	**them**	**every**	**ever**

The following simple story was constructed to drill on the student's error words. The missed words have been highlighted so the student is on alert for them when reading the passage. In some cases, forms of the word (e.g., *correcting/correct*) are used. These should be pointed out to the student.

The teacher told **them** she would **correct** their papers **instead** of going out to the playground with **them**. **Then** she wouldn't have to take the papers home to **correct them** like she does **every** day. If she **ever** gets done **correcting** the papers in class, **then** she can do something fun at night. She might take her dogs to the park and let **them** run **instead** of letting them out in her little backyard like she does **every** night. **Then** the dogs would be as happy as they have **ever** been.

Computer Games

The chart reflects computer games that address sight word development.

Games	Sight words	Timed
Lexia PB—Level 1 Match It	X	
Lexia PB—Level 2 Spin It	X	
Lexia SOS—Level 1 Short vowel spin	X	
Lexia SOS—Level 2		
Picture It	X	
Search & Spell	X	
Reading Blaster—Ages 6-7 Marbles	X	X

For information on where to obtain these materials, see the Resources list on pages 260-262.

Other Materials

This chart reflects other materials that address sight word development.

Games	Sight words
100 Write-and-Learn Sight Word Practice Pages	X
Beginning and Advanced Sight Word Flash Cards	X
Easy Sight Words Sets 1 & 2	X
Quizmo? Sight Word Sets 1 & 2	X
Sight Word Books - Level 1	X
Sight Word Flash Cards	X
Sight Word Fun	X
Spectrum Dolch Sight Word Activities Vol. 1 & 2	X
Success with Sight Words	X

For information on where to obtain these materials, see the Resources list on pages 260-262.

Chapter 8

Word Retrieval, Semantics, and Vocabulary

What do depth of vocabulary, a rich store of word meanings, and the ability to retrieve words have to do with reading fluently? Many reading specialists believe that skillful reading of words requires not only good understanding of orthography and phonology, but also of meaning and context. Having a good grasp on meaning is easier for a student who has adequate word retrieval skills and a good understanding of multiple meanings of words. Wolf and Segal (1999) point out the interrelationship between vocabulary and retrieval:

- A well-established vocabulary enhances the student's ability to retrieve specific words.
- Speed of retrieval facilitates word recognition processes.

It is presumed that students can read faster when they can efficiently retrieve specific words as they encounter them in text. Remember the Chaucerian example provided in Chapter 1? Imagine how much more quickly you could read that passage if you knew the meaning of each of those words.

The connectionist model (Seidenberg 1990) also stresses the importance of word meaning. The connectionist model indicates that reading occurs when there is parallel activation of three subsystems:

- phonological—the sounds of the language
- orthographic—rules of the printed word
- semantic—the meaning of the words

The process starts when the brain receives an image of a printed letter string through visual processing. The brain recognizes this string by activation of appropriate codes in phonological and orthographic systems. These systems then activate the semantic system.

Wolf (1997) states, "Fast and accurate retrieval, whether for oral or written language, occurs best for words that are highly familiar and that possess rich associations for the reader, whether he is able or impaired." Some researchers have wondered whether a naming-speed deficit is actually a reflection of a broader word-finding problem, one that might be exhibited on a test of confrontation naming (i.e., naming when shown a picture). Research has yielded mixed results in an attempt to answer this question. Bowers et al. (1994) hypothesized that reduced rapid automatized naming may be a cause for children not developing sight word vocabulary and instead having to continue to rely on decoding. Their view is that children with word-finding difficulties may be poor readers and slow on RAN, but the converse may not be true.

Children with reading impairments often have better receptive vocabularies than expressive vocabularies (Haynes 1994, Swan and Goswami 1994). This suggests that their retrieval difficulties are due to limitations in processing rather than limitations in vocabulary. However, Wolf and Segal (1999) indicate that this generalization is not always true, especially given the heterogeneity in the population and the developmental changes that take place. They also indicate that retrieval problems are more prevalent than vocabulary issues at younger ages. Thus, these authors argue for the need to work simultaneously on vocabulary and retrieval processes in a variety of linguistic contexts. Based on the premise that retrieval can only occur after a word is in a child's vocabulary, Bjork and Bjork (1992) designed treatment so that retrieval activities always followed vocabulary activities. The child's basic knowledge of the word was established before he was expected to retrieve it.

Some studies have been done to determine if working to improve a student's knowledge of vocabulary and word retrieval can have an impact on his reading skills. In one of Wolf's studies (Wolf and Segal 1992), the authors worked on word specific and general strategies that were designed to aid flexibility during word finding problems. Their conclusion was that some aspects of word retrieval problems in dyslexic readers will respond to treatment, and that these gains might even generalize to other naming-speed tasks. Fawcett and Nicolson (1991) demonstrated that adolescents with dyslexia could improve lexical accuracy and speed with some generalization to untrained words when they were trained by their parents using principles of vocabulary development.

In their description of their pilot intervention program entitled *Retrieval Rate, Accuracy, and Vocabulary Elaboration (RAVE) in Reading-impaired Children*, Wolf and Segal (1999) discussed the importance of increasing speed and accuracy of naming, or what they described as lexical retrieval skills. They also discussed the importance of developing vocabulary depth. This was based on the awareness of the close relationship between word knowledge and the speed with which a word can be retrieved. Their study found significant gains on word retrieval accuracy and vocabulary. They also found a significant generalization to an untrained naming-speed task.

In their program entitled *Retrieval, Automaticity, Vocabulary Elaboration, and Orthography (RAVE-O)*, Wolf et al. (2000) discuss the importance of addressing semantic facilitation. Their program introduces core words, particularly those that have multiple meanings. They indicate that most core words have three or more common meanings. They state it is important to work on multiple meanings because many children with reading impairments are inflexible concerning the meaning of words. In addition, some children with reading disorders have word-finding problems, or dysnomia. They point out that slow readers don't have the time to process alternative meanings to words when they read.

Wolf et al. also teach a meta-cognitive approach to word retrieval. When a student can't retrieve the specific word he needs, he is encouraged to use a detective approach, asking himself the following questions:

- What sound does the missing word start with?
- What known word does it sound like? What is the rime inside it?
- What word has a similar meaning?
- Is it a short word or a long word?

In light of all these findings, it seems that to improve skills students need to work on:

- building vocabulary
- understanding words with multiple meanings
- retrieving meanings quickly

Building vocabulary

There are a multitude of products designed to improve vocabulary skills. These can be found in catalogs of materials for communication disorders, as well as in school supply catalogs and bookstores. A more practical approach to vocabulary development is to use the glossary sections from the student's textbooks, such as social studies or science. Lists of vocabulary words can also be developed from fiction the child has been assigned to read.

Another activity for developing vocabulary is the use of word webs. This technique helps the student make rich associations between words with similar meanings. A word is placed in the middle of the web, and the student is encouraged to think of words related to that word. It is helpful to make the student explain how the word is related. A blank word web can be found in Appendix 8A (page 215).

See Appendix 8A.

Word Web

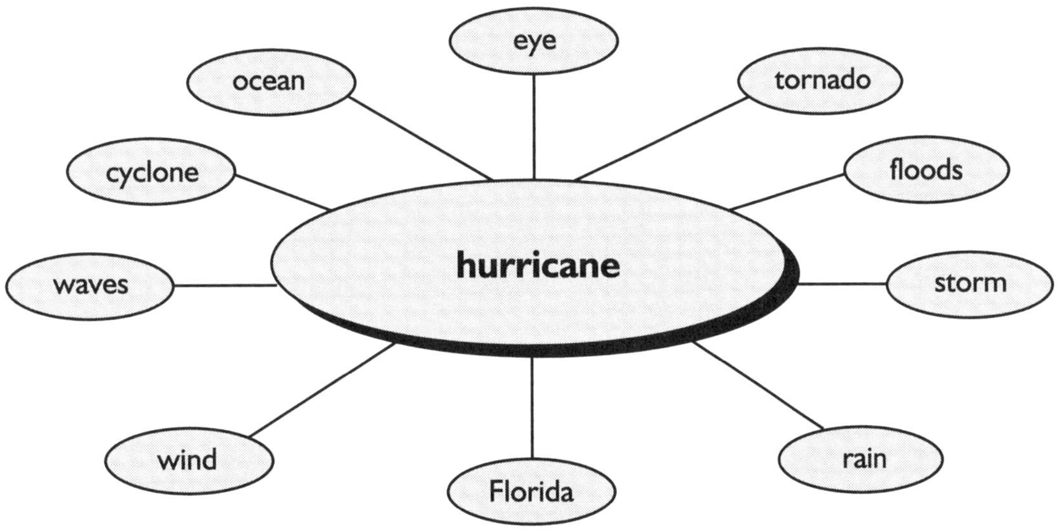

Students may also use a more advanced form of the word web in which they extend more words from any of the words on the web. This is called Web Plus. The student has to justify why the word he is putting on the extended web is related to the word on the web. For example, the student might extend a line from the word *waves* and write *surf*. This has nothing to do with *hurricane*, but it is related to *waves*. The diagram on the following page demonstrates the Web Plus.

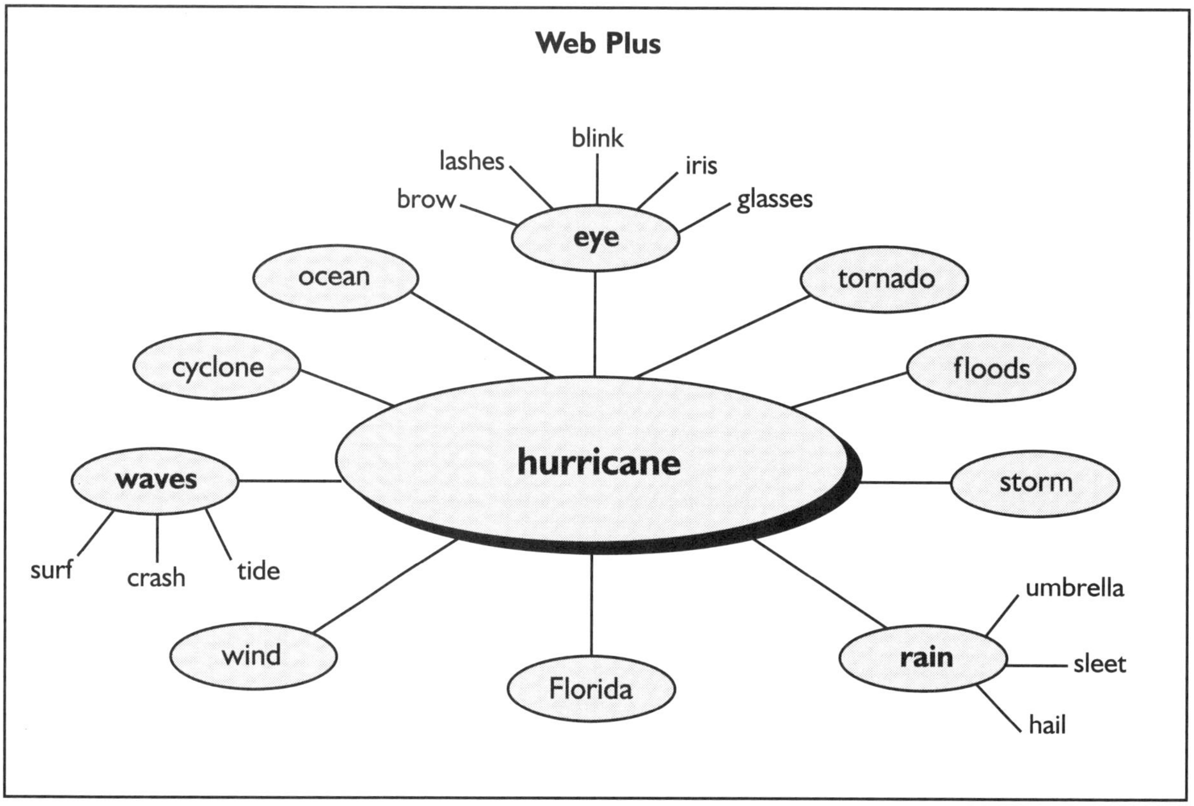

Use the information provided in Chapters 5 and 6 about root words to build your student's vocabulary. You can diagram this on a Word Root Tree to help the student see the relationships between a word root and its derivatives. For example, write the Latin root *struct* on the trunk of the tree. The student will tell you which words to write on the branches (e.g., *construct*, *destruct*, *destruction*) and why each word belongs by explaining how it is related to the root. You can use Anglo-Saxon, Latin, and Greek prefixes and suffixes as well. For example, if you write the Latin prefix *bi-* on the trunk of the tree, the student can add *biceps*, *bicycle*, and *biped* to the branches. *Bison* or *bite* do not belong because they do not use the meaning "two" for the *bi* that occurs in the word. In case the student can't think of any related words, you can write the words and have the student figure out their meanings. A blank Word Root Tree can be found in Appendix 8B, page 216.

See Appendix 8B.

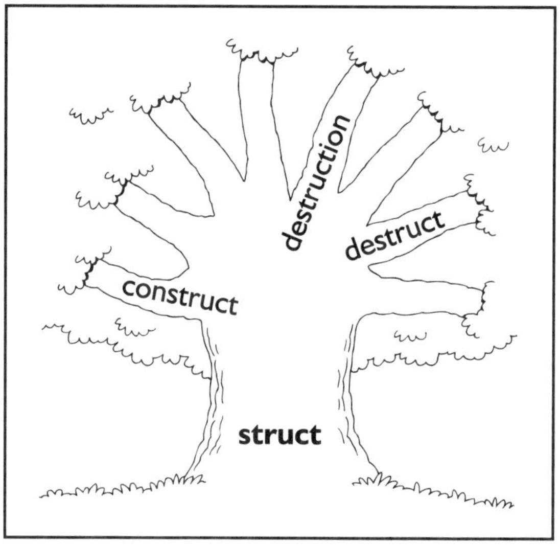

Understanding words with multiple meanings

The most common type of word with multiple meanings that causes students difficulty is a *homograph*, a word that looks the same as another but has a different meaning. It may or may not be pronounced the same. For example, *block* can mean a child's toy, a city block, or a defensive move. *Entrance*, with the stress on the first syllable, means a point of entry. However, when the stress is on the second syllable, *entrance* means to fill with delight.

Another type of word with multiple meanings is the *homophone*, a word that sounds the same but differs in meaning and often has a different spelling. For example, *block* would be considered a homophone as well as a homograph. Other examples of homophones that are not spelled the same are the words *eight* and *ate* or *weak* and *week*.

Yet a third category of confusing words is the *homonym*, a word that is pronounced the same and spelled the same but has a different meaning (e.g., *duck*, *date*). Some reference books use the term *heteronym* to mean a word (typically a noun, adjective, or verb) that is spelled the same but has a different meaning depending on how you pronounce it (i.e., where the stress is placed). Note: Different dictionaries define *homograph*, *homophone*, and *homonym* in slightly different ways. These definitions are from Webster's Dictionary.

Features	Homograph	Homophone	Homonym	Heteronym
Different meaning	X	X	X	X
Sounds same	X	X	X	
Sounds different	X (most often)			X
Spelled same	X	X	X	X
Spelled different		X (most often)		

It is important for students to be able to understand that homographs, homophones, and homonyms will cause confusion for reading and spelling. Students need to know the different spellings and meanings of these types of confusing words. They don't, however, need to know the name of the categories (e.g., homonym or homograph) because even the dictionaries can't agree on that! To recognize the different meanings and spellings, students typically have to have a good visual orthographic image (Hultquist 1997) and also an understanding of the different meanings. Ways to help students understand and practice using words with multiple meanings are discussed in Appendix 8C (pages 217-219). Appendix 8C also includes lists of homographs, homophones, and homonyms.

See Appendix 8C.

Retrieving meanings quickly

As students develop improved skills in vocabulary and semantics, push the student to increase the speed and efficiency of retrieving these meanings. Any activities can be timed to encourage the student to retrieve the word more quickly.

This chapter has not provided many practice activities for vocabulary, semantics, and word retrieval because there are so many readily available materials. When using such materials, be sure to incorporate the printed word whenever possible. Computer games and other materials for practice are listed in Appendices 8D (page 220) and 8E (page 221).

See Appendices 8D and 8E.

List of Appendices for Chapter 8

Word Web

Write a word in the center of the word web. Then write words related to that word in the circles around it.

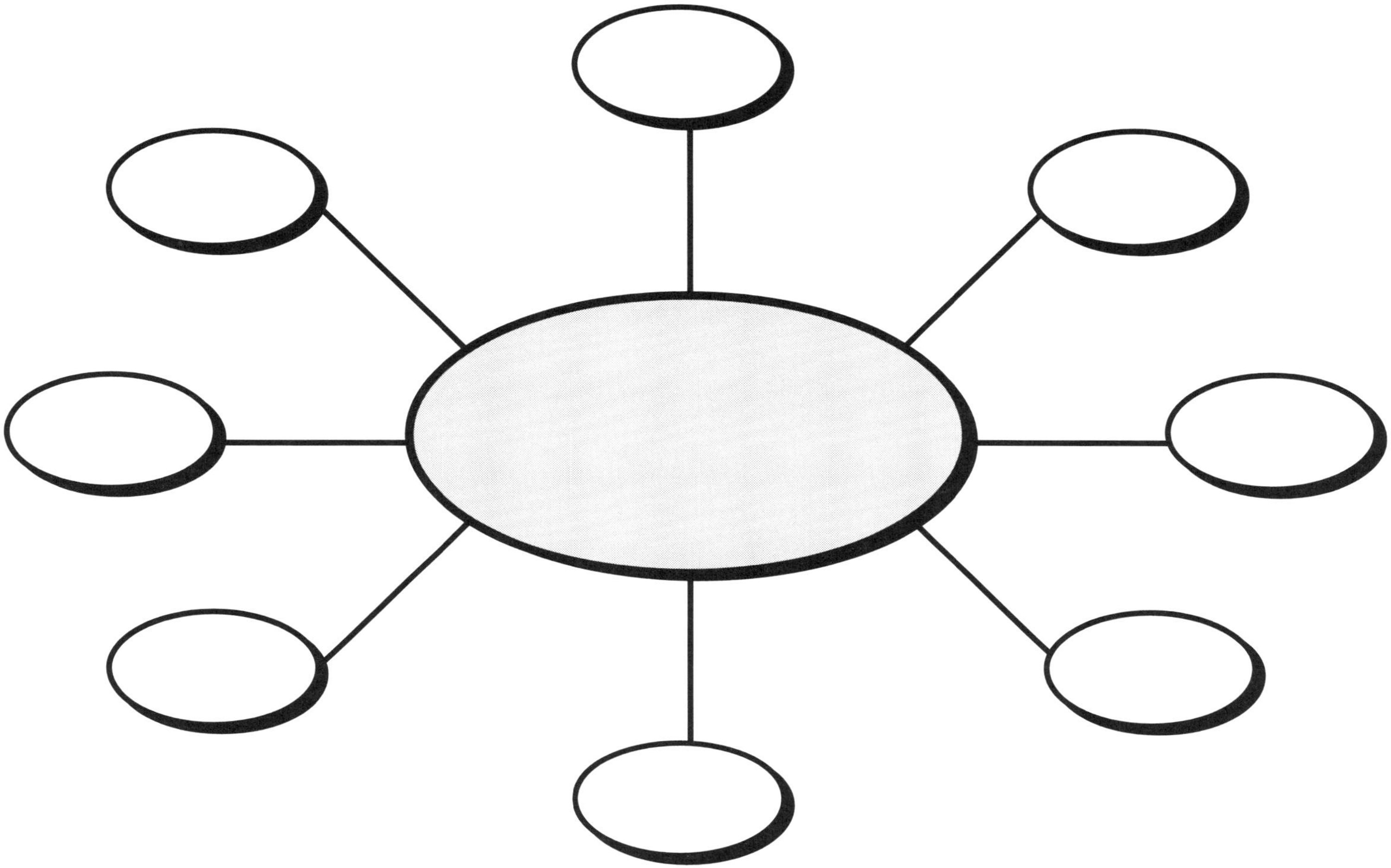

Word Root Tree

Write a root word on the trunk. Then write derivatives of the root word on the branches.

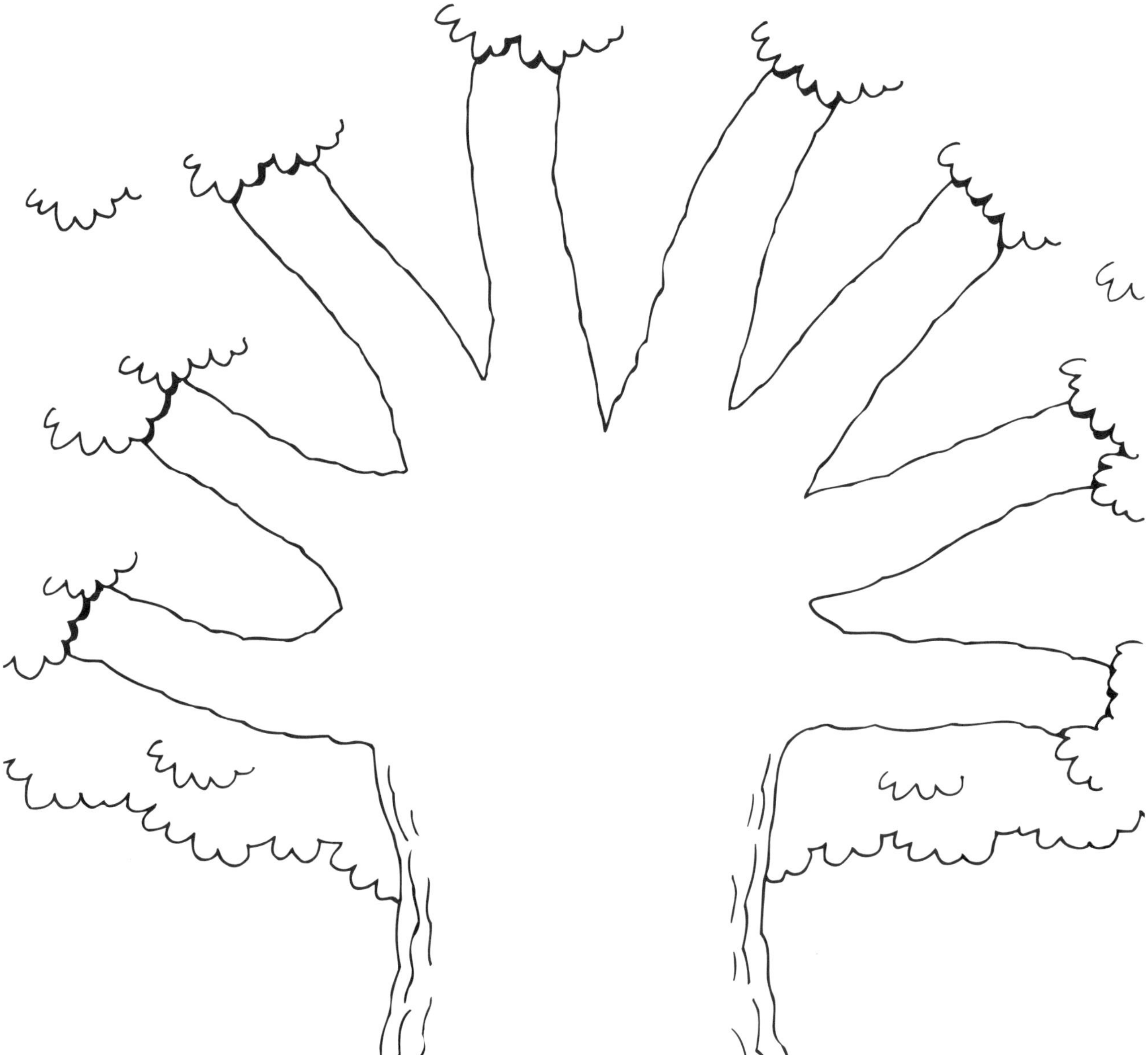

Homographs, Homophones, and Homonyms

The chart on pages 218-219 summarizes the characteristics of homographs, homophones, homonyms, and heteronyms. Because sorting into these categories would be very confusing for students (most dictionaries don't even agree on differences between these words!), lists of words on pages 218 and 219 are organized by:

- words that sound the same and are spelled the same, but have different meanings
- words that sound different, but are spelled the same and have different meanings (Note: To make the words sound different, you have to change the accent/stress.)
- words that sound the same, but are spelled differently and have different meanings

Use the lists in the following ways:

- Have the student tell as many meanings as possible for the word.
- Have the student construct a sentence with each meaning.
- Write the words on index cards. Make a duplicate copy. Play *Go Fish*. When the player asks for a card, he has to read the word and tell one of the meanings. For example, the student might have the word *two* in his hand. He would have to ask, "Do you have *two* that means the number two?"
- Spread out on the table some of the homophone index cards that are spelled differently (e.g., *scent*, *cent*, *sent*). Give the student a hint, such as "I am thinking of a word that means the smell of something." The student would have to find *scent* and not *cent* or *sent*.
- Write silly stories that contain the word used in multiple ways.

Sample silly stories

I went to the store with one dollar and one cent. That was enough to buy a valentine with a special scent. It smelled like roses. I sent the scented valentine to my grandmother.

When I was riding my bike around the block, I saw a car blocking our neighbor's driveway. It was parked there so the driver could pick up the building blocks the little boy had spilled.

Homographs, Homophones, and Homonyms, *continued*

Words that: • sound the same • are spelled the same • have different meanings	Words that: * • sound different • are spelled the same • have different meanings	Words that: • sound the same • are spelled differently • have different meanings		
block	entrance	ate	eight	
duck	advocate	bear	bare	
act	aggregate	beat	beet	
arms	animate	be	bee	
buck	complement	break	brake	
blue	consummate	blew	blue	
box	delegate	board	bored	
base	desolate	buy	by	
back	duplicate	cell	sell	
bank	estimate	cent	sent	scent
ball	graduate	close	clothes	
bright	implement	dear	deer	
bat	intimate	dew	do	due
bill	isolate	die	dye	
bed	moderate	doe	dough	
coat	separate	fair	fare	
court	supplement	flea	flee	
change	syndicate	flu	flew	flue
can	conduct	flour	flower	
corn	convert	fore	fore	four
date	convict	hay	hey	
dull	defect	hear	here	
draw	digest	knot	not	
ear	discharge	know	no	
fly	extract	mail	male	
fall	object	meat	meet	
fast	permit	nose	knows	
foot	produce	pail	pale	
ground	rebel	pair	pare	pear
hit	survey	peace	piece	
hard	record	rain	rein	reign
ice	address	read	red	
jar	content	right	rite	write
jam	contrast	road	rode	rowed

* To make the words sound different, change the accent/stress.

Chart continued on next page.

Homographs, Homophones, and Homonyms, *continued*

Words that: • **sound the same** • **are spelled the same** • **have different meanings**	**Words that: *** • **sound different** • **are spelled the same** • **have different meanings**	**Words that:** • **sound the same** • **are spelled differently** • **have different meanings**		
kid	present	sew	so	sow
key	project	son	sun	
letter	subject	steal	steel	
light		tail	tale	
mine		aisle	I'll	isle
miss		hair	hare	
nail		pole	poll	
nap		rap	wrap	
pen		knead	need	
point		maid	made	
quack		would	wood	
rare		week	weak	
roll		vane	vein	vain
rock		berry	bury	
run		bass	base	
strike		bite	bight	
shine		chute	shoot	
stick		earn	urn	
trip		except	accept	
tip		bored	board	
well		flour	flower	
wave		eye	I	
watch		creak	creek	

* To make the words sound different, change the accent/stress.

Computer Games

The chart reflects computer games that teach semantics and vocabulary.

Game	Semantics		Vocabulary
	Affix meaning	Synonyms	
Lexia SOS—Level 5			
Greek	X		
Meaning Structures	X		
Reading Blaster—Ages 7-8			
Geyser 4		X	
Volcano Climb 2 & 3			X

For information on where to obtain these materials, see the Resources list on pages 260-262.

Other Materials

The chart reflects other games and materials that teach word retrieval, semantics, and vocabulary.

Materials	Word Retrieval	Semantics	Vocabulary
100% Curriculum Vocabulary		X	X
100% Vocabulary Primary & Intermediate		X	X
125 Vocabulary Builders	X	X	X
50 Quick-Play Language Games			X
Basic Vocabulary		X	X
Curriculum Vocabulary Game, The		X	X
HELP Elementary	X		
HELP for Middle School			X
HELP for Vocabulary	X	X	X
HELP for Word Finding	X		
Idiom Game, The		X	
Idioms Workbook, The - Second Edition		X	
It's on the Tip of My Tongue	X		
LanguageBURST: A Language and Vocabulary Game		X	X
More Semantically Speaking		X	X
Multiple Word Meanings		X	X
No-Glamour Language Cards		X	
No-Glamour Language Elementary		X	X
No-Glamour Language Game		X	X
No-Glamour Language Middle School		X	X
No-Glamour Reading: Content Vocabulary			X
No-Glamour Vocabulary		X	X
Patty's Cake: A Describing Game	X		
Plunk's Pond: A Riddles Game for Language	X		X
Rocky's Mountain: A Word Finding Game	X		
Scissors, Glue, and Vocabulary, Too!		X	X
Semantically Speaking		X	X
SPARC for Vocabulary		X	X
Tic-Tac-Language & Match		X	X
VocabOPOLY: A Play with Words Game		X	X
WordBURST: A Word Recall Game	X		
Word Finding Intervention Program	X		
Workbook for Synonyms, Homonyms, and Antonyms		X	X

For information on where to obtain these materials, see the Resources list on pages 260-262.

Chapter 9

Increasing Reading Rate in Context

The ultimate goal of reading intervention is to assure that the student understands what she has read and can read things in a reasonable amount of time. Improving fluency of connected text reading will not only result in a faster rate of reading, but will improve comprehension as well. Reading 95 words per minute is the minimum a student will need to complete most standardized tests of proficiency within the time limit (Meyer and Felton 1998). This chapter describes ways to increase reading rate and accuracy in connected text. The student who comprehends text and reads efficiently will be able to complete school assignments accurately and in a reasonable amount of time.

Relationship of reading rate and short-term memory

Breznitz and Share (1992) have performed multiple studies in which the reading rate was manipulated. The studies "consistently supported the hypothesis that accelerated reading rate increased the level of comprehension and reduced decoding errors." Breznitz et al. conclude that these gains may be due at least in part to:

- lower distractibility
- how the words sound when read more quickly, matching more closely the stored pronunciations

However, this 1992 study concluded that the improvements in comprehension that resulted from accelerated reading were "primarily attributable to changes in short-term memory processing."

Breznitz (1997) later tested this hypothesis among children with dyslexia. He found that "reading acceleration significantly enhances reading performance in specifically disabled readers. Dyslexic children can read faster than they normally do and, by doing so, increase decoding accuracy and comprehension." However, he found that short-term memory resources may be used differently by readers with dyslexia than by novice readers (those novice readers which were reported in the 1992 study). One of those differences was that individuals with dyslexia were much more dependent on context. Breznitz concluded: "For dyslexic children, the effects of reading acceleration may enhance processing operations, whereas for normal readers acceleration may increase capacity."

Short-term memory and working memory are assumed to play an important role in reading. When a student has limitations in short-term memory, there is likely to be an impact on reading. Reading requires that the word or phrase being decoded be retained in temporary storage while a student decodes it into a meaningful part of the text (Perfetti and Lesgold 1977). Perhaps the processing operations Breznitz refers to are the use of working memory for decoding.

Other explanations have been proposed for improved comprehension with increased reading rate. Based on Swanson's description (1994) of the relationship between short-term and working memory, one interpretation is that fast-paced reading may improve reading effectiveness because it facilitates the interaction between short-term and long-term memory storage functions. That interaction would allow better integration between top-down and bottom-up processing.

Individuals use a variety of strategies to minimize the limitations of short-term memory (e.g., the information can be retained typically for about 30 seconds, and only a limited amount of information can be held in working memory). They do this by organizing the information into chunks, rehearsing information, and parsing (Caplan 1972, Jarvella 1971, Kimball 1973, and Miller 1956). Other researchers (Dempster 1981, Torgesen and Houck 1980) have found that increasing the stimulus presentation rate helps to overcome the limitations of short-term memory.

Connectionist theory and reading rate

The connectionist theory discussed in Chapter 8 (page 209) provides another explanation for why fast-paced reading would help individuals with dyslexia (Seidenberg 1990). According to the connectionist model, reading occurs when there is parallel activation of three subsystems:

- phonological
- orthographic
- semantic

The brain receives an image of a printed letter string through visual processing and recognizes this string by activation of appropriate codes in phonological and orthographic systems. Then the meaning of the letter string is extracted from the semantic system.

Perhaps working memory is the coordinating mechanism for information that arrives from each of those three subsystems. Breznitz (1997) hypothesizes that perhaps the fast-paced reading forces information to arrive in working memory at a faster rate, making it more likely that the corresponding information from the three subsystems will present at the same time.

We know that reading acceleration permits more efficient use of other cognitive abilities such as attention. Breznitz hypothesizes that this faster-paced reading forces children with dyslexia to use other available cognitive resources more extensively.

Breznitz (1997) also hypothesizes that acceleration might shift the emphasis away from the slow phonological route to other, possibly compensating, routes for processing information during reading. Perhaps it forces the students to compensate for their phonological impairments by increasing their reliance on orthographic and contextual cues.

What happens when children read faster?

When children read faster, they:

- make fewer pauses
- make shorter pauses
- vocalize at faster rate
- speak in longer units

Corrective feedback during reading

Most researchers agree that corrective feedback must be given when a student makes an error when reading aloud. If not, the student retains the wrong information about the word just misread. Some might think that stopping to correct the student would be detrimental. Any negative reaction to providing feedback during oral reading generally is related to one of three concerns:

- Frequent interruptions may make the reader rely on the external monitor, and this might discourage self-monitoring.
- Emphasizing error word recognition might detract from an emphasis on meaning.
- Feedback might be disruptive and interfere with the reader's attention to the story and therefore impair comprehension.

One study by Pany et al. (1981) demonstrates that corrective feedback is not detrimental to reading comprehension. Another study of third graders with learning disabilities (Pany and McCoy 1988) found that when corrective feedback was given after every oral reading error, children made significant improvements. The students were also able to retell more story units.

Results of corrective feedback

- significantly fewer overall errors
- significantly fewer meaning change errors
- significantly fewer errors on lists of error words
- significantly fewer errors on passage comprehension questions

Most times, corrective feedback is simply stating the correct word when the student reads it incorrectly. However, a more detailed cueing and correction system could be used.

Hansen and Eaton (1978) summarized a study in which a hierarchy of corrective feedback cues was used. If a lower level cue did not work, the teacher provided a higher level cue. The chart on the next page shows the hierarchy used in the study.

Hierarchy of Corrective Feedback Cues

No.	Cue	Explanation	Rationale
1	Try another way.	Cue the student that he has read a word incorrectly.	The student should be allowed to first choose his own method of correction.
2*	Finish the sentence and guess the word.	Cue the student to use the context for correction.	Syntax and semantics are the basic methods of word recognition.
3	Break the word into parts and pronounce each one.	Cue the student to analyze the segments of the word.	Morphological elements are the largest meaning bearing units of words.
4	The teacher covers parts of the word and asks the child to decode each part.	Provide the student with an aided visual cue to decrease the amount of stimuli.	Aided visual cues provide a transition between morphological and phonological cues.
5	What sound does "____" make?	Provide the student with a phonic cue to indicate the location of his error within the word.	Phonological elements are the smallest sound bearing units in words.
6	The word is _______.	Provide the student with the correct word.	After the word has been analyzed unsuccessfully, it should be provided by an outside source.

* Note: Though Hanson and Eaton used guessing as a cueing strategy, guessing from context does not help a student improve phonological processing and is not recommended.

Reprinted with permission from Hansen, C.L. & Eaton, M.D. *Reading*. In Haring, N.G., Lovitt, T.C., Eaton, M.D., & Hansen, C.L. (eds.) "The Fourth R: Research in the classroom." Columbus: Charles E. Merrill Publishing Company, 1978.

This study was on a small sample of children. However, Hanson and Eaton found that when they used the hierarchy while the children read, the children used a higher level word attack skill when requested. They found an increase in both self corrections and in accuracy, as well as a decrease in omission errors. They concluded this may indicate that when alternative strategies are practiced in a formal situation, children can internalize these strategies and then begin to use them independently.

Several studies posit that the most effective method of correction when a student misses a word in reading is word drill (Jenkins and Larson 1979). Word drill involves noting any errors the student makes when reading and then drilling on those words in mass practice at the end of the reading session (Chapter 7, pages 188-190).

Jenkins et al. (1982) investigated what effect single word error correction had on comprehension. They compared two strategies: word supply and word drill. In word supply, the instructor states the correct word after the student has made an error. The student then repeats the word and continues reading. In the word drill method the word is also supplied, but, in addition, the student drills by practicing the words printed on index cards. This study concluded that the drill correction, which affects word recognition, also helps to improve comprehension of text that contains the original error words. The authors pointed out, however, that these were not large changes in comprehension, and other more specific activities for improving comprehension should be used if that is the goal.

Repeat and paired reading

Repeat reading is a technique in which the child reads the same passage several times in an attempt to increase speed and accuracy. Corrections are given when errors are made. Echo reading, or paired reading, is a variation of repeat reading. Repeat reading is designed to:

- increase reading speed
- transfer that improvement in speed to subsequent material
- enhance comprehension with each successive reading of text

Appendix 9A (page 237) describes repeat reading, and should be used as a handout for parents. Appendices 9B through 9E (pages 238-241) describe four types of repeat reading used with a "count up" method (i.e., seeing how long it takes to read a selected passage). The *Reinforcement Page for Repeat Reading* (Appendix 9F, page 242) can be used to track progress of the count up method. Any of the four types of reading can also be used with a "count down" method (i.e., read a passage within a time limit) as described in Appendix 9G (page 243). The descriptions overlap, but this was done intentionally so a page can be copied and given to a parent to fully explain the technique. If you send any of these appendices home, be sure to include Appendix 9A as the information on that sheet is not repeated in Appendices 9B, 9C, 9D, or 9E. The reinforcement page *How Far Can You Go?* (Appendix 9H, page 244) can be used to track the "count down" method.

See Appendices 9A through 9H.

The *Student Progress Chart for Repeat Reading* (Appendix 9J, page 246) can be used to record results of repeat reading tasks. (A sample progress chart can be found in Appendix 9I, page 245). You can also used the *Reading Fluency Chart* in Appendix 9L (page 248) as another way to chart progress. (A sample reading fluency chart can be found in Appendix 9K, page 247).

See Appendices 9I through 9L.

To determine a student's reading rate (i.e., compute words read per minute), use Appendix 9M (page 249).

See Appendix 9M.

It is important to use materials that the student can read with good accuracy. Most studies indicate that the student should be 90 to 95 percent accurate on the first read-through of the passage. Young and Bowers (1995) found that poor readers declined in reading rate, accuracy, and fluency as the text became more difficult. Therefore, in order for the student to concentrate on improving rate and fluency, the passages need to be easy enough that the student is not worrying about decoding and accuracy.

Does repeat reading help the student transfer this fluency to other text? Meyer and Felton (1999) describe this as a complicated issue. It may be the number of shared words in the text and it may be shared content that influences the transfer fluency (Rashotte and Torgesen 1985, Faulkner and Levy 1994).

> When selecting text for the student to read, consider that most reading programs describe text at three different levels according to how accurate the child can be:
>
> - Independent reading level 95% to 100%
> - Instructional level 90% to 94%
> - Frustration/hard level 89% or below
>
> For repeat reading and other activities to build fluency, select text in the independent level.

Providing correction of errors during repeat reading seems to be important. The correction can simply be the instructor saying the word the student has missed as soon as the error occurs. It can also involve drill activities on those missed words in between each repeat reading.

Meyer and Felton (1999) indicate that answering the question of whether repeated reading improves comprehension is difficult. That is because many of the studies that have assessed this have used different methods for measuring comprehension. Many of the researchers hypothesize that the reading practice helps the poor reader to become more efficient. This in turn enables her to shift her processing resources to comprehension. O'Shea et al. (1985) found that there was a difference when the instructor directed the student to pay attention to fluency or comprehension. If the student was asked to pay attention to fluency, she showed improvement in fluency but not as much in comprehension. If the student was asked to pay attention to meaning, she improved her comprehension and was better able to retell the story. These authors suggest that a combination of cueing the student for both fluency and comprehension would be ideal.

Meyer and Felton provide an excellent review of repeated reading in an article entitled, "Repeated Reading to Enhance Fluency: Old Approaches and New Directions." They report that repeated reading is based on the information processing model. This is the model that suggests that fluent readers can decode text automatically and leave their attention free for comprehension.

Samuels (1979) was one of the first to describe the method of repeated reading. He listed three goals:

1. Increase reading speed.
2. Transfer improvement in speed to other material.
3. Improve comprehension with each successive rereading of the text.

Repeat reading may also increase accuracy. There are a number of studies that report improvement in word recognition accuracy as a result of repeat reading activities.

Several research studies with both normal and disabled readers indicate that the most improvement in reading rate occurs after three or four readings. Beyond that number of readings, no significant change takes place (O'Shea et al. 1985, Bowers 1993).

Meyer and Felton also indicate that most researchers recommend spending about 15 minutes a day in repeat reading. This time may include not only the fluency training, but activities for correction of errors and testing for outcomes.

Topping (1987) found that paired reading can significantly improve the student's reading fluency and overall proficiency. Rasinski (1995) describes how paired reading is used. Each night the parent reads a brief poem or passage to her children. This is followed by the parent and child reading the text together several times. Then the child reads the text to the parent. Rasinski found that children who engage in this form of paired reading make significant gains (in as little as five weeks) over children who get tutoring without this paired reading support.

If there is a question as to whether silent reading will also improve the student's reading performance, a study by Wilkinson et al. (1988) showed that silent reading does not have a significant effect on post-test reading performance.

Improving attention to the details of text

Recalling Berninger's et al. (2001) hypothesis of three types of non-fluent readers (processing rate/efficiency impaired, automaticity impaired, executive coordination impaired) reminds us that different students may need different activities to improve fluent reading of text. Students with executive coordination impairment demonstrate:

- inattention to orthography
- inattention to morphology
- inattention to serial order of words
- inattention to self-monitoring of meaning
- inattention to prosody
- inattention or lack of awareness of syntactic structure, including inattention to punctuation.

Inattention to orthography

Students who don't attend to orthography may misread small words in the text (e.g., *if* for *of*, *this* for *that*). They may also skip words in the text or insert words that do not belong in the text. According to Berninger's et al. (2001) description, this type of student needs strategies for improving self-monitoring (i.e., to improve her attention to the actual words on the page). She needs to learn to look very carefully at the text and read only what is printed on the page.

One way to help a student pay closer attention to the words as they are written on the page is to have her read sentences from back to front. The sentences may sound silly, but the student won't be as tempted to change the words as she reads. After the student has read the sentence back to front, have her read it front to back to see if she can still get all of the words exactly as they are printed on the page.

Another way for students to practice reading word-for-word is to use an index card with a small window (rectangle) cut in the middle. The window should only be as tall as the line of text across which you're going to pass it. You won't want any words from the line above or the line below to show in the window. Since words are of differing lengths, there is no way you can cut the window so that only one word will show at a time. Make the window long enough for the longest word in the text to show.

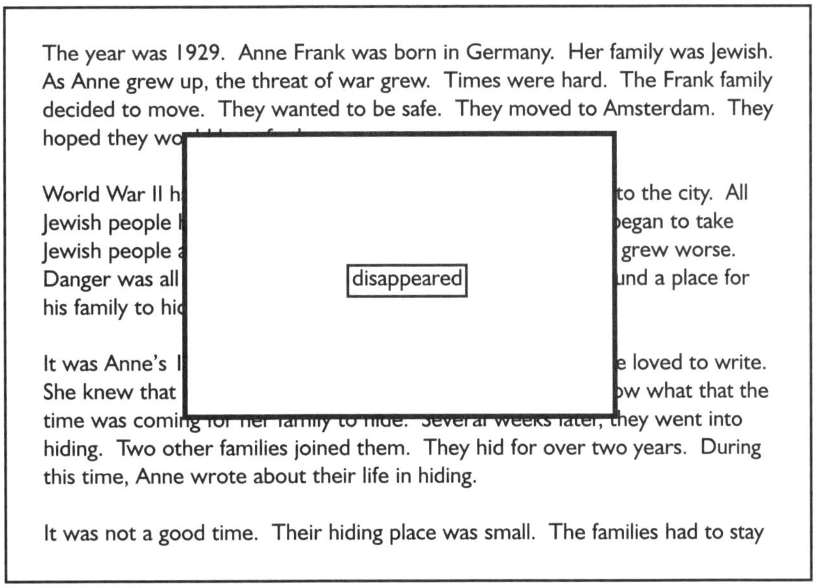
The year was 1929. Anne Frank was born in Germany. Her family was Jewish.
As Anne grew up, the threat of war grew. Times were hard. The Frank family
decided to move. They wanted to be safe. They moved to Amsterdam. They
hoped they wo
World War II h
to the city. All
Jewish people
egan to take
Jewish people
grew worse.
Danger was all
disappeared
nd a place for
his family to hi
It was Anne's
e loved to write.
She knew that
w what that the
time was comi
hey went into
hiding. Two other families joined them. They hid for over two years. During
this time, Anne wrote about their life in hiding.
It was not a good time. Their hiding place was small. The families had to stay

Inattention to morphology

Appendices 5K through 5M (pages 140-142) and Appendices 6H-6N (pages 162-176) provide multiple practice activities for improving student's understanding of morphology.

Inattention to serial order of words

Some students move words around in the sentence, insert words, and skip words. This can indicate inattention to orthography but also an inattention to the serial order of words. Reading through the window and reading from back to front will help these students.

Inattention to self-monitoring of meaning

Some poor readers stop and question when what they are reading does not make sense. Others continue to read and seemingly fail to realize that what they have just read does not make sense. If the student is not monitoring meaning, stop frequently and ask her to paraphrase what she has just read and answer questions about that sentence or group of sentences.

Some non-fluent readers who do not self-monitor as they read (Berninger's et al. Type 3, 2001) may not even be aware that they are changing words in the text. Often they are still able to understand the passage and answer questions accurately because they have not drastically changed the meaning of what they've read. Other times, the word they have changed does alter the meaning, and the text doesn't make sense to them. The activity in Appendix 9N (page 250) will demonstrate to students that changing even one word in a sentence can totally change the meaning.

See Appendix 9N.

Inattention to prosody and syntactic structure

Of the deficits listed on page 228, much has been written about inattention to prosody and syntactic structure. Many authors believe that the student's inability to grasp the underlying syntactic structure and rhythmic characteristics of written language is a cause of dysfluency. In particular, Schreiber (1980) suggested that if the reader can understand the underlying syntactic structure, then she can read more automatically.

Reading run-on sentences compared to appropriately punctuated sentences can be useful in helping students recognize the importance of punctuation. Appendix 9O (page 251) provides practice reading run-on sentences. You may want to use a highlighter to mark the punctuation and discuss what the student should do when encountering such punctuation marks.

See Appendix 9O.

Prosody includes suprasegmental features

- intonation
- stress
- duration (including pause and juncture)
- rhythm
- timing

Meyer and Felton (1999) suggest that for students with lack of sensitivity to prosodic cues, work should include helping the student recognize phrases within sentences. They suggest using techniques such as:

- parsing exercises (separating noun and predicate phrases)
- modeling prosody (listening to a fluent reader who is using good phrasing)

Some students show inattention to phrasing and sentence structure. They become bound reading one word at a time. This results in slow, plodding reading. The following activities and the parsing activity in Appendix 9P (pages 252-254) are designed to help students begin to see bigger chunks of the text at a time.

See Appendix 9P.

Cut and Scramble

Handwrite or type sentences the student has practiced reading onto a sheet of paper. Cut them into strips with three to four words per strip, depending on the length of the words. Mix up the strips and place them faceup on the table. Then have the student pick up each strip and read all of the words on it. Do not have her read the words one by one. Instead, have her read the three or four words as a phrase. Model for the student as needed.

every day after school	to eat apples	Amanda really likes

After the student has completed the task, reassemble the strips in their correct order and have the student read the sentence again, still attending to the phrases.

Amanda really likes	to eat apples	every day after school

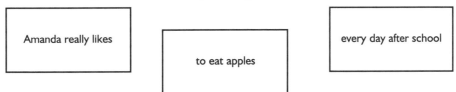

Telegram Game

Often in a sentence, there is one piece, or chunk, that carries the most important information. In sentences in textbooks read by older students (third grade and up), there are often multiple phrases or chunks that are important for carrying meaning. The following activity can be used to help students understand the meaning of what they read and improve prosody by picking out the most important information.

You will need a reading passage on which the student is 90 to 95% successful and a highlighter marker. Make a copy of the material so you can highlight sentences directly on the reading material. Have the student read the passage one sentence at a time so you can find the word, phrase, or phrases that seem to be the most important in each sentence. As she reads, highlight the important words or phrases with the marker. Explain that if the right word and phrases are selected, she will be able to read only those phrases and still get the meaning of what the author was trying to say.

After the important words and phrases are highlighted, have the student re-read the passage, but have her read the highlighted phrases all together rather than word-by-word.

Examples:

Pedro knew as soon as he **hit the ground** that things were **not good**. He had made a **great save**. The **soccer ball** was coming directly **toward the goal**. Pedro **jumped** in the air and **blocked the ball** with his body. Then he **fell** to the ground. He **landed** directly on his **right elbow**. He heard a **sickening crack**. Pedro had **never** had a **broken bone** before, but he was sure he **had one now**.

Magda **hated spaghetti**. It was really the **only food she hated**. Her mother **fixed it all the time**. Her mother fixed it **with red sauce**. Her mother fixed it **with cheese**. Her mother even made it **with olive oil**. Magna **hated them all**. She **hated** it if it was **long**, **thin** spaghetti or if it was **flat**, **fat** spaghetti. It **didn't matter what shape** it was, it was **still spaghetti**.

Jessica's team was the **worst** one **in the league**. They **hadn't won a game** yet, and there were **only two games to go** in the season. Jessica's **coach said** they should **keep trying hard**, but Jessica **didn't see the point**. **Trying hard for what?** **Losers were losers**! And there was no doubt about it, **Jessica's team was a loser**!

Chunking Machine

Hook and Jones (2002) indicate that students who read word-for-word also need help with phrasing. They suggest starting with the alphabet, having the student say or read the alphabet three letters at a time: *abc*, *def*, *ghi*, *jkl*, etc. They also describe a *tachistoscope*, a chunking machine that allows the student to see chunks of the text through a window. Use Appendix 9Q (page 255) to write in phrases from a passage you want the student to practice. Cut a window in an index card that will allow the student to only see one phrase at a time. The student is to read each phrase smoothly, not word-by-word. The diagram below shows how it will look. Hook and Jones suggest that the same set of phrases be read until the student can pull the card quickly over the phrases and answer comprehension questions.

See Appendix 9Q.

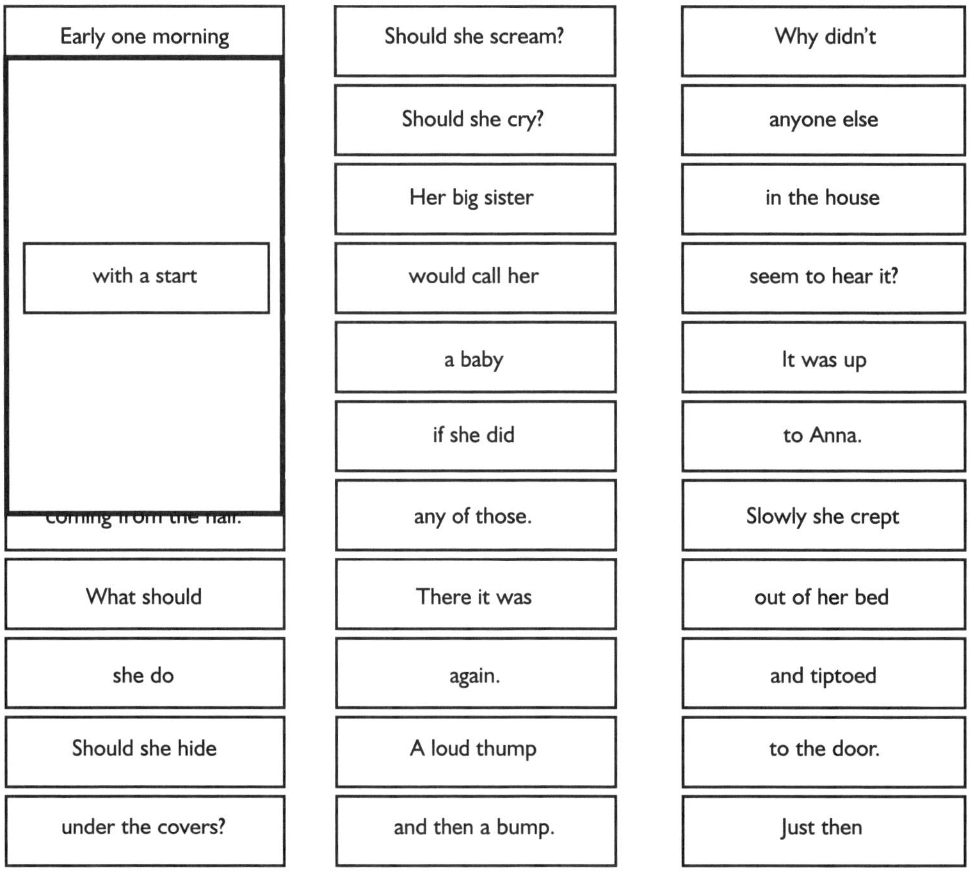
Early one morning
with a start
What should
she do
Should she hide
under the covers?
Should she scream?
Should she cry?
Her big sister
would call her
a baby
if she did
any of those.
There it was
again.
A loud thump
and then a bump.
Why didn't
anyone else
in the house
seem to hear it?
It was up
to Anna.
Slowly she crept
out of her bed
and tiptoed
to the door.
Just then

Scooping

Hook and Jones also describe two methods to mark phrasal boundaries in short passages. Slash marks can be placed between phrases. They also describe a method called *scooping*. You can pre-mark the boundaries or let the student help you decide where to mark them. When using scooping, the student uses a finger or pencil to mark the phrases with a scoop mark. Hook and Jones (2002) suggest a hierarchy for teaching scooping:

1. Begin with baseline reading of the passage without scooping.
2. Practice selected phrases with scooping.
3. Practice selected sentences with scooping.
4. Practice paragraphs with scooping of sentences and pauses between.
5. Read again with scooping.

Example of scooping in a passage

The student makes the scoop marks with her finger on the passage and reads the chunk as marked.

Renata was next | up at bat. | She had been | practicing her swing

all week | with her brother. | Now it was time | to see

if she could deliver.

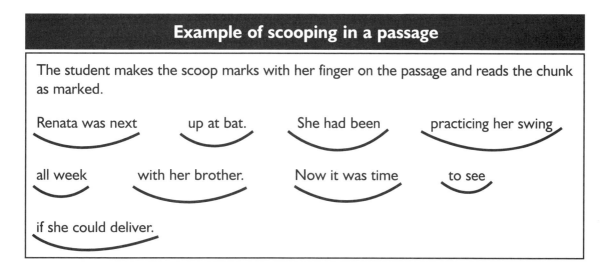

As students become more fluent readers, they recognize larger chunks of text at one time and move beyond the point of having to look word-by-word as they read. Some research has focused on what readers' eyes do as they read a line of text (Samuels 1992). The methodology for this research is to record the number of fixations, or stops, the eye makes when recognizing words. This research actually calculates the duration of the eye fixation, or the amount of time it takes the reader to identify and understand a segment of text before moving on. This research also analyzes the number of times the eye regresses, working back to a previously encountered portion of the text. The researchers found that as automaticity improved the fixations were few, the durations were short, and there were few regressions. Therefore, helping students to recognize phrases and larger portions of text above the word level might be one of the reasons that there were fewer fixations in readers who had achieved automaticity.

Poetry and dialogue

Rasinski (2000) suggests that the use of poetry can help students attend to syntax and promote fluency. He thinks it is important that the repeat readings the child has to complete have a real reason. For instance, the student might have to read a passage several times in preparation of helping a younger student read it. Otherwise, the repeat readings may seem artificial and laborious.

One study investigated using a reader's theater approach with second graders. In a ten-week implementation of this approach, small groups of second grade students were introduced to, practiced, and performed a new script each week. The students made significant gains in reading rate and overall reading achievement (Martinez et al. 1999). Using this repeat reading approach, the students made an average rate gain of 17 WPM. Rasinski (1999) reported that 17 WPM is about the gain that can be expected in an entire year, so this change in ten weeks was significant.

If you can't use a full-theater approach, have students read small dialogues to help with prosody. Appendix 9R (page 256) provides sample dialogues for students to practice. You can also use children's books with a lot of dialogue. Remind the student that what she is reading is really what someone is saying. Have the student choose which character she would like to portray. You be the other character. It's often a good idea after the first reading for you and the student to switch characters and reread the dialogue. That way, the student has heard you modeling the dialogue of the first character.

See Appendix 9R.

Contrastive stress

Drills for contrastive stress (Appendix 9S, page 257) are another excellent way to demonstrate to the students that intonation (in this case, stress) can change the meaning and intent of the utterance. In contrastive stress drills, the student reads the same response several times as you ask questions.

See Appendix 9S.

Intonation

Rasinski (2000) also likes to model expressive reading for the students. After he reads the passage to the student expressively, he asks questions such as:

- What did the long pauses make you think of?
- Why did I read that part in a quiet voice?
- When I read this section fast, did it affect how you understood the story?

Rasinski also sometimes reads a sentence or passage from different perspectives; such as with an angry, sad, or surprised tone. Then he discusses the passage with the students. He states this helps the students by:

- developing meta-cognitive understanding that the meaning of the passage is carried not only in the words, but also the way the words are read
- providing the model for students of what reading for meaning sounds like

To model different intonations for your students, use the activity in Appendix 9T (page 258).

See Appendix 9T.

If your student is having a very hard time imitating or using correct intonation, you might try reading sentences or paragraphs to the student, sometimes using correct intonation and sometimes reading with incorrect intonation. The following activity will give the student practice discriminating between correct intonation and incorrect intonation.

You'll need any printed material and two index cards. One on index card, draw a facial expression indicating that the sentence makes sense as read (i.e., correct stress and intonation). On the other index card, draw a facial expression indicating that the sentence did not make sense (i.e., incorrect stress and intonation).

Explain to your students that you'll be reading a sentence to them. They need to decide if the sentence has meaning based on how you read it. If you use correct intonation and stress, have students point to the card that indicates "makes sense." If you use incorrect intonation and stress, have students point to the card that indicates "doesn't make sense."

The tricky part of this activity is reading with incorrect intonation. Remember that in English we often put the stress on the noun or verb, or sometimes on the object of the prepositional phrase. We rarely stress articles or pronouns. Therefore in order to read with incorrect stress, you need only select a small word and stress it. Another incorrect stress pattern that you can model for the student is to read with flat intonation with no stress at all. This, unfortunately, is a pattern that many non-fluent readers use. They need to be made aware of how boring it is to listen to such reading, and how hard it is to discern meaning when there is no intonation.

Importance of prosodic cues

Perhaps part of the reason that some children have difficulty reading with expression is that the text has no markings to indicate what these prosodic features should be. More than 40 years ago, Fries (1963) pointed out that, "In the graphic representation of language there are left out such language signals as intonation and stress and pause."

Schreiber (1980) hypothesized that the child's ability to compensate for the lack of prosodic cues may be what enables her to become a fluent reader. He proposes that the reason repeat reading works is that it gives the child the opportunity to recognize the importance of attending to this lack of prosodic cues. He indicates that it helps the student learn to rely on morphological and syntactic cues to parse the sentence into the appropriate phrases. The repeat reading, Schreiber states (1991), "affords readers the opportunity to perceive the syntactic organization of sentences."

Schrieber points out that there are many morphological, syntactic, and semantic cues within the sentence that help determine what the prosody should be. For example, the use of the word *those* in a sentence indicates that the noun is likely to be plural. It also gives information about the verb form which will appear. Schreiber states that the improvement in repeat readings is due to the child's ability to make better use of signals such as these in order to understand the prosodic cues. Although this hypothesis has not been fully substantiated in later studies, there is certainly some logic to the rationale that improving the student's understanding of and recognition of prosodic cues can only help to make her a more fluent reader

In later work Schreiber (1987) continues to discuss this hypothesis that fluency can only be obtained as the student masters recognizing and using prosodic cues. In earlier chapters we discussed the importance of recognition of individual letters, letter patterns, syllables, and then whole words. A logical extension of this would be for the student to learn to recognize syntactic phrases. Gibson and Levin (1975) suggest that part of what makes the difference between good and poor readers is the reader's ability to segment written sentences into units such as phrases.

Note: Computer games for increasing reading rate in context can be found in Appendix 9U, page 259.

See Appendix 9U.

List of Appendices for Chapter 9

Appendix 9A

General Instructions for Repeat Reading

All repeat reading is designed to:

- increase reading speed
- transfer that improvement in speed to subsequent material
- enhance comprehension with each successive reading of text

For all types of repeat reading, keep the following in mind:

- The student should use a finger to follow along under the line of text to help the student's eyes follow along.
- For students who are very distracted, you may need to cover the remaining lines of text with a card or paper.
- Use materials that the student can read with good accuracy (90 to 95% accuracy on first read-through of the passage). If the student has more errors than that, the passage is too difficult. The goal of this activity is not to work on decoding.
- Correct any errors that occur by immediately saying the word correctly. You may ask the student to stop and repeat the word correctly, or you may let her go on reading. Some students become too frustrated when they are made to repeat.
- Read the passage three or four times to get the most benefit.
- Record the student's accuracy as well as rate.
- Use a visible measure of progress. (See Appendices 9F, page 242, and 9H-9L, pages 244-248.)
- Use different types of repeat reading practice for different students. (See Appendices 9B-9G, pages 238-243 for descriptions.)
- Practice 15 to 20 minutes daily with repeat reading.
- Ask comprehension questions to remind the student to pay attention to the content of what is read.

Echo (Paired) Reading Instruction Sheet

This technique is best used with beginning readers who read accurately, but slowly (less than 45 wpm). In echo reading, you can use your finger to follow the line of text, as the student may not move her finger along quickly enough.

1. Have the student read the passage while you time the baseline reading. Use a highlighter to mark any errors. If there are more than 10 percent of words in error, choose another passage. Discuss any words the student missed. Then tell the student that you are going to read together. Tell her that she is to try to keep up with you and say the words at the same time. Remind her that you will be reading the story with "feeling," and she should do the same.

2. Time the second reading (which is now in unison) and count the number of errors. With unison reading, it is very difficult to stop and supply a correct word. It is more efficient to wait until the end of the passage and then go back over any words missed. Read the passage a third and fourth time, increasing your speed slightly each time. Remember to read with good expression.

3. Praise the student for how much time has been taken off from the baseline reading to the last reading. Discuss how the errors have decreased. If there are words that consistently caused problems for the student, write these down for later practice. Point out to the student how much smoother the reading sounded as the rate increased.

4. To assure comprehension of the passage, ask a few questions about the content. It is important that the student understand that even though you are working on increasing speed, you are also concerned with how much she understood.

Reference: Young, Bowers, and MacKinnon 1996; Dowhower 1994

Sprint Repeat Reading Instruction Sheet

1. Have the student read the passage while you time the baseline reading. Use a highlighter to mark any errors. If there are more than 10 percent of words in error, choose another passage. Discuss any words the student missed.

2. Tell the student that if she makes an error you will correct her. Then have the student read the passage, telling her to read as quickly as she can. If the student makes an error, immediately say what the word should have been. You can decide if you want the student to repeat the correct word. If there is a major error, turn off the stopwatch, discuss what was wrong with the word, and then continue the timed reading. You must count each error as it occurs. You can do this by making a mark on the corner of the passage, counting on your fingers, or using any method which will help you remember the total number of errors. An easy way to do this is to make two copies of the passage. As the student reads one, note the errors on the other copy. Write a small 1 above errors the student makes during baseline reading, a 2 for errors in the next trial, etc. This way, you can review all the errors with the student.

3. At the end of the passage, tell the student her time and the number of errors. Ask her what her goal is for the next reading. How much faster does she think she can read, and how many errors can she eliminate? Then reset the stopwatch and have her read again. Follow the guidelines described above. At the end of the passage, record the time and errors. Have the student set the goals for time and errors for the next reading and repeat.

4. Praise the student for how much time has been taken off from the baseline reading to the last reading. Discuss how the errors have decreased. If there are words that consistently caused problems for the student, write these down for later practice. Point out to the student how much smoother the reading sounded as the rate increased.

5. To assure comprehension of the passage, ask a few questions about the content. It is important for the student to understand that even though you are working on increasing speed, you are also concerned with how much she understood.

Reference: Samuels 1979

Appendix 9D

Sprint + Drill Repeat Reading Instruction Sheet

1. Have the student read the passage while you time the baseline reading. Use a highlighter to mark any errors. If there are more than 10 percent of words in error, choose another passage. Write one error word on each index card. Complete a variety of activities to drill the student on recognition of the words.

   Activity 1: Turn the cards over quickly and have the student say them.
   Activity 2: Place all the cards facedown on the table and have the student turn one over and read it.
   Activity 3: Hold two cards facing you and randomly turn one to face the student for her to read. Then turn the other card to face the student. Repeat turning cards around, alternating between words. Sometimes turn the same card around two times in a row. When you are confident that the student recognizes these words, continue with the repeat reading.

2. Tell the student that if you hear an error sometime during the reading, you will say the word correctly. You can decide if you want the student to repeat the word correctly before going on with reading. Then have the student read the passage, telling her to read as quickly as she can. If the student makes an error, immediately say what the word should have been. If there is a major error, turn off the stopwatch, discuss what was wrong with the word, and then continue the timed reading. You must count each error as it occurs. You can do this by making a mark on the corner of the passage, counting on your fingers, or using any method which will help you remember the total number of errors. An easy way to do this is to make two copies of the passage. As the student reads one, note the errors on the other copy. Write a small 1 above the errors that the student makes during baseline reading, a 2 for errors in the next trial, etc. This way, you can review all the errors with the student. If any of the words are new errors (i.e., those not identified on the baseline reading and drilled), make a card and add it to those made previously. You can drill again between trials.

3. At the end of the passage, tell the student her time and the number of errors. Ask her what her goal is for the next reading. How much faster does she think she can read, and how many errors can she eliminate? Then reset the stopwatch and have the student read again. Follow the guidelines described above. At the end of the passage, record the time and errors. Have the student set the goals for time and errors for the next reading and repeat.

4. Praise the student for how much time has been taken off from the baseline reading to the last reading. Discuss how the errors have decreased. If there are words that consistently caused problems for the student, write these down for later practice. Point out to the student how much smoother the reading sounded as the rate increased.

5. To assure comprehension of the passage, ask a few questions about the content. It is important for the student to understand that even though you are working on increasing speed, you are also concerned with how much she understood.

Reference: Schreiber 1980

Sprint + Style Repeat Reading Instruction Sheet

1. Have the student read the passage while you time the baseline reading. Use a highlighter to mark any errors. If there are more than 10 percent of words in error, choose another passage. Discuss any words the student missed. Highlight any areas you think would help the student to sound more fluent. You might mark all the punctuation, or just those being ignored by the student. You might highlight a phrase or two and help the student practice reading/saying those phrases with meaning. You can even read the whole passage for the student, modeling good phrasing and expression.

2. Tell the student that if you hear an error during the reading, you will say the word correctly. You can decide if you want her to repeat the word correctly before going on with reading. Then have the student read the passage, telling her to read as quickly as she can. If the student makes an error, immediately say what the word should have been. If there is a major error, turn off the stopwatch, discuss what was wrong with the word, and then continue the timed reading. You must count each error as it occurs. You can do this by making a mark on the corner of the passage, counting on your fingers, or using any method which will help you remember the total number of errors. An easy way to do this is to make two copies of the passage. As the student reads one, note the errors on the other copy. Write a small 1 above errors that the student makes during baseline reading, a 2 for errors in the next trial, etc. This way, you can review all the errors with the student.

3. At the end of the passage, tell the student her time and the number of errors. Point out whether or not she attended to the syntactic and rhythmic cues you had discussed. Ask her what her goal is for the next reading. How much faster does she think she can read, and how many errors can she eliminate? Then reset the stopwatch and have the student read again. Follow the guidelines described above. At the end of the passage, record the time and errors. Have the student set the goals for time and errors for the next reading and repeat.

4. Praise the student for how much time has been taken off from the baseline reading to the last reading. Praise the student for more expressive reading. Point out phrases or sentences that were read well with meaning. Discuss how the errors have decreased. If there are words that consistently caused problems for the student, write them down for later practice. Point out to the student how much smoother the reading sounded as the rate increased.

5. To assure comprehension of the passage, ask a few questions about the content. It is important for the student to understand that even though you are working on increasing speed, you are also concerned with how much she understood.

Reference: Schreiber 1980

Reinforcement Page for Repeat Reading

Name ______________________________ Date ______________________________

Today I used Repeat Reading technique:

Echo _____ Sprint _____ Sprint + Drill _____ Sprint + Style _____

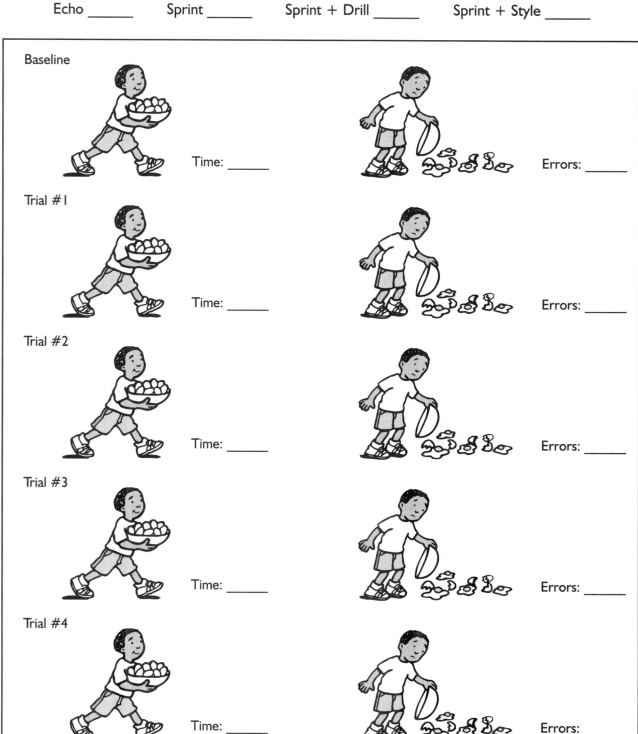

Baseline

Time: _____

Errors: _____

Trial #1

Time: _____

Errors: _____

Trial #2

Time: _____

Errors: _____

Trial #3

Time: _____

Errors: _____

Trial #4

Time: _____

Errors: _____

Count Down Method Repeat Reading Instruction Sheet
(How Far Can You Go?)

A different way to approach repeat reading is to have the child try to read farther in a passage within a time limit (usually one minute). When using this technique, you will need a timer that counts down to one minute and rings when the minute is reached. The goal is to have the student get further in the passage each time with fewer errors. This is a very easy way to determine WPM, since the number of words read is the WPM. You can also give the student a words correct per minute (WCPM) score by deducting the number of errors.

The student must be able to read the selected passage with 90 to 95 percent accuracy on the baseline read-through. If there are more errors than that, the passage selected is too difficult.

1. Have the student read the passage while you time the baseline reading. Use a highlighter to mark any errors. If there are more than 10 percent of words in error, choose another passage. Discuss any words the student missed.

2. Tell the student that if you hear an error during the reading, you will say the word correctly. You can decide if you want her to repeat the word correctly before going on with reading. Set the timer for one minute. Remind the student to read as quickly as she can, and have her read until the timer rings. If the student makes an error, immediately say what the word should have been. If there is a major error, turn off the timer, discuss what was wrong with the word, and then continue the timed reading. You must count each error as it occurs. You can do this by making a mark on the corner of the passage, counting on your fingers, or using any method which will help you remember the total number of errors. An easy way to do this is to make two copies of the passage. As the student reads one, note the errors on the other copy. Write a small 1 above errors that the student makes during baseline reading, a 2 for errors in the next trial, etc. This way, you can review all the errors with the student.

3. When the timer goes off indicating that a minute has passed, mark the last word read. Ask the student what her goal is for the next reading. How much further does she think she can read, and how many errors can she eliminate? Then reset the timer and have the student read again. Follow the guidelines described above. At the end of the minute, record the number of words and errors. Have the student set the goals for words (how far in the passage) and errors for the next reading and repeat.

4. Praise the student for how much further in the passage she read each time. Discuss how the errors have decreased. If there are words that consistently caused problems for the student, write them down for later practice. Point out to the student how much smoother the reading sounded as the rate increased.

5. To assure comprehension of the passage, ask a few questions about the content. It is important for the student to understand that even though you are working on increasing speed, you are also concerned with how much she understood.

Reference: Schreiber 1980

How Far Can You Go?

Name: ______________________________

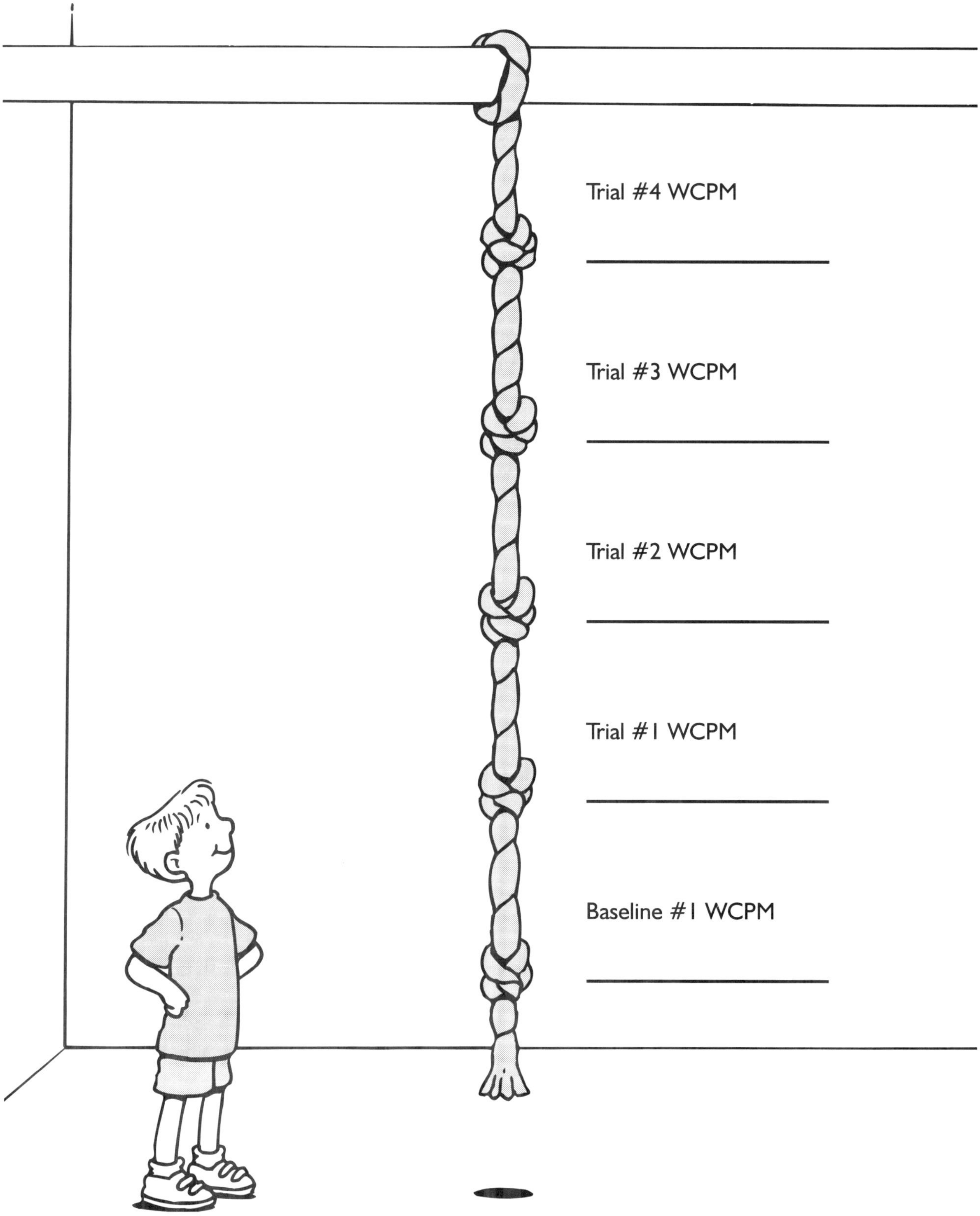

Trial #4 WCPM

____

Trial #3 WCPM

____

Trial #2 WCPM

____

Trial #1 WCPM

____

Baseline #1 WCPM

____

Sample Student Progress Chart for Repeat Reading

Student: *Carmen*

Date	Method/ # words	Baseline time	Errors	WPM/ WCPM	#1 time	Errors	WPM/ WCPM	#2 time	Errors	WPM/ WCPM	#3 time	Errors	WPM/ WCPM	Words to practice or notes
3-5	S / 45	:78 seconds	4	34/30	:76 seconds	3	35/32	:65 seconds	2	41/39	:58 seconds	0	46/46	their
3-5	S+D / 79	3:30 210 seconds	12											new passage; too difficult
3-5	S+D / 68	1:45 105 seconds	5	38/33	1:20 80 seconds	1	51/50	1:12 72 seconds	0	56/56	1:01 61 seconds	0	66/66	The drill really helped her.
* 3-9	CD / 1:00	56 words	3	56/53	59 words	2	59/57	64 words	0	64/64	66 words	1	66/65	

Echo (E) Sprint (S) Sprint + Drill (S+D) Sprint + Style (S+S) Count Down Method (CD)

* Note: When using this form to record results using the Count Down method, you will need to record the time (which is constant at 1:00) in the second column instead of # words. Also, the number of words read should be recorded in the 3rd, 6th, 9th, and 12th columns instead of time.

Appendix 9J

Student Progress Chart for Repeat Reading

Student: ______________________

Date	Method/ # words	Baseline time	Errors	WPM/ WCPM	#1 time	Errors	WPM/ WCPM	#2 time	Errors	WPM/ WCPM	#3 time	Errors	WPM/ WCPM	Words to practice or notes

Echo (E) Sprint (S) Sprint + Drill (S+D) Sprint + Style (S+S) Count Down Method (CD)

Note: When using this form to record results using the Count Down method, you will need to record the time (which is constant at 1:00) in the second column instead of # words. Also, the number of words read should be recorded in the 3rd, 6th, 9th, and 12th columns instead of time.

Sample Reading Fluency Chart for Repeat Reading

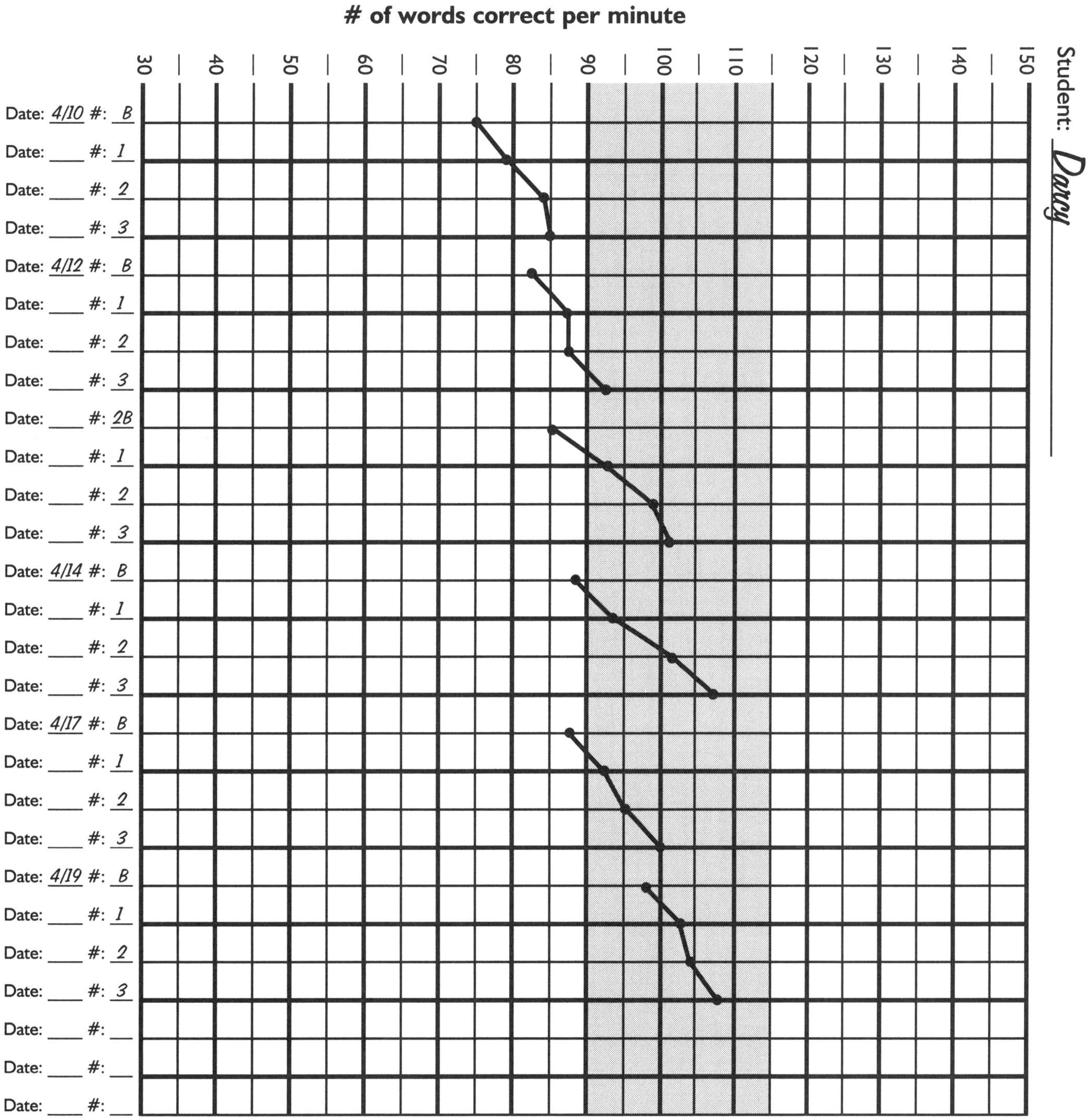

You can highlight a target reading rate range (see Chapter 2, page 21). You might select the range between the 50th and 75th percentiles. You could also select a specific target, such as 50 WCPM, and then a range around that target (e.g., 40 to 60 WCPM). For students for whom that is an unrealistic target, you might select the 25th percentile as the target and choose a range of 10 WCPM in either direction. When the student is in the target range on 2 to 3 consecutive baseline readings, you might select a harder level text. However, the student still needs to be 90 to 95% correct on the baseline reading. Record the number of words correct per minute on the baseline reading and each subsequent reading. See Appendix 9N for the formula to calculate WPM and WCPM.

In the example above, on 4/12, two separate passages were used. Also, on 4/19, the student achieved baseline reading in the target range. If this occurs on two more consecutive readings, try selecting a harder passage (but the student should still be able to read it with 90-95% accuracy).

Appendix 9L

Reading Fluency Chart for Repeat Reading

# of words correct per minute

30 | 40 | 50 | 60 | 70 | 80 | 90 | 100 | 110 | 120 | 130 | 140 | 150

Student: ____________

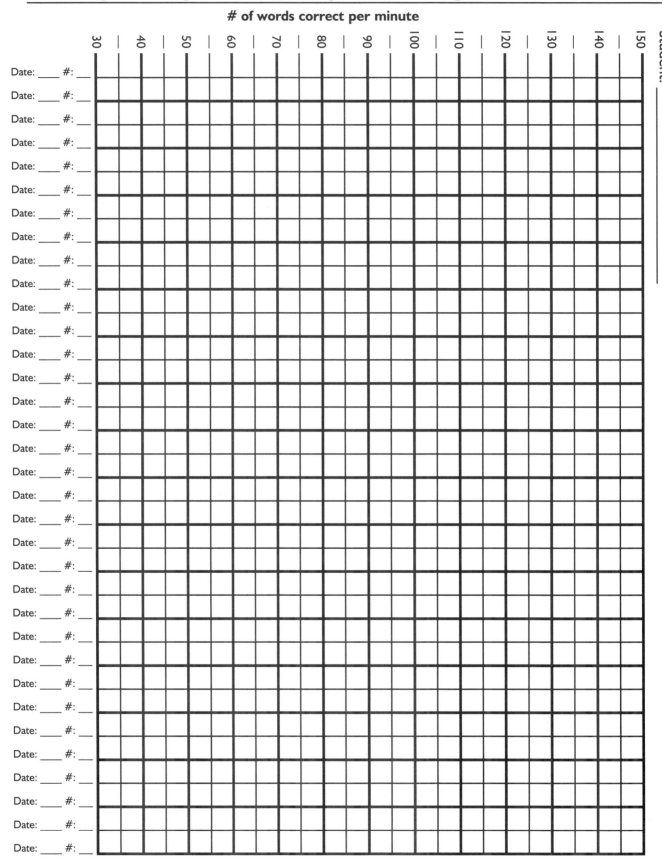

Date: ____ #: ___
Date: ____ #: ___
Date: ____ #: ___
Date: ____ #: ___
Date: ____ #: ___
Date: ____ #: ___
Date: ____ #: ___
Date: ____ #: ___
Date: ____ #: ___
Date: ____ #: ___
Date: ____ #: ___
Date: ____ #: ___
Date: ____ #: ___
Date: ____ #: ___
Date: ____ #: ___
Date: ____ #: ___
Date: ____ #: ___
Date: ____ #: ___
Date: ____ #: ___
Date: ____ #: ___
Date: ____ #: ___
Date: ____ #: ___
Date: ____ #: ___
Date: ____ #: ___
Date: ____ #: ___
Date: ____ #: ___
Date: ____ #: ___
Date: ____ #: ___
Date: ____ #: ___
Date: ____ #: ___
Date: ____ #: ___
Date: ____ #: ___
Date: ____ #: ___
Date: ____ #: ___

Formula for Computing Words per Minute

An easy way to figure the words per minute (WPM) is to use one of the following formulae:

Take the number of words read divided by the seconds needed to read the passage. This yields the number of words per second. Then multiply by 60 for the number of words per minute.

FORMULA 1

☐ ÷ ☐ = ☐ X 60 = ☐

words read | # seconds to read | # words/second | # words/minute

Example A: Student reads a 100 word passage in 1:35 (95 seconds).
100 divided by 95 = 1.05 (words per second) X 60 = 63 WPM

Example B: Student reads 100 word passage in 45 seconds
100 divided by 45 = 2.22 (words per second) X 60 = 133 WPM

This formula works with any number of words read.

Example C: Student reads a 225 word passage in 3:25 (205 seconds)
225 divided by 205 = 1.09 (words per second) X 60 = 65 WPM

Another way to perform the same calculation to determine reading rate follows:

FORMULA 2

☐ X 60 = ☐ ÷ ☐ = ☐

words read | # seconds to read | # words/minute

Using the same information in Example C above, the second formula works this way:
225 words X 60 = 13500 divided by 205 seconds = 65 WPM

WORDS CORRECT PER MINUTE

After obtaining a words per minute count, subtract the number of errors. The remainder equals words correct/minute (WCPM).

In the example above, if the student had 5 errors, the WCPM would be 60.

Sentences with One Word Changes

Read these sentences to demonstrate how changing even one word in a sentence can totally change the meaning.

Original sentence	Changing one word
Their house isn't on fire.	Their house is on fire.
Henry got the highest grade in the class.	Henry got the lowest grade in the class.
Her sister was on the bus this morning.	Her sister was beside the bus this morning.
Javier was the most helpful member of the team.	Javier was the least helpful member of the team.
You didn't believe his story, did you?	You didn't believe her story, did you?
The westerly winds blew in a snowstorm.	The westerly winds blew in a rainstorm.
The big, brown dog ate my homework.	The big, brown dog ripped my homework.
The weather is supposed to be nice tomorrow.	The weather is supposed to be stormy tomorrow.
My mom's favorite color is bright pink.	My mom's favorite color is pastel pink.
Jane likes to eat apples with peanut butter.	Jane hates to eat apples with peanut butter.
The baseball game ended in a tie.	The baseball game ended in a forfeit.
The paved road was covered with snow.	The paved road was covered with water.
Martin's friends were mean to the new girl in their class.	Martin's friends were nice to the new girl in their class.
The cow ate all the grass.	The horse ate all the grass.
The red candle lasted for two days.	The red candle lasted for two hours.
Whitney sang her favorite song at a school play.	Whitney sang her favorite song at a wedding.

Run-on Sentences

These sentences will help the student understand the importance of paying attention to punctuation when she reads. Use a sheet of paper to cover the second sentence in each pair. Have the student read the first sentence in the pair (the run-on sentence). Then ask questions to demonstrate how hard it is to understand the meaning when the two sentences run together. For instance, after the student reads the first sentence, ask, "Did the boy eat the banana at the mall?" or "Did the friend buy shoes at the mall?" Then uncover the second sentence in the pair and have the student read it. Discuss how much easier it is to understand when the punctuation is present.

1. The boy ate the banana at the mall his friend bought a new pair of shoes.
   The boy ate the banana. At the mall, his friend bought a new pair of shoes.
2. Tim hit the boys bikes are fun to ride.
   Tim hit the boys. Bikes are fun to ride.
3. Sally likes to stand by the pond snakes are long and slimy.
   Sally likes to stand by the pond. Snakes are long and slimy.
4. The boy sang his favorite song at school the teacher read a story.
   The boy sang his favorite song. At school the teacher read a story.
5. The weather changed from cold to hot soup is my favorite meal.
   The weather changed from cold to hot. Soup is my favorite meal.
6. Bob played on the playground at the park the slide was covered with snow.
   Bob played on the playground. At the park, the slide was covered with snow.
7. The cow ate the dead grass on the hill Jack played with his tools.
   The cow ate the dead grass. On the hill, Jack played with his tools.
8. Red is my favorite color of the three cars the blue is the best.
   Red is my favorite color. Of the three cars, the blue is the best.
9. The puppies were born yesterday in the basket were three apples.
   The puppies were born yesterday. In the basket were three apples.
10. The road was covered in ice storms are bad for old trees.
    The road was covered in ice. Storms are bad for old trees.
11. The swimming pool was used for training camps are several weeks long.
    The swimming pool was used for training. Camps are several weeks long.
12. The third grader won all three spelling bees flying is the quickest way to travel.
    The third grader won all three spelling bees. Flying is the quickest way to travel.
13. John drank two glasses of water a day to lose weight Sally doesn't eat candy.
    John drank two glasses of water a day. To lose weight, Sally doesn't eat candy.
14. The bridge was used for traveling in a small car you have to talk quietly.
    The bridge was used for traveling. In a small car, you have to talk quietly.
15. Maggie's friends were mean to the shy girl in town jewelry is very expensive.
    Maggie's friends were mean to the shy girl. In town, jewelry is very expensive.

Parsing Sentences

This activity is designed to help the student begin to see bigger chunks of the text at a time.

- **Materials needed:**
  Index cards of different colors

- **Directions for preparing your materials:**
  Use one color card for each column. Write the table letter (e.g., A, B) and the row number (e.g., 1, 2, 3) on the back of each card. On the front of each card, write one of the phrases.

  For example, from Table A, row 1, write: "The boy" on the front of a yellow card and on the back write "A-1." Write "and his brother" on the front of a blue card and on the back write "A-1." On the front of a green card write "were climbing" and on the back write "A-1." On the front of five orange cards write "under the fence, over the fence, on the ladder, on the roof," and "in the tree" and on the back of each write "A-1." These letter-number codes will allow you to keep each set together.

  The words from row 2 will also go on yellow cards for the first column, blue cards for the second column, green cards for the third column, and orange cards for the fourth column. On the back of each of those, write "A-2." This will make it easy to sort the cards when they get mixed up.

  Of course, it may be fun for the students to mix the different sets for some nonsensical sentences. For example, using rows 1 and 2, you might have silly sentences such as these:

  Tom and his brother were climbing to school.
  The boy and his dog were climbing on the ladder.
  Tom and his sister were running on the roof.
  The boy and Chip were climbing to school.

  These silly sentences will still accomplish having the student look at the phrase and attend to the prosody. Many students will enjoy telling what was silly about the sentence.

- **Say the following instructions to the student:**
  This activity is to help you practice reading parts of the sentence together rather than reading word-by-word. I have written the parts of the sentence on index cards. I'll put them on the table in a straight line. You can turn over the cards in stacks that contain more than one card and read how the sentence has changed. Sometimes we will mix up the cards so that we can make silly sentences.

Parsing Sentences, *continued*

Write these phrases on separate index cards so students can see and then read the chunks of text.

Table A: Sentences with verb phrases and prepositional phrases

	Column 1 (yellow)	Column 2 (blue)	Column 3 (green)	Column 4 (orange)
1	The boy	and his brother	were climbing	under the fence over the fence on the ladder on the roof in the tree
2	Tom	and his dog and his friend and his sister and Chip	were running	around the house in the yard up the steps to school past the store
3	The fat cat	and Bob	were sleeping were sitting were standing	on the couch on Bob's bed on the floor in the grass
4	The cardinal	and the bluejay	were flying	around the tree in the sky past the window to Florida to the birdbath

Table B: Sentences with introductory phrases and prepositional phrases

	Column 1 (yellow)	Column 2 (blue)	Column 3 (green)	Column 4 (orange)
1	In the summer When it was warm When they had time	Don and Dan Mary and Dan Don and Sue	went swimming went wading hunted for shells looked for rocks	in the pond in the lake every day each morning every afternoon
2	On a school day On Monday On a rainy day	all the students only the boys only the girls the fourth graders the third graders	like to go want to go never get to go walk quietly	to the library to the cafeteria to the playground to recess

Parsing Sentences, *continued*

Table C: *When* question with verb phrases and prepositional phrases

	Column 1 (yellow)	Column 2 (blue)	Column 3 (green)
1	When	is it time are we going are we happy	to go to school? to go home? to do our homework? to go to practice?

Table D: *Where* question with verb phrases and prepositional phrases

	Column 1 (yellow)	Column 2 (blue)	Column 3 (green)
1	Where	in the world in the state in the school in this store	can I find new shoes? can he be hiding? can the teacher be? is the bathroom? is the fastest person?

Table E: *Why* question with phrases

	Column 1 (yellow)	Column 2 (blue)	Column 3 (green)
1	Why	did you go did the boys go did your mother go is your sister going	to school today? fishing after school? to the birthday party? to shop alone?

Table F: Sentences with commands

	Column 1 (yellow)	Column 2 (blue)	Column 3 (green)	Column 4 (orange)
1	Look	in the basket on the floor under the bed in the bathroom	for the socks for the cats for the shoes for the pants	that are gray that are black that are missing that are lost
2	Read	the homework the book the magazine the letter	that is assigned of your choice from your brother with the red ink	on your bed under a tree in the car with a friend

Chunking Machine*

Write in the phrases of the passage you want the student to practice. Cut a window in an index card that will only allow the student to see one line of text at a time.

* For more information on how to use a chunking machine, see pages 231-232.

Prosody—Dialogue

Read these dialogues aloud with a student to practice reading with emotion and intonation.

Scene: Two boys talking before class starts about why their homework isn't done
Characters: Justin and Lamar

Justin: Did you finish your homework?
Lamar: No, I only got half of it done.
Justin: I didn't finish mine either.
Lamar: I didn't start on my homework until nine o'clock, and then my mom made me go to bed at 9:30.
Justin: My brother promised to help me with my homework, but he was too busy watching the game.
Lamar: This is the second time this week that I didn't get my math homework done. I bet Ms. Stanley is really going to be mad.
Justin: She will probably make us stay after school to do this homework.

Scene: A girl talking to her mother in the car on the way home from school
Characters: Mother and Sylvia

Mother: How did you do on your spelling test?
Sylvia: I only missed two of the words.
Mother: Which words did you miss?
Sylvia: I missed *fight,* and I missed the bonus word.
Mother: What did you forget about the word *fight*?
Sylvia: I spelled it *f-i-t-e*.
Mother: Yes, those words that end in *-ight* are tricky, aren't they?

Scene: Two friends talking about a birthday party
Characters: Jed and Sachi

Sachi: Does she have a birthday party every year?
Jed: Well, at least for the last five years!
Sachi: Where was the party last year?
Jed: You won't believe it! She had it on a boat on the river.
Sachi: Well, not many people would fit on a boat.
Jed: No, I mean a BIG boat. There were 25 kids invited and a bunch of adults.
Sachi: I can't wait to see where this year's party will be!

Scene: Standing in line at the cafeteria
Characters: Renata and Theo

Renata: Not pizza again! Do we have pizza every day?
Theo: No, it just seems that way because the pizza is so bad.
Renata: I know. Why can't they just order in pizza, like we do at home?
Theo: Yeah, that would be a lot better. Their pizza tastes like cardboard.
Renata: Yeah, cardboard with fake cheese on top!

Prosody—Contrastive Stress

Give the student a sentence and ask questions about it. The student should answer only using the sentence she is given but she should change the word she stresses, depending on the question.

Phrase for student	Your question to be read with stress on the bold word	Student's reply with correct stress in bold
Jack plays soccer.	Does **Fred** play soccer? Does Jack **like** soccer? Does Jack play **baseball**?	**Jack** plays soccer. Jack **plays** soccer. Jack plays **soccer**.
Mary eats cookies.	Does Mary eat **bananas**? Does Mary **throw** cookies? Does **Jerry** eat cookies?	Mary eats **cookies**. Mary **eats** cookies. **Mary** eats cookies.
The teacher is strict.	Is the teacher **easy**? Is the **principal** strict?	The teacher is **strict**. The **teacher** is strict.
His mother drove this morning.	Did his **father** drive this morning? Did his mother **walk** this morning? Did his mother drive this **evening**?	His **mother** drove this morning. His mother **drove** this morning. His mother drove this **morning**.
Peter never feeds the dog in the morning.	Does Peter **always** feed the dog in the morning? Does Peter never feed the **cat** in the morning? Does Peter never feed the dog in the **evening**? Does Peter never **pet** the dog in the morning?	Peter **never** feeds the dog in the morning. Peter never feeds the **dog** in the morning. Peter never feeds the dog in the **morning**. Peter never **feeds** the dog in the morning.
Father remembered to pick up the milk.	Did father remember to pick up the **juice**? Did father **forget** to pick up the milk? Did **mother** remember to pick up the milk? Did father remember to **drop** the milk?	Father remembered to pick up the **milk**. Father **remembered** to pick up the milk. **Father** remembered to pick up the milk. Father remembered to **pick up** the milk.

Appendix 9T

Prosody— Changing the Meaning through Intonation

Each of the sentences below can be read with a different intonation to indicate that the reader is mad, glad, or surprised. Use these sentences to model how intonation can change the meaning of a sentence.

- **Materials needed:**
  Emotion cards (index cards with a symbol drawn on each to represent *glad, mad,* or *surprised.* Label the cards as indicated.)

mad

glad

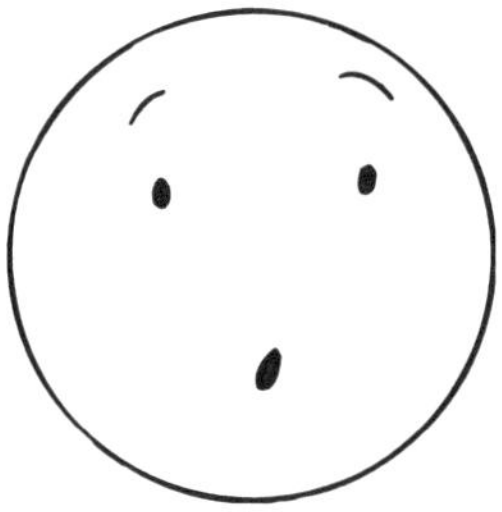

surprised

Say the following to the student: "I'm going to read a sentence to you using one of the emotions indicated on these cards. You repeat (re-read) the sentence with the same emotion (intonation)." Note: As the student gets better at this task, ask her to read the sentences without your model.

Select one of the emotion cards and place it on the table. Then read one of the following sentences with intonation to indicate that emotion.

1. Can you believe they won the soccer game?
2. The girls never get to go first.
3. The whole fourth grade has to stay after school.
4. He told me middle school wasn't as hard as he thought.
5. The Tigers won the football game again this year?
6. His mother lets him drive to school?
7. The dog ate his homework.
8. He stepped in the mud in his brand new shoes.
9. Maria wasn't invited to the sleepover.
10. When his friend stayed over, they got to stay up until midnight.
11. Sheron's dog is faster than Jamal's dog.
12. Penny makes more money than her sister.
13. It is raining really hard.
14. We were out of school for a week when it snowed.
15. That little dog barks really loudly.
16. Tim's brand new watch stopped working.
17. Shanika never helps me with my homework.
18. There are five pickle slices on this sandwich.
19. Janet's mom didn't buy her those new shoes.
20. Their basketball team won three games in a row.

Computer Games

The chart reflects computer games for increasing reading rate in context.

Games	Sentence level	Story level	Prosody word & sentence
Lexia PB—Level 2			
Word Hunt	X		
Lexia SOS—Level 2			
Picture It	X	X	
Lexia SOS—Level 3			
Trails West		X	
Lexia SOS—Level 4			
Winners Old & New		X	
Lexia SOS—Level 5			
Special Accents			X
Reading Blaster—Ages 6-7 Treasure Room—			
Story Room (All levels)		X	
Reading Blaster—Ages 7-8			
Geyser Valley (Level 5)	X		
Mumbler Maze (All levels)		X	
Ski Bum Mumbler (All levels)		X	

For information on where to obtain these materials, see the Resources list on pages 260-262.

Resources

Creative Teaching Press
PO Box 2723
Huntington Beach CA 92647-0723
1-800-444-4CTP (4287)
www.creativeteaching.com
Sight Word Books Level 1
Success with Sight Words

Didax
395 Main Street
Rowley MA 01969
1-800-458-0024
www.didaxinc.com
Compound Words Puzzles

Don Johnston Incorporated
26799 West Commerce Drive
Volo IL 60073
1-800-999-4660
www.donjohnston.com
Making Big Words
Making Words

Earobics
990 Grove Street Ste 300
Evanston IL 60201
888-328-8199
www.cogcon.com
Earobics

Gander Educational Publishing
412 Higuera Street, Ste 200
San Luis Obispo CA 93401
1-800-233-1819
1-805-541-3836
www.LindamoodBell.com
www.ganderpublishing.com
Lindamood Phoneme Sequencing Program (LiPS)
Seeing Stars

Judy/Instructo
A Division of Frank Schaffer Publications, Inc.
23740 Hawthorne Boulevard
Torrance CA 90505-5927
1-310-378-1135
www.school-tools.com/Judy-Instructo.htm
Compound Word Memory Match
Easy Sight Word Sets 1& 2

Knowledge Adventure, Inc.
4100 West 190th Street
Torrance CA 90504
1-818-246-4400
1-800-556-6141
www.adventure.com
Reading Blaster

Lakeshore
2695 E. Dominguez St
Carson CA 90810
1-800-421-5354
1-310-537-8600
www.lakeshorelearning.com
Word Families (Flip Books, Pocket Charts, Sliders set)
Write/Wipe

LDA
4156 Library Road
Pittsburgh PA 15234-1349
1-412-341-1515
1-412-344-0224
www.ldanatl.org
Dog Bones!

Learning Resources
380 N. Fairway Drive
Vernon Hills Illinois 60061
1-847-573-8400
1-800-222-3909
www.learningresources.com
Pharaoh's Phonics
Snap It Up

Lexia Learning Systems, Inc.
2 Lewis Street
PO Box 466
Lincoln MA 01773
1-800-435-3942
www.lexialearning.com
Lexia PB/Lexia SOS

LocuTour Multimedia
1130 Grove Street
San Luis Obispo CA 93401
1-800-777-3166
www.Locutour.com
Literacy: Rules, Rules, Rules

McGraw-Hill
PO Box 182604
Columbus OH 43272
1-877-833-5524
www.mcgraw-hill.com
Easy Sight Words Sets 1 & 2
Sight Word Fun
Spectrum Word Study and Phonics
Spectrum Dolch Sight Word Activities Vol. 1 and 2

Pro-Ed
8700 Shoal Creek Blvd.
Austin TX 78757
1-800-897-3202
Fax 1-800-397-7633
www.proedinc.com
Multiple Word Meanings
More Semantically Speaking
Semantically Speaking
The Idioms Workbook—Second Edition
Workbook for Synonyms, Homonyms, and Antonyms
Word Finding Intervention Program

Remedia Publications
15887 N 76th Street
Suite 120
Scottsdale AZ 85260
1-800-826-4740
www.rempub.com
COMPOUNDS
SYLLABLES

Scholastic Professional Books
2931 East McCarty Street
Jefferson City MO 65101
1-800-246-2986
www.scholastic.com
100 Write-and-Learn Sight Word Practice Pages
Phonemic Awareness Activities

School Zone
1819 Industrial Drive
Grand Haven MI 49417
1-800-253-0564
www.schoolzone.com
Beginning and Advanced Sight Word Flash Cards

Smart Kids LTD
158-2680 Shell Road
Richmond BC CANADA
V6X 4C9
1-604-207-0150
1-604-207-0156
www.smartkidscatalog.com
Syllabification

Sound Reading Solutions
379 Turkey Hill Road
Ithaca NY 14850
1-800-801-1954
1-607-273-1370
www.SoundReading.com

Teacher Created Materials, Inc.
6421 Industry Way
Westminster CA 92683
1-800-858-7339
www.teachercreated.com
Phonics—Phonemic Awareness Word Recognition

The Learning Company
6493 Kaiser Drive
Fremont CA 94555
1-510-792-2101
www.learningcompanyschool.com
Reader Rabbit

The Psychological Corporation
19500 Bulverde
San Antonio TX 78259
1-800-872-1726
www.psychcorp.com
It's on the Tip of My Tongue

The Word Workshop
1317 Shawnee Drive
Yellow Springs OH 45387
1-937-767-1142
www.thewordworkshop.com
Word Workout

Thinking Publications
424 Galloway Street
Eau Claire WI 54703
1-800-225-GROW (4769)
www.ThinkingPublications.com
Silly Sounds Playground

Trend Enterprises, Inc.
Customer Service
PO BOX 64073
St. Paul MN 55164
1-800-328-5540
www.trendenterprises.com
Sight Word Flash Cards

Twin Sisters Publications
2680 West Market Street
Akron OH 44333
1-800-248-TWIN (8946)
www.twinsisters.com
Advanced Phonics Activity Book

World Class Learning Materials
111 Kane Street
Baltimore MD 21224
1-800-638-6470
www.wclm.com
Quizmo? Sight Word Sets 1 & 2

LinguiSystems, Inc.
3100 4th Avenue
East Moline IL 61244-9700
1-800-776-4332
www.linguisystems.com
100% Curriculum Vocabulary
100% Reading: Decoding & Word Recognition
100% Vocabulary Primary & Intermediate
125 Vocabulary Builders
50 Quick Play Language Games
Basic Vocabulary
Blend It, End It
Curriculum Vocabulary Game, The
HELP Elementary
HELP for Middle School
HELP for Vocabulary
HELP for Word Finding
Idiom Game, The
Just for Me: Phonological Awareness
LanguageBURST: A Language & Vocabulary Game
No-Glamour Language Cards
No-Glamour Language Elementary
No-Glamour Language Game
No-Glamour Language Middle School
No-Glamour Reading: Content Vocabulary
No-Glamour Reading: Syllables
No-Glamour Vocabulary
Patty's Cake: A Describing Game
Plunk's Pond: A Riddles Game for Language
Rocky's Mountain: A Word Finding Game
Scissors, Glue, and Vocabulary, Too!
Sounds Abound
SPARC for Vocabulary
Tic-Tac-Language & Match
Tic-Tac-Read and Match
VocabOPOLY
WordBURST: A Word Recall Game

References

Abbott, S.P., & Berninger, V.W. (1999). It's never too late to remediate: Teaching word recognition to students with reading disabilities in Grades 4-7. *Annals of Dyslexia*, 49, 223-250.

Adams, M. (1990). *Beginning to read: Thinking and learning about print.* Cambridge, MA: MIT Press.

Adams, M., & Henry, M. (1997). Myths and realities about words and literacy. *School Psychology Review,* 26, 425-36.

Allington, R., & Cunningham, P. (1996). Using Running Records. In I.C. Fountas & G.S. Pinnell (Ed.), *Guided reading: Good first teaching for all children.* 89-96.

Anderson, J.R. (1980). *Cognitive psychology and its implications*. San Francisco: Freeman.

Anglin, J.M. (1993). Vocabulary development: A morphological analysis. *Monographs of the Society for Research in Child Development.* Chicago, IL: University of Chicago Press; Serial No. 238.

Apel, K., & Swank, L.K. (1999). Second chances: Improving decoding skills in the older student. *Speech and Hearing Services in Schools*, 30, 231-42.

Balmuth, M. (1982). *The roots of phonics.* New York, NY: Teachers College Press.

Berninger, V.W. (1987). Global, component, and serial processing of printed words in beginning reading. *Journal of Experimental Child Psychology*, 43, 387-418.

Berninger, V., Abbott, R., Billingsley, F., & Nagy, W. (2001). Process underlying timing and fluency of reading: efficiency, automatically, coordination, and morphological awareness. In M. Wolf (Ed.), *Dyslexia, fluency, and the brain.* Timonium, MD: York Press.

Berninger, V., Abbott, R., Brooksher, R., Lemos, Z., Ogier, S., Zook, D., & Mostafapour, E. (2000). A connectionist approach to making the predictability of English orthography explicit to at-risk beginning reader: Evidence for alternative effective strategies. *Developmental Neuropsychology,* 17-2, 21-71.

Berninger, V., Vaughan, K., Abbot, R., Brooks, A., Abbott, S., Reed, E., Rogan, L., & Graham, S. (1998). Early intervention for spelling problems: Teaching spelling units of varying size within a multiple connections framework. *Journal of Educational Psychology,* 90, 587-605.

Berninger, V.W., Yates, C., & Lester, K. (1991). Multiple orthographic codes in reading and writing acquisition. *Reading and Writing: An Interdisciplinary Journal*, 3, 115-149.

Beimiller, A. (1977-1978). Relationships between oral reading rates for letters, words, and simple text in the development of reading achievement. *Reading Research Quarterly,* 13, 223-253.

Bjork, R., & Bjork, L. (1992). A new theory of disuse and an old theory of stimulus fluctuation. In A.F. Healy, S.M. Kosslyn, & R.M. Shiffrin (Eds.), *From Learning Processes to Cognitive Processes: Essays in Honor of William K. Estes.* Mahwah, NJ: Lawrence Erlbaum Associates, Inc., 2, 35-67.

Bowers, P.G. (1993). Text reading and rereading: predictors of fluency beyond word recognition. *Journal of Reading Behavior,* 25, 133-153.

Bowers, P.G. (2001). Exploration of the basis for rapid naming of the relationship to reading. In M. Wolf (Ed.), *Dyslexia, fluency, and the brain.* Cimonium, MA: York Press.

Bowers, P.G., Golden, J., Kennedy, A., & Young, A. (1994). Limits upon orthographic knowledge due to processes indexed by naming speed. In V.W. Berninger (Ed.), *The Varieties of Orthographic Knowledge I: Theoretical and Developmental Issues.* Dordrecht, The Netherlands: Kluwer Academic Press.

Bowers, P.G., Steffy, R., & Tate, E. (1988). Comparison of the effects of IQ control methods on memory and naming speed predictors of reading disability. *Reading Research Quarterly,* 23, 304-309.

Bowers, P.G., & Wolf, M. (March 1993). *A double-deficit hypothesis for developmental reading disability.* Paper presented to the meetings of the Society for Research in Child Development, New Orleans.

Bowers, P.G., & Wolf, M. (1993b). Theoretical links between naming speed, precise timing mechanisms and orthographic skill in dyslexia. *Reading and Writing: An Interdisciplinary Journal*, 5, 69-85.

Breznitz, Z. (1990). Vocalization and pauses in fast-paced reading. *Journal of General Psychology*, 117, 153-159.

Breznitz, Z. (1997). Effects of accelerated reading rate on memory for text among dyslexic readers. *Journal of Educational Psychology*, 89, 289-297.

Breznitz, Z., & Share, D.L. (1992). The effect of accelerated reading rate on memory for text. *Journal of Educational Psychology*, 84, 193-200.

Caplan, D. (1972). Clause boundaries and recognition latencies for words in sentences. *Perception & Psychophysics,* 12, 73-76.

Carnine, D., Filbert, J. & Kame'enui, E.J. (1990). *Direct instruction reading, 2nd Edition*, Columbus, MD: Prentice Hall.

Catts, H.W., & Hogan, T.P. (November 2002). *At what grades should we assess phonological awareness?* Presented at ASHA National Convention, Atlanta, GA.

Chabot, R.J., Zehr, H.D., Prinzo, O.V., & Petros, T.V. (1984). The speed of word recognition subprocesses and reading achievement in college students. *Reading Research Quarterly,* 19, 147-161.

Chaucer, G. (1968). *Canterbury tales.* In *The Norton Anthology of English Literature: Major Authors Edition*; New York, NY: W.W. Norton & Company, Inc.

Clark, D.B. (1988). *Dyslexia: Theory and practice of remedial instruction.* Parkton, MD: York Press.

Clay, M. (1993). *An observation survey of early literacy achievement: Taking records of reading continuous texts*. Auckland, NZ: Heinemann.

Collins, A.M., & Loftus, E.F. (1975). A spreading-activation theory of semantic processing. *Psychological Review,* 82, 407-428.

Coltheart, M. (1978). Lexical access in simple reading tasks. In G. Underwood (Ed.), *Strategies of Information Processing.* New York: Academic Press, 112-174.

Cornwall, A. (1992). The relationship of phonological awareness, rapid naming, and verbal memory to severe reading and spelling disability. *Journal of Learning Disabilities,* 25, 532-38.

DeJong, P.F., & Van der Leij, A. (1999). Specific contributions of phonological abilities to early reading acquisition: Results from a Dutch latent variable longitudinal study. *Journal of Educational Psychology,* 91, 450-476.

Dempster, F.N. (1981). Memory span sources of individual and developmental differences. *Psychological Bulletin,* 89, 63-100.

Denckla, M.B. (1972). Color-naming defects in dyslexic boys. *Cortex,* 8, 164-176.

Denckla, M.B., & Cutting, L.E. (1999). History and significance of rapid automatized naming. *Annals of Dyslexia,* 49, 29-42.

Denckla, M.B., & Rudel, R.G. (1974). Rapid automatized naming of pictured objects, colors, letters, and numbers by normal children. *Cortex,* 10, 186-202.

Denckla, M.B., & Rudel, R.G. (1976a). Naming of objects by dyslexic and other learning-disabled children. *Brain and Language,* 3, 1-15.

Denckla, M.B., & Rudel, R.G. (1976b). Rapid automatized naming (R. A. N.): Dyslexia differentiated from other learning disabilities. *Neuropsychologia*, 14, 471-479.

Dolch, E.W. (1948). *Problems in reading.* Champaign, IL: Garrard Press.

Dowhower, S. (1987). Aspects of repeated reading on second-grade transitional readers fluency and comprehension. *Reading Research Quarterly,* 22, 389-406.

Dowhower, S. (1994). Repeated reading revisited: Research into practice. *Reading and Writing Quarterly: Overcoming Learning Difficulties,* 10, 343-358.

Ehri, L.C. (1992). Reconceptualizing the development of sight word reading and its relationship to recoding. In P.B. Gough, L.C. Ehri, & R. Treimen (Eds.), *Reading Acquisition.* Mahwah, NJ: Lawrence Erlbaum Associates, Inc., 107-143.

Ehri., L.C., & Wilce, L.S. (1983). Development of word identification speed in skilled and less skilled beginning readers. *Journal of Educational Psychology,* 75, 3-18.

Elbro, C. (1990). *Differences in dyslexia: A study of reading strategies in a linguistic perspective.* Copenhagen, Munksgaard.

Erekson, J. (1999). *Sound meanings: The role of prosody in children's comprehension of text and developing sense of voice.* National Reading Conference Symposium on Reconciling the Cognitive and the Social in Conceptualizations of Reading.

Faulkner, H.J., & Levy, B.A. (1994). How text difficulty and reader skill interact to produce differential reliance on word and content overlap in reading transfer. *Journal of Experimental Child Psychology,* 58, 1-24.

Fawcett, A., & Nicolson, R. (1991). Vocabulary training for children with dyslexia. *Journal of Learning Disabilities,* 24, 379-383.

Felton, R.H., Naylor, C.E., & Wood, F.B. (1990). Neuropsychological profile of adult dyslexics. *Brain and Language,* 39, 485-497.

Fisher, P. (1995). *Speed drills for decoding automaticity.* Farmington, ME: Oxton House Publishers.

Fisher, P. (1999). Getting up to speed. *Perspectives,* 25-2, 12-13.

Fleisher, L.S., Jenkins, J.R., & Pandy, D. (1979). Effects on poor readers' comprehension of training in rapid decoding. *Reading Research Quarterly*, 15, 30-48.

Forster, K.I. (1976). Accessing the mental lexicon. In E.C.T. Walker & R.J. Wales (Eds.), *New Approaches to Language Mechanisms.* Amsterdam: North Holland, 257-287.

Fries, C.C. (1963). *Linguistics and Reading.* New York: Holt, Rinehart & Winston.

Fry, E. (1994). *1000 instant words: The most common words for teaching reading, writing and spelling.* Laguna Beach, CA: Laguna Beach Educational Books.

Geschwind, N., & Fusillo, M. (1966). Color-naming defects in association with Alexia. *Archives of Neurology,* 15, 137-46.

Gibson, E.J., & Levin, H. (1975). *The psychology of reading.* Cambridge, MA: MIT Press.

Goodman, Y.M., & Burke, C.L. (1972). *Reading miscue inventory: Procedure for diagnosis and correction.* New York: Macmillan.

Goswami, U. (1993). Toward an interactive analogy model of reading development: Decoding vowel graphemes in beginning reading. *Journal of Experimental Child Psychology*, 56, 443-475.

Hansen, C.L., & Eaton, M. (1978). *Reading.* In N. Haring, T. Lovitt, M. Eaton, & C. Hansen (Eds.), *The Fourth R: Research in the Classroom.* Columbus, OH: Merrill, 41-93.

Haring, N.G., Lovitt, T.C., Eaton, M.D., & Hansen, C.L. (1978) *The fourth R: Research in the classroom.* Columbus, OH: Merrill, 41-93.

Harris, T.L., & Hodges, R.E. (1981). *A dictionary of reading and related terms.* Newark, DE: International Reading Association.

Hasbrouck, J.E., & Tindal, G. (1992). Curriculum-based oral reading fluency norms for students in grades 2 through 5. *Teaching Exceptional Children,* 24.3, 41-44.

Haynes, C. (1994). Differences between name recognition and name retrieval abilities in relationship to reading performance. *Doctoral Dissertation.* Harvard University, Cambridge MA (unpublished).

Heibert, E.H. (2003). *Quick reads: A research-based fluency program.* Lebanon, IN: Pearson Learning Group.

Henderson, E. (1990). *Teaching spelling.* Boston, MA: Houghton-Mifflin.

Henry, M.K. (1998). Beyond Phonics: Integrated decoding and spelling instruction based on word origin and structure. *Annals of Dyslexia,* 38, 258-75.

Henry, M.K. (1990). *Words: Integrated decoding and spelling instruction based on word origin and word structure.* Austin, TX: Pro-Ed.

Hook, P. & Jones, S.D. (2002). The importance of automaticity and fluency for efficient reading comprehension. *Perspectives,* 28, 9-14.

Hoyt, L. (2000). *Snapshots.* Portsmouth, NH: Heinemann Publishing.

Hultquist, A.M. (1997). Orthographic processing abilities of adolescents with dyslexia. *Annals of Dyslexia,* 47, 69-88.

Jarvella, R.J. (1971). Syntactic processing of connected speech. *Journal of Verbal Learning and Verbal Behavior,* 10, 409-16.

Jenkins, J., & Larson, K. (1979). Evaluating error-correction procedures for oral reading. *Journal of Special Education,* 13, 145-156.

Jenkins, J.R., Larson, K., & Fleisher, L.S. (1982). Effects of error correction on word recognition and reading comprehension. *Learning Disability Quarterly,* 6, 139-154.

Johnson, M.S., Kress, R.A., & Pikulski, J.J. (1987). *Informal reading inventories, 2nd edition*, Newark, IL: International Reading Association.

Kame'enui, E.J., Simmons, D.C., Good, R.H. & Harn, B.A. (2001). The use of fluency-based measures in early identification and evaluation of intervention efficacy in schools. In M. Wolf (Ed.), *Dyslexia, Fluency, and the Brain,* 307-331.

Kaminski, R.A., & Good, R.H. III. (1996). Toward a technology for assessing basic early literacy skills. *School Psychology Review,* 25.2, 215-227.

Kimball, J.P. (1973). Seven principles of surface structure parsing in natural language. *Cognition,* 2, 15-47.

LaBerge, D., & Samuels, S.J. (1974). Toward a theory of automatic information processing in reading. *Cognitive Psychology,* 6, 293-323.

Leu, D., & Kinzer, C. (1987). *Effective reading instruction in the elementary grades.* Westerville, OH: Merrill.

Levy, B.A., Abello, B., & Lysynchuk, L. (1997). Transfer from word training to reading in context: Gains in reading fluency and comprehension. *Learning Disability Quarterly,* 20, 173-88.

Lindsay, P.H., & Norman, D. (1977). *Human Information Processing.* San Diego, CA: Academic Press.

Lindamood, P., & Lindamood, P. (1998). *The LiPS Program.* Austin, TX: Pro-Ed.

Lovett, M.W. (1987). A developmental approach to reading disability: Accuracy and speed criteria of normal and deficient reading skills. *Child Development,* 58, 234-260.

Lovett, M., Borden, S., DeLuca, T., Lacerenza, L., Benson, N., & Brackstone, D. (1994). Treating the core deficits of developmental dyslexia: Evidence of transfer of learning after phonologically and strategy-based reading training programs. *Developmental Psychology,* 30, 805-22.

Lovett, M.W., Warren-Chaplin, P.M., Ransby, M.J., & Borden, S.L. (1990). Training the word recognition skills of reading disabled children: Treatment and transfer effects. *Journal of Educational Psychology,* 82, 769-780.

Manis, F.R. (1985). Acquisition of word identification skills in normal and disabled readers. *Journal of Educational Psychology,* 77, 78-90.

Manis, F.R. & Freedman, L. (2001). The relationship of naming speed to multiple reading measures in disabled and normal readers. In M. Wolf (Ed.), *Dyslexia, fluency, and the brain.* Timonium, MD: York Press, Inc.

Manis, F., Doi, L., & Bhada, B. (2000). Naming speed, phonological awareness and orthographic knowledge in second graders. *Journal of Learning Disabilities,* 33, 325-333.

Manis, F.R., Seidenberg M.S., & Doi, L.M. (1999). See Dick RAN: Rapid naming and the longitudinal prediction of reading skills in first and second graders. *Scientific Studies of Reading*, 3, 129-157.

Martinez, M., Roser, N., & Strecker, S. (1999). I never thought I could be a star: A reader's theatre ticket to fluency. *The Reading Teacher,* 52, 326-334.

McClelland, J.L., & Rumelhart, D.E. (1981). An interactive activation model of context effects in letter perception: Part 1. An account of basic findings. *Psychological Review,* 88, 375-407.

Meyer, M.S., & Felton. R.H. (1998). *Evolution of fluency training: Old approaches and new directions.* Paper presented at the meeting of International Dyslexia Association, San Francisco, CA.

Meyer, M.S., & Felton, R.H. (1999). Repeated reading to enhance fluency: Old approaches and new directions. *Annals of Dyslexia,* 49, 283-306.

Meyer, M.S., Wood, F.B., Hart, L.A., & Felton, R.H. (1998). Selective predictive value of rapid automatized naming in poor readers. *Journal of Learning Disabilities,* 31, 106-117.

Miller, G.A. (1956). The magical number seven, plus or minus two: Some limits on our capacity for processing information. *Psychological Review,* 63, 81-97.

Moats, L.C., & Smith, C. (1992). Derivational morphology: Why it should be included in language assessment and instruction. *Language, Speech, and Hearing Services in Schools,* 23, 312-319.

Naslund, J.C., & Smolkin, L.B. (1997). Automaticity and phonemic representations: Perceptual and cognitive building blocks for reading. *Reading and Writing Quarterly,* 13, 147-169.

National Center for Educational Statistics (1995). Washington, D.C.: Office of Educational Research and Improvement, U.S. Department of Education.

National Assessment of Educational Progress (NAEP) Technical Report. (1992). Princeton, NJ: Educational Testing Service.

Nigg, J.T., Hinshaw, S.P., Carte, E.T., & Treuting, J.J. (1998). Neuropsychological correlates of childhood attention-deficit/hyperactivity disorder: Explainable by co-morbid disruptive behavior or reading problems? *Journal of Abnormal Child Psychology,* 107, 468-80.

O'Shea, L., Sindelar, P., & O'Shea, D. (1985). The effects of repeated readings and attentional cues on reading fluency and comprehension. *Journal of Reading Behavior,* 17, 129-142.

Pany, D., & McCoy, K.M. (1988). Effects of corrective feedback on word accuracy and reading comprehension of readers with learning disabilities. *Journal of Learning Disabilities,* 21, 546-550.

Pany, D., McCoy, K. M., & Peters, E. E. (1981). Effects of corrective feedback on comprehension skills of remedial students. *Journal of Reading Behavior*, 13, 131-143.

Perfetti, C.A. (1985). *Reading ability.* New York: Oxford University Press.

Perfetti, C.A. (1992). The representation problem in reading acquisition. In P.B. Gough, L.C. Ehri, R. Treimen (Eds.), *Reading Acquisition.* Mahwah, NJ: Lawrence Erlbaum Associates, Inc., 145-174.

Perfetti, C.A., & Lesgold, A.M. (1977). Discourse comprehension and sources of individual differences. In M.A. Just, & P.A. Carpenter (Eds.), *Cognitive Processes in Comprehension.* Mahwah, NJ: Lawrence Erlbaum Associates Inc., 144-183.

Pinnell, G.S., Pikulski, J.J., Wixson, K.K., Campbell, J.R., Gough, P.B., & Beatty, A.S. (1995). *Listening to children read aloud.* Washington, DC: Office of Educational Research and Improvement, U.S. Department of Education.

Rashotte, C., & Torgesen, J. (1985). Repeated reading and reading fluency in learning disabled children. *Reading Research Quarterly,* 20, 180-88.

Rasinski, T.V. (2000). Speed does matter in reading. *The Reading Teacher,* 54, 146-151.

Rasinski, T.V. (1995). Fast Start: A parent involvement reading program for primary grade students. In W. Linek & E. Sturtevant (Eds.), *Generations of Literacy: The 17th Yearbook of the College Reading Association.* Harrisonburg, VA: College Reading Association, 301-312.

Rasinski, T.V. (1999). Exploring a method for estimating independent, instructional, and frustration reading rates. *Reading Psychology: An International Quarterly,* 20, 61-69.

Rasinski, T.V., & Padak, N. (1998). How elementary students referred for compensatory reading instruction perform on school-based measures of word recognition, fluency, and comprehension. *Reading Psychology: An International Quarterly,* 19, 185-216.

Reitsma, P. (1983). Printed word learning in beginning readers. *Journal of Experimental: Child Psychology,* 36, 321-339.

Report of the National Reading Panel: Teaching Children to Read. National Reading Panel (December 2000). National Institute for Literacy. Rockville, MD: MICHD Clearinghouse.

Samuels, S.J. (1979). The method of repeated readings. *The Reading Teacher*; 32-4, 403-408.

Samuels, S.J. (1985). Automaticity and repeated reading. In J. Osborn, P.T. Wilson, & R.C. Anderson (Eds.), *Reading Education: Foundations for a Literate America*, Lexington, MA: Lexington Books, 215-230.

Samuels, S.J. (1992). *What research has to say about reading instruction.* Newark, DE: International Reading Association.

Samuels, S.J., LaBerge, D., & Bremer, C. (1978). Units of word recognition: Evidence for developmental changes. *Journal of Verbal Learning and Verbal Behavior,* 17, 715-720.

Schreiber, P.A. (1980). On the acquisition of reading fluency. *Journal of Reading Behavior,* 12, 177-186.

Schreiber, P.A. (1987). Prosody and structure in children's syntactic processing. In R. Horowitz ,& S.J. Samuels (Eds.), *Comprehending Oral and Written Language.* New York: Academic Press.

Schreiber, P.A. (1991). Understanding prosody's role in reading acquisition. *Theory Into Practice,* 30-33, 158-164.

Seidenberg, M.S. (1990). Dyslexia in a computational model of word recognition in reading. In P.B. Gough, L.C. Ehri & R. Treiman (Eds.), *Reading acquisition.* Mahwah, NJ: Lawrence Erlbaum Associates, Inc., 243-73.

Seidenberg, M.S., & McClelland, JL. (1989). A distributed, developmental model of word recognition and naming. *Psychological Review*, 96, 523-568.

Shiffrin, R., & Schneider, W. (1977). Controlled and automatic information processing: II. Perceptual learning, automatic attending, and a general theory. *Psychological Review,* 84, 120-90.

Shinn, M.R., Good, R.H., Knutson, N., Tilly, W.D., & Collins, V.L. (1992). Curriculum-based measurement of oral reading fluency: A confirmatory analysis of its relation to reading. *School Psychology Review,* 21, 45-79.

Spring, C., & Capps, C. (1974). Encoding speed, rehearsal and probed recall of dyslexic boys. *Journal of Educational Psychology,* 66, 780-86.

Stanovich, K.E. (1986). Matthew effects in reading: Some consequences of individual differences in the acquisition of literacy. *Reading Research Quarterly,* 21, 360-407.

Steere, A., Peck, C.Z., & Kahn, L. (1998). *Solving language difficulties: Remedial routines.* Cambridge, MA: Educators Publishing Service, Inc.

Swan, L., & Goswami, U. (1994). *Picture naming deficits in developmental dyslexia.* Paper presented at the Society for Scientific Study of Reading. New Orleans, LA.

Swanson, H.L. (1994). Short-term memory and working memory: Do both contribute to our understanding of academic achievement in children and adults with learning disabilities? *Journal of Learning Disabilities,* 27, 34-50.

Tan, A., & Nicholson, T. (1997). Flashcards revisited: Training poor readers to read words faster improves their comprehension of text. *Journal of Educational Psychology*, 59, 276-288.

Tannock, R., Martinussen, R., & Frijters, J. (2000). Naming speed performance and stimulant effects indicate effortful, semantic processing deficits in attention-deficit/hyperactivity disorder. *Journal of Abnormal Child Psychology,* 28, 237-53.

Topping, K. (1987). Paired reading: A powerful technique for parent use. *The Reading Teacher*, 40, 608-614.

Torgesen, J.K. (2002). *Reading Fluency: Conceptual and Instructional Issues.* Presentation at 53rd Annual IDA Conference. Atlanta, GA. November 13-16.

Torgesen, J.K., & Houck, D.G. (1980). Processing deficiencies in learning-disabled children who perform poorly on the Digit Span test. *Journal of Educational Psychology*, 72, 141-160.

Torgesen, J.K., Wagner, R.K., Rashotte, C.A., Burgess, S., & Hecht, S. (1997). Contributions of phonological awareness and rapid automatic naming ability to the growth of word-reading skills in second-to-fifth grade children. *Scientific Studies of Reading*, 1, 161-185.

Treiman, R. & Cassar, M. (1997). Spelling acquisition in English. In C.A. Perfetti, L. Rieben, M. Fayol (Eds.), *Learning to Spell: Research Theory and Practice Across Languages.* Mahwah, NJ: Lawrence Erlbaum Associates, Inc.

van den Bosch, K., Van Bon, W.H., & Schreuder, R. (1995). Readers' decoding skills: Effects of training with limited exposure duration. *Reading Research Quarterly*, 30, 110-125.

van der Sloot, M, Licht, R., Horsley, T.M. & Sergeant, J.A. (2000) Inhibitory deficits in reading disability depend on subtype: Guessers but not spellers. *Neuropsychology, Development, and Cognition. Sec C, Child Neuropsychology: A Journal on Normal and Abnormal Development in Childhood and Adolescence,* 4, 297-312.

Waber, D. (2001). Aberrations in timing in children with impaired reading reading. In M. Wolf (Ed.), *Dyslexia, Fluency, and the Brain.* Timonium, MD: York Press.

Weaver, C. (1988). *Reading process and practice: From socio-psycholinguistics to whole language.* Portsmouth, NH: Heinemann Educational Books, Inc.

Wilkinson, I., Wardrop, J.L., & Anderson, R.C. (1988). Silent reading considered: Reinterpreting reading instruction and its effects. *American Educational Research Journal,* 25, 1, 127-144.

Windsor, J., & Hwang, M. (1997). Knowledge of derivational suffixes in students with language learning disabilities. *Annals of Dyslexia,* 47, 57-68.

Wolf, M. (1984). Naming, reading, and the dyslexias: A longitudinal overview. *Annals of Dyslexia,* 34, 87-115.

Wolf, M. (1991). Naming speed and reading: The contribution of the cognitive neurosciences. *Reading Research Quarterly,* 26, 123-141.

Wolf, M. (1997). A provisional, integrative account of phonological and naming-speed deficits in dyslexia: Implications for diagnosis and intervention. In B. Blachman. (Ed.), *Cognitive and Linguistic Foundations of Reading Acquisition: Implications for Intervention Research.* Mahwah, NJ: Lawrence Erlbaum Associates, Inc.

Wolf. M. (Ed.) (2001). *Dyslexia, fluency, and the brain.* Timonium, MD: York Press, Inc.

Wolf, M., Bally, H., & Morris, R. (1986). Automaticity, retrieval processes, and reading: A longitudinal study in average and impaired readers. *Child Development*, 96, 988-1005.

Wolf, M., & Bowers, P. (1993). Theoretical links among naming speed, precise timing mechanisms and orthographic skill in dyslexia. *Reading and Writing: An Interdisciplinary Journal,* 5, 69-85.

Wolf, M., & Bowers, P. (1999). The double-deficit hypothesis for the developmental dyslexias. *Journal of Educational Psychology,* 91, 415-438.

Wolf, M., & Katzir-Cohen, T. (2001). Reading fluency and its intervention. *Scientific Studies of Reading,* 5, 3, 211-239.

Wolf, M., Miller, L., & Donnelly, K. (2000). Retrieval, automaticity, vocabulary elaboration, and orthography (RAVE-O). *Journal of Learning Disabilities,* 33, 4, 375-386.

Wolf, M., & Obregon, M. (1992). Early naming deficits, developmental dyslexia, and a specific deficit hypothesis. *Brain and Language,* 42, 219-247.

Wolf, M., & Segal, D. (1992). Word finding and reading in the developmental dyslexias. *Topics in Language Disorders,* 13,1, 51-65.

Wolf, M., & Segal, D. (1999). Retrieval-rate, accuracy and vocabulary elaboration (RAVE) in reading-impaired children: A pilot intervention program. *Dyslexia*, 5, 1-27.

Wood, F.B., Flowers, L., & Grigorenko, E. (2001). On the functional neuroanatomy of fluency or why walking is just as important to reading as talking is. In Wolf, M. (Ed.), *Dyslexia, Fluency, and the Brain.* Timonium, MD: York Press.

Young, A., & Bowers, P. (1995). Individual difference and text difficulty determinants of reading fluency and expressiveness. *Journal of Experimental Child Psychology,* 60, 428-454.

Young A., Bowers, P., & MacKinnon, G. (1996). Effects of prosodic modeling and repeated reading on poor readers' fluency and comprehension. *Applied Psycholinguistics*, 17, 59-84.

Young A., Bowers, P., & MacKinnon, G. (1996)

19-05-9876543

